HISTORIC TEXAS

An Illustrated Chronicle of Texas' Past

By Archie P. McDonald

Published for Preservation Texas, Inc.

Historical Publishing Network
A division of Lammert Publications, Inc.
San Antonio, Texas

Texas Front Gate. *Texas scene painting of a West Texas landscape by William Alexandre Hogue.*

Printed in Dallas, Texas by Taylor Publishing Company.
Color scans by Taylor Publishing Company.

ISBN: 0-9654999-0-1

Library of Congress Catalog Card Number: 96-79257

author: Archie P. McDonald

publisher: Ron Lammert

photo editors: R.G. Dean & Oiuda Dean

cover artist: Gordon Snidow

designer: Charles Newton

project coordinator: Barry Black

"Sharing the Heritage"
representatives: Sydney McNew

Barbara Frank

Helen Carr

Gene Peeples

Jim Heath

administration: Stefanie Stevenson

Dee Steidle

Michèle Newton

Rob Friedrich

contributing writers for
"Sharing the Heritage":   Sally Bell

Verone M. Travis

Betty T. Chapman

Anne Feltus

Marcy Meffert

Diana J. Kleiner

Patricia L. Spence

Randall Reed

Steven LeMons

Kirsten Jonrowe Coats

Cristine S. Davila

726

CONTENTS

"Burro Party." Taking a break near Mineral Wells, Texas.

INTRODUCTION & ACKNOWLEDGMENT

Why Another History of Texas?

Opposite: Roaming herds of animals were forced to discover the best places to cross rivers and other streams. Indians, and later other men, located and used the same crossings. The Old Pinta Crossing on the Guadalupe [River], *painted by Hermann Lungkwitz (1813-1891), depicts such a site.* COURTESY, THE TORCH COLLECTION, HOUSTON, TEXAS.

Why write another history of Texas? This is a reasonable question and a particularly appropriate one for me because library shelves already strain under the weight of thousands of previous histories of Texas, and I am to blame for some of them. Histories of Texas range from multi-volume, or at least plural-volume narratives such as *The Saga of Texas* and John Henry Brown to bulging single-volume surveys by T.R. Fehrenbach; traditional texts by Rupert Richardson, the "dean" of earlier Texas historians and now revised by Ernest Wallace and Adrian Anderson, later works by Seymour V. Connor and by Robert A. Calvert and Arnoldo DeLeon, and the most recent by David G. McComb; sleek, easy-to-read narratives by Joe B. Frantz and by that East Texan who wrote *Texas: All Hail The Mighty State*; and stacks of biographies, monographs, ethnic and gender studies, local history, memoirs, periodicals with even more specific articles, the published papers of the mighty—and lording over all, the venerable and indispensable *Handbook of Texas* and *The Texas Almanac*.

One could safely suggest that everything that could be said about Texas—at least everything really worth saying—has been included somewhere among the items cited. But we have to tell the story anew for these reasons: no matter how much we study the history of Texans we continue to learn more about them; the style of books and reinterpretations of long established stories, like neckties and hem lines, change frequently; and finally, we are presented with wonderful anniversaries such as the 150th year since the beginning of the Texas Revolution in 1986 and a similar milestone that commemorates the merging of the Texas Republic with the other United States.

This book, then, is prompted by the sesquicentennial of statehood. Anson Jones pronounced the conclusion of our predecessors' experiment with independence, saying, "The Republic of Texas is no more," and Sam Houston clutched the Lone Star flag as that standard descended the pole to make room for the Stars and Stripes with a bright, new, twenty-eighth star on its field of blue.

Over the past 150 years Texas and Texans changed much. At the beginning of statehood native Texans were few, even including *tejano* and Native Americans, and the whole of them numbered only a few hundred thousand; many still "join up" to become Texans when war or economic reversal at home catches our state on the upsweep of the curve of opportunity, but by now some of us have been around long enough to count ourselves unto the sixth or seventh generation, and we amount to approximately eighteen million souls in the third largest accumulation of Americans within a single state.

Texans were exclusively "horse and buggy" people for approximately the first half of their experience in the Union, but now operate as many automobiles, airplanes, and boats as do the citizens of other states, probably more than most. And we host the nerve center of all of our country's space exploration. We have gone from the horse to horse-power to rockets in an accumulation of change so rapid and so complete that it spins the head to remember that persons of my parents' generation grew up in times not much different from those experienced by Sam Houston, and that persons of my generation actually can remember a time without air conditioning and television, circumstances of hardship unimaginable and unacceptable to our children. Or our grandchildren, who will not know a time without computers. Who knows what awaits *their* children?

So, for these, it is appropriate to take another look at the history of Texas, to preserve for them the old stories of Indians, Spanish explorers and missionaries, Mexican nationalists, Anglo settlers, warriors of our uncivil conflicts, entrepreneurs and laborers, women, reformers, cowboys, drillers, athletes, criminals—the whole lot of us who bear the label of Texan. Some of us have been posi-

Right: Primitive half-dugout structure serving Happy Jack School teacher and students, probably near Canyon, Texas.

MRS. EDWARD W. THORPE COLLECTION ALBUM. COURTESY, PANHANDLE-PLAINS HISTORICAL MUSEUM, CANYON, TEXAS.

Below: African-American wedding party, Lubbock.

COURTESY, SOUTHWEST COLLECTION, TEXAS TECH UNIVERSITY, LUBBOCK, TEXAS.

Bottom: Ice sailing, Amarillo, Texas, January, 1912.

MRS. EDWARD W. THORPE COLLECTION ALBUM. COURTESY, PANHANDLE-PLAINS HISTORICAL MUSEUM, CANYON, TEXAS.

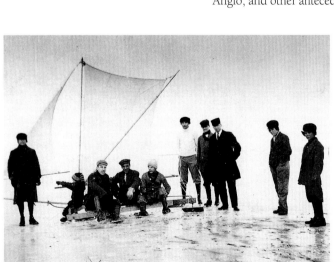

tive forces and some have not, but we all have played a role in making Texas whatever it is. As students and as citizens we must understand how Texas came to be as it is before we can do anything to make it better.

In publicly-supported institutions in Texas, all students must take a course in Texas and/or United States history. I think students deserve to know why this is required, and there are several answers, all correct. An Official Reason: because we were concerned about communist subversion immediately after World War II, we wanted to ground our young in the fundamentals of their state's and nation's history so they would not even consider this alien and errant political creed. I am not sure any course could really do that, but I am pleased with the requirement because it has guaranteed me a certain level of job security for over three decades. A Better Or Maybe At Least An Equally Good Reason: because each generation in turn takes its place in the ballot booth and in the jury room and on the councils, boards, and elected positions that govern our lives, and they serve best who understand how things came to be. Then they have the guide of the past to chart the future.

So that is why we are here once more to roam the path trod by our Indian, Spanish, Mexican, Anglo, and other antecedents; to apologize when necessary for having made a mess some of the time; to bluster a little when things went well; and—with whatever grace we can muster—to "pass it on" to Kelly Marie McDonald and to your grandchildren and pray they will make Texas an even better place for all.

In the main chapters of this book you will find a series of lessons that much resemble a college-level course in Texas history. There will be no need to take notes because there are no examinations, or to tape record the lectures because you will have a verbatim account in these pages. And you will find less personal intrusion from the lecturer. Here, however, it is necessary to explain that few history teachers generate original ideas. I have known one: Walter Prescott Webb, author of *The Great Plains* and *The Great Frontier*, whose books launched great debates and eventually won armies of disciples (and a few critics). Most of us "pass it on" from idea people such as Webb or from earlier and often quite gifted narrators who got the story first. We learn it from them, then pass it on to those we teach and hope that we inspire them to learn more, or, when we do our job badly, kill or suppress their interest in our past.

So before I pass along the story of Texas as I have received it, let me confess that about as close as I ever came to an original idea is the explanation of immigration that appears in Chapter Two, and even that is the product of reading such works as James A. Michener's *Centennial* and Barnes Lathrop's study of Anglo immigration into East Texas. So it is with all I know about the state of the state before I became its native citizen in 1935.

My formal education in Texas studies began in the seventh grade under Mrs. Heinrich, who masked a soft heart with stern discipline and took a shine to someone who demonstrated interest in her subject. Mrs. Heinrich bullied me and babied me but the sum of it was the beginning of a lifetime of interest in Texas even though my original professional goals focused on the Civil War, and

especially on Virginia, not Texas, in that awe-filled time. Truth is, I never took a formal course in Texas history after leaving French Junior High School in Beaumont; the subject was not offered at the Rice Institute or Louisiana State University. It is also true that the Texas history teacher retired before the Civil War historian at Stephen F. Austin State University, and as senior of the junior profs, the cup passed to me.

I paid more than a passing interest in the current events that have now become modern Texas history and became active (and lucky) in researching, writing, and speaking on the adopted field that became my own. And I read. And read. My teachers included all those mentioned in the second paragraph of this introduction, but more must be said of some of them, especially Ted Fehrenbach. His *Lone Star* had just appeared when I inherited the Texas history course. It was a rule in those days that you "borrowed" your notes from one book and used another for a text. Ted "loaned" me the

first set of notes I used in class, quite without knowing it, of course, but I got the chance to thank him for this and many other kindnesses later and acknowledge him now for the role he has played in my efforts to become more knowledgeable about Texas history. Debt to Richardson, Connor, Calvert, DeLeon, and McComb is confessed, with gratitude, as well as to the developers of the great *Handbook of Texas* and its *Supplement*, especially Walter Webb, L. Tuffly Ellis, Eldon Branda, and to Ron Tyler, Tom Cutrer, and Doug Barnett for *The New Handbook of Texas* whose gestation I have observed at first hand.

Appreciative acknowledgment

Above: Judge Roy Bean's Justice of the Peace office and billiard hall in the trans-Pecos region near Langtry.

COURTESY, TEXAS DEPARTMENT OF TRANSPORTATION.

Below: "Big Tex" and a "wanna be" Tex extend an invitation to the 1952 State Fair in Dallas.

FROM THE COLLECTIONS OF THE TEXAS/DALLAS HISTORY AND ARCHIVES DIVISION, DALLAS PUBLIC LIBRARY.

"Cattle Trails," map of the three main routes along which herds of cattle were driven from Texas ranges to the American Plains: the Chisholm, the Western, and the Goodnight-Loving trails.

MAP BY BARBARA WHITEHEAD.
COURTESY, SOUTHWESTERN WRITERS COLLECTION, SAN MARCOS, TEXAS.

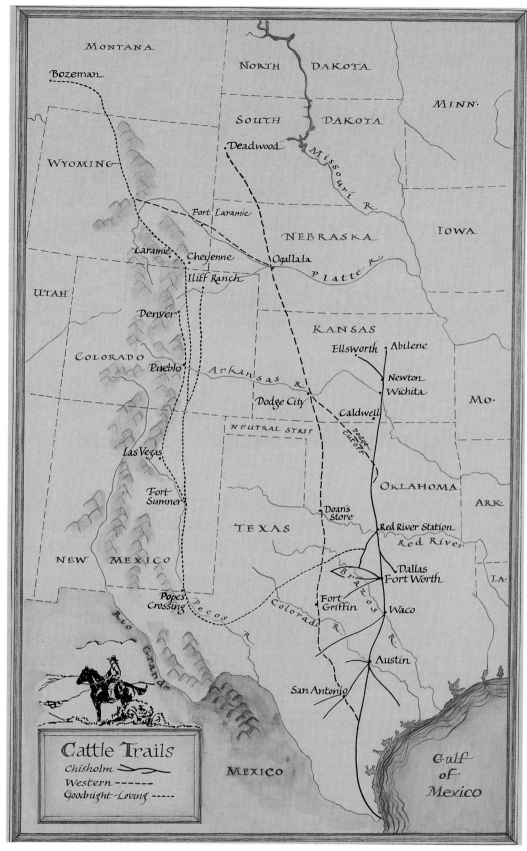

is also extended to A. C. Greene and Don Graham, who taught me the culture of Texas. And to Ben Procter, the dean and guru of Texas historians past and present, who showed me by example that the historian must be a friend as well as a teacher, and to F. E. Abernethy, who corrects me and directs me to follow the muse; and to gifted lay historians, F. Lee Lawrence, Max S. Lale, J. P. Bryan, Jenkins Garrett, and Clifton Caldwell, who remind me by their devotion to Texas and knowledge of its history that a Ph.D. is but one avenue to Clio's heart.

I'll not put down my union, though, for some wonderful folks have endured graduate school and turned out just fine, among them Jim Reese, my former boss and current colleague, who knows more about Texas history than I do. O. Bill Brophy, Ken Hendrickson, Mike Campbell, Bill O'Neal, Jim Pohl, Ray Stephens, Frank Vandiver, Cary Wintz, and Ralph Wooster are wonderful teachers of Texas history, although some of them started life elsewhere.

So, in a way, all of these plus quite a few others bear the blame for the "course" which follows because they have taught me what I now pass along to you—and if I get anything dreadfully wrong, we can correct that the next time. That is one of the marvelous things about teaching and about writing of Texas once more: someone will come along to do it better next time.

Let us begin.

THE EVOLUTION OF THE TEXAS FLAG.

(From Wm. G. Scarff's "Comprehensive History of Texas.")

No. 1.—Flag of San Jacinto.
No. 2.—National Standard of Republic (January 24, 1839), present State Flag.
No. 3.—Flag of the Alamo.
No. 4.—San Felipe Flag (February 29, 1836).
No. 5.—Flag of Goliad and Velasco (Brown's).
No. 6.—McGahey Flag (1835).
No. 7.—Flag of Ward's Georgia Battalion.
No. 8.—Captain Dodson's Flag (September, 1835).
No. 9.—Naval Flag (April 9, 1836).
No. 10.—Captain Burroughs's Flag (1836).
No. 11.—National Standard of Republic (December 10, 1836).

EARLY TEXANS, THEIR GEOGRAPHY, AND THE FIRST EUROPEANS

REGIONS

The story of Texas begins with the land. James A. Michener began his novel *Texas* with a chapter titled "Land of Many Lands" and T.R. Fehrenbach's first sentence in *Lone Star* is "In the beginning, before any people, was the land...." So, with these preceptors providing our guide, we begin with geography. In the most precise sense, ultimately geography determines whether or not people can inhabit any place, and if they can, how they shall live.

We take geography as we find it, for ultimately humans cannot change it permanently, or at least they cannot do so positively. We alter it with air conditioning and irrigation but when the electricity fails or the source of water is exhausted, nature prevails; unfortunately, we foul the land with toxins and pollutants sufficiently to make it unusable for a long, long time.

Texas contains forests, prairies (plains), and mountains, the three basic land forms, and does so abundantly. The Southern Forest extends into eastern Texas for approximately 100 miles before merging into prairie; eastward to the Atlantic, except for the Mississippi delta, soils, trees, and other life forms are so similar that an East Texan waking up in Monroe County, Alabama, or Carroll County, Georgia, might think himself at home. Central Texas hosts the prairie and rolling hills, some quite dramatically high, and the trans-Pecos area features the promontories of the lower Rockies as well as the desert.

Precipitation grids extend north to south, or vertically, with the greatest abundance falling on eastern Texas, and descend to the west, so Newton, Jasper, or Orange counties receive upwards of fifty inches each year while El Paso County is lucky to receive as much as eight inches. Twenty inches of precipitation is the minimum annual requirement for predictable row-crop agriculture without irrigation. West of that line—somewhere to the west of Fort Worth—where the water runs low the crop growing stopped and grazing began, at least until what Don Green called "the underground rain" was pumped to the surface to quicken the fertile soils of the upper prairie.

Temperature grids run horizontally. The growing season in the Panhandle averages between 200 and 250 days annually, but some years never ends in the lower regions of the Río Grande Valley. "Growing season" means the time between the last killing frost of spring and the first in the fall; that is the time span for most row-crop agriculture.

The combination of these two grid systems determined what could be grown and established or limited human endeavor, at least until technology contributed irrigation, hot houses, or other artificial adjustments to nature. The combination of temperature and precipitation is important; the richer soils of the upper prairie could not grow the corn or cotton so abundant in the twentieth century without irrigation; and citrus might be irrigated in the Panhandle but could never survive the sustained temperatures below freezing that occur there each winter.

Assuming the alignment of temperature and precipitation, and some artificial help to nature such as irrigation, cultivating and later technological societies could and do exist throughout Texas, and each stamps the economy and society so uniquely that they are called regions.

Although Texans often speak of East, West, North, and South Texas, only the first really is a region. The rest are compass directions confounded by politics. How else could one explain the Texas legislature locating The University of North Texas in Denton, considerably south of Canyon, which hosts West Texas A&M, formerly known as West Texas State University. East Texas differs in

that it extends eastward from the Sabine River for approximately 100 miles, and in that its predominate Anglo population mostly originated in the same part of the American South. Once in Texas, these immigrants replicated the cotton culture of that area once they felled the trees. East Texas does not extend all the way to the Gulf of Mexico; for about fifty miles from the seashore, the Coastal Plains intrude and continue along approximately 370 miles of coastline to the Río Grande. Formal geographers think that nearly all of East Texas qualifies as Coastal Plains, but true East Texans never agree. For them, the Coastal Plain begins at the water's edge and extends inland for approximately fifty miles of wetlands, rich salt grasses, savannahs, and scrub growth trees too gnarled to become lumber. Much of the upper Coastal Plains can be used for grazing; the lower portion and westward along the Río Grande the area competes with Florida and California in the production of citrus and truck crops. In some areas the Continental Shelf, or the area near the shore submerged under the Gulf, is rich in minerals and in most areas is equally rich in marine life.

Continuing around the clock-face of Texas, along the Río Grande and northwest of the Valley appear the lower regions of the Edwards Plateau, which is separated from the lower plains by the Balcones Escarpment. This is dry country, but not as dry as the mountains and basins of the Trans-Pecos region. On the plateau, early humans hunted the buffalo; later immigrants raised sheep and goats for wool and mohair and meat.

Above, or northward from the plateau and divided by the Cap Rock Escarpment, lies the greatest natural grazing country in the world ever turned under by the plow to be made into farms by the miracle of the underground rain. Once the home of buffalo, antelope, and jackrabbits, in modern times it produces an abundance of cotton and corn. Treeless, the victim of wind, and lacking much precipitation except snow, the High Plains was adapted by technology, especially windmills and barbed wire, from grazing to growing.

Each of the regions has been subdivided into smaller units that reflect unique settlement patterns, less broad geographic land forms, or just the muse of the populations they host. So we speak of a Hill Country and a Cross Timbers and other sub-regions to accommodate the interests of Texans, for not all the stubborn ones live in East Texas.

EARLY TEXANS

To date, no theologian or archeologist has claimed that human life originated in the Western Hemisphere, as one or the other has for Africa, Asia, Europe, or what is called presumptively the "Middle East." Assuming, then, that human life originated somewhere else, it must be assumed further that humans first left their origination points to live elsewhere because of some change that made residence in former homelands no longer palatable or possible. In time, once word of better or at least different circumstances returned, some might have responded to attraction, but in the beginning immigration must have begun as blind or unwitting emigration. And in more time, from either stimulus, immigrants came from everywhere to become Americans and Texans. And it must be presumed further that they came aggressively and acquisitively, for neither nature nor Indians, Spaniards, or Mexicans surrendered to the next wave easily.

The first to make this emigration-immigration trek are called the Old People by some, or Paleo Americans more formally. Artifacts they left behind indicate singleness of movement, cultural unity, and sparseness of settlement. None of the artifacts testify to motivation for coming to Texas or explain why they perished or perhaps were absorbed by waves of later immigrants called Indians by generations of Americans and now known as Native Americans. The latter term is polite but not accurate if the assumption in the previous paragraph that none are native is true.

Probably the Old People were not Texans for long, but they were here a long time ago, at least before the arrival of the Indians, which most scientists date back 25,000 years or so. The Old People's artifacts indicate that they hunted and did so communally and at least some of the time successfully, that they employed symbols and fire ceremonially and functionally, and fashioned garments of fur. Then they vanished or were absorbed by other groups.

About Indians, more is known. Since they came in waves of migration from the western Pacific to the Western Hemisphere over a great many years, several avenues of travel were available to them. Some could have walked the land bridge that appeared during the Ice Age when the frozen sea stilled the waves in the north and reduced the volume of the ocean; others may have walked on that sea itself while in a firm state; and still others might have made the journey in vessels sufficient for the narrows where the hemispheres nearly kiss, even when the sea swelled to its present size.

Once in the Western Hemisphere, the Indians fanned out across the continent, generation by generation, some stopping to adapt to the geography they found, others moving southward to warmer climes and more abundant food sources before congregating at the waistline of the hemisphere, then spread out again to occupy South America.

Those who remained in North America and in Texas never achieved high population density, and eventually so adapted to the geography they inhabited that they lost the ability to communicate orally with neighboring groups. Indeed, the change was so thorough, their separation so complete, that in time their meetings often were characterized by confrontation rather than cooperation, although trade alliances always existed. Now we think of them as Forest Indians, Plains Indians, and Mountain and Desert Indians to reflect the three land forms they occupied; again, geography—nature—prevails. And since Texas contained all three land forms, it also hosted all three cultures of North American Indians.

Many "tribes" and "subtribes," or large, extended families, lived in Texas. As with the regions, the Forest Indians lived in eastern Texas. The Caddo claimed the upper and middle portions of East Texas and portions of Louisiana, Arkansas, and Oklahoma as well. Caddo lived in villages that stretched along streams and they rarely built their large, conical dwellings and service buildings far from

Mammals capable of flight, bats emerge at dusk like a black cloud for their nocturnal activities. They sleep during the day and hibernate in winter in dark places such as the James River Bat Cave in Mason County, photographed August 1993. Flying by echolocation, bats devour tons of night-flying insects, including mosquitoes and crop pests. Fossil remains of bats from over sixty million years ago have been found in Texas.
PHOTO BY LEROY WILLIAMSON.

Hernán Cortés (1485-1547) established Vera Cruz, Mexico in 1519, conquering the wealthy Aztec empire for Spain. Cortés brought the first horses to the mainland of North America, where they were effectively used in overthrowing Montezuma.

COURTESY, ARCHIVES DIVISION - TEXAS STATE LIBRARY.

Opposite, bottom: Gregorio de Villalobos brought the first cattle to the New World, an event depicted in this painting by Tom Lea, Unloading the First Cattle in North America, Vera Cruz, 1521. *Both horses and cattle spread rapidly across Texas. They were dispersed by the migrating Indians; they strayed from missionaries driving stock for food; and they were intentionally left at water crossings by explorer Juan de Oñate, who crossed the Rio Grande at El Paso del Norte in 1598 to search for gold and claim land for Philip II of Spain.*

COURTESY, DALLAS MUSEUM OF ART, DALLAS, TEXAS, AND THE SOUTHWESTERN WRITERS COLLECTION, SAN MARCOS, TEXAS.

water. They hunted and fished, and because their forests and streams contained much food for those with skills to obtain it, they did not have to roam far from their villages to do so. Caddo were not as war-like as the Indians who lived on the coast or the plains but not all their encounters with other Indians or the first Europeans who came to Texas were peaceful. Still, they are remembered more as traders than as fighters. Long before the arrival of Europeans they had made the great leap from hunting and gathering into the Agricultural Revolution, although they still practiced both.

Following the clock, to the south of the Caddo lived the Atakapa, who also extended eastward along the Gulf through Louisiana—and also the Karankawa. The latter group early were branded as cannibals, and did practice it, as did most Texas Indians, or, for that matter, as did the Europeans, at least in ritual. Coastal Indians anointed their bodies with a foul-smelling grease composed of animal fats to ward off mosquitoes and perhaps because they valued the decoration. They were not always hostile, but as late as the arrival of Anglo colonists in the nineteenth century they sometimes were.

Coahuiltecan Indians lived in South Texas, and, as the occupiers of an area that yielded food sparely, were perhaps Texas' poorest. This also made them the best candidates for missions when the Spaniards founded them because the missionaries had food to share.

Apaches occupied the western portions of Texas and the High Plains, at least until the Comanche, who were pushed down from eastern Colorado by a then-stronger foe, obtained the horse culture from the Spaniards and became the Lords of the Plains. Even the Apaches moved aside from the Comanche. The Kiowa joined the Comanche in hunting for buffalo on the plains and also in the final resistance to the advance of Anglo settlers.

Before and during the occupation of Texas by Europeans, other Indians, Cherokee, Creek, Choctaw, and Chickasaw among them,

were forced westward into eastern Texas by westering Anglo-Americans determined to remove them from their path. Texans did the same, pushing these groups westward or northward into Indian Territory, or Oklahoma. By the later decades of the twentieth century only the Alabama-Coushatta in eastern Texas and the Tigua in western Texas remained together as a people on lands occupied by their ancestors. How many Indians lived in Texas at the time of the European Intervention is difficult to determine. Surely fewer than 100,000, with even these spread thinly because of the struggle for survival. In the 1990s, perhaps a few more than 50,000 persons of total Indian descent lived in Texas; the number of those of partial Indian descent is much larger.

SPANISH BEGINNINGS

Christopher Columbus led Europeans to Texas without personally seeing its shore. His voyage of discovery in 1492 demonstrated access to a whole new world that attracted first a trickle and then a torrent of Old World citizens who explored and then exploited the New World. Efforts to celebrate the 500th anniversary of Columbus' extraordinary achievement in 1992 failed to produce the bonanza for Spain its various promoters had envisioned because not all the consequences of the explorer's connection of the two worlds were positive. The destruction, suppression, or submergence of virtually all Western Hemisphere Indian cultures, considered justified previously because Europeans brought them Christianity and other Old World institutions, was questioned and criticized by twentieth-century descendants and allies. The introduction of diseases new to the Indians sometimes eliminated whole tribes and decimated others, and the loss of separate cultures, personal freedom, and ethnic purity did not make the Colombian Exchange a complete bargain for Indians.

From the beginning Spaniards concerned themselves with defining the proper "place" of Indian groups. In the time of the early explorers, Europeans usually did not boldly admit that they sought land and riches;

instead, their confessed motivation for conquest involved sharing Christianity according to the Great Commission in the Book of St. Matthew. From the earliest times, then, plural motivation characterized Spanish conquerors: they hungered for personal fame and riches; since the union of Ferdinand and Isabella had created modern Spain, they burned with desire to expand the power and the glory of their nation; and many sincerely wanted to share the Good News of Jesus Christ with the Indians—even if this resulted in the destruction of the Indians' culture, although eventually a compromise produced a blend of Old and New World faiths with the Old dominant in outward appearances.

Above: Waters of Falcon Lake rise around an old church in Guerrero, Mexico, between present-day Zapata and Río Grande City, Texas. The Spanish flag flew over the Río Grande at Guerrero on January 1, 1700, and missions San Juan Bautista, San Francisco Solano, and San Bernardo—and Presidio San Bernardo— were built on the southern side of the river. One of the earliest crossings into Texas, Guerrero has become known as the "Gateway to Texas." There, Franciscans operated a college and seminary, and from there accompanied New Spain expeditions along the frontier trails into Texas, establishing the missions east of the Pecos River and north to the Red River, including the East Texas missions around Nacogdoches and the founding of San Antonio.

Above: Map of Texas and the Countries Adjacent (Carte Contenant le Royaume du Mexique et la Floride), by Henri Abraham Chatelain. This 1718 map is based on La Salle's claim for France of all the lands draining to the Mississippi. Indian villages as well as Spanish towns were mapped by the French cartographer.

COURTESY, CARTOGRAPHIC COLLECTIONS OF MRS. JENKINS GARRETT, FORT WORTH; HOUSED AT THE SPECIAL COLLECTIONS DIVISION, THE UNIVERSITY OF TEXAS AT ARLINGTON LIBRARIES, ARLINGTON, TEXAS.

Below: Caddoan Mounds State Historical Park exhibit at the George C. Davis site in East Texas near the Neches River and the town of Alto. The Early Caddos selected the site about AD 800 because the alluvial prairie offered ideal qualities for a village and ceremonial center. Known for their mound building and sturdy conical shaped buildings, the Caddos dominated life in the region for 500 years. Caddoan Mounds flourished until the 13th century, when they suddenly abandoned the site.

COURTESY, TEXAS DEPARTMENT OF TRANSPORTATION.

Spain began the process of accommodating Indians into their system that eventually reached Texas as soon as they reached the Caribbean. *Conquistadores* became administrators of land units known as *encomiendas*, including authority over Indians who resided there. The commission of these *encomienderos* was to make the land productive through the labor of the Indians and to create a "pacified land" that remained peaceful because the overwhelming power of the Spaniards made resistance by Indians or invasion by other European nations difficult.

The conquest proved easy, but making the Caribbean or later mainland Mexico productive with Indian labor, did not. The Indians did not overtly resist forced labor so much as their culture, which utilized male energy as warriors and hunters rather than as workers, rendered them unable to comply satisfactorily. Too, there was the question of salvation: if the Spaniards succeeded in saving the Indians' souls, was it proper to enslave them? Little enough work from the Indians and growing concerns about theological propriety produced a solution: import Africans to do the manual labor and continue to teach the catechism to the Indians.

Then Hernán Cortés carried Spanish conquest on to Mexico and Almagro and Pizarro did the same in Peru; both expeditions stumbled into the territory of American Indian civilizations that most resembled their own in development. Aztecs and Incas long before had discovered gold, and while neither regarded it as having intrinsic value it was a most precious commodity to the Spaniards. Until they proved otherwise, Spaniards assumed that the remainder of America harbored gold.

Cortés and Almagro and Pizarro commanded only a few hundred men, yet they conquered many thousands of Indians. The numbers defy creditability until the Spaniards' advantages are appreciated. These advantages were both practical and psychological, and thus were of short tenure; once the Indians acquired them or lost their awe of them, many more Spanish soldiers were required to hold them in line or to conquer more. Horses, guns, armor, dogs, and attitude provided the edge. Horses gave the Spanish greater mobility, and since Indians had never seen horses before, these large, noisy animals frightened them. Guns lent their destructive powers in practical ways, added the mystery of the stick that exploded and injured or killed, and retained a psychological advantage even after the Indians understood them, even as modern people, shy from others wielding firearms because they know too well what they can do. Armor that shined in the sun and deflected arrows added the sense of immortality to the Spaniards. Indians knew about dogs, but not the trained animals the invaders employed to maim. But perhaps the Spaniards' greatest advantage was their attitude: within one people they combined what they accepted without doubt was the best ethnicity and the one and only True Faith, so they went forth convinced of the inevitability of victory.

So the Spaniards spread across Central America and began the southward penetration that eventually gave them control of most of South America, and moved northward through Mexico toward Texas. Alonzo Álvarez de Piñeda first saw what later generations defined as Texas, and did so about the same time Cortés conquered the Aztecs. His expedition sailed the rim of the Gulf of Mexico, mapped the area, and made landfall near a river he called Río de los Palmos, or the Río

Grande. He referred to the area he surveyed as Amichael; later it would be called the New Philippines, then *Tejas*, and finally Texas.

After Piñeda came Diego de Camargo, who would have planted a colony in south Texas except for the forceful objection of Cortés, who wanted no neighbors. So the first Spaniards who spent significant time in Texas did so involuntarily. They were members of an expedition sent to explore Florida led by Pánfilo de Narváez, and they missed the rendezvous with ships that would have taken them back to Cuba safely. Not knowing if other ships would return for them, the stranded explorers constructed crude, unseaworthy crafts, made sails from their clothes, and tried to hug the Gulf Coast around to Spanish developments in Mexico rather than risk the open sea to reach Cuba.

Along the upper Gulf Coast they made landfall, probably on an island or peninsula near present-day Galveston, but their vessels could not carry them farther. Several score of men reached the island, but within a year exposure reduced their numbers to a handful. They crossed the bay to the mainland but the attrition continued, and in the end only four—Alvar Núñez, Cabeza de Vaca, Alonso de Castillo Maldonao, Andrés Dorantes de Carranza, and a Moor named Estavánico

(Stephen)—survived to tell of their adventures among the Indians of Texas, where they had heard stories of golden cities located somewhere to the north. Searching for those golden cities, or any gold, motivated all Spanish interest in Texas for decades, and failure to find it shaped Spanish policy toward the area as long as they controlled it.

Cabeza de Vaca's ordeal is the first significant European adventure in Texas. Descended from minor nobility and an officer of Narváez's expedition, his position made him the leader of the survivors. All of them were more captives than guests of various groups of Karankawa, perhaps of other Indians. They were not always together, but met periodically when their "hosts" gathered to harvest the hip of the prickly pear blossoms or other food. Survival depended on cooperation, which included what amounted to "faith healing" and other services, plus their curiosity quotient. After wandering over much of central Texas and then New Mexico, they encountered a patrol of Spaniards who first mistook them for Indians because all evidence of Spanish dress had vanished after several years among the Indians. Once the survivors' identities were established, they were a great prize. They alone had viewed the mysteries of the north. And the marvelous stories they

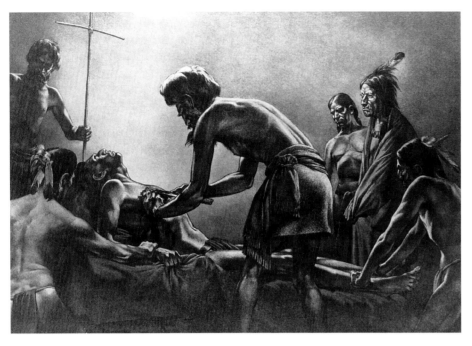

Cabeza de Vaca removing an arrow from the chest of an Indian, 1535. In 1542, Cabeza de Vaca first published La Relación y Comentarios, *the account of his eight-year journey from Florida across Texas into northern Mexico in which he described many of his experiences among the Indians. He made medical history with his account of the surgery, in which he used sutures made out of deer skin and a needle made of deer bone. El Paso artist Tom Lea commemorated the event in "The first Recorded Surgical Operation in North America." Copies of Lea's painting hang in medical schools throughout the nation.*

repeated about golden cities excited all who heard them. When Viceroy Mendoza decided to check on the truth about the gold, Cabeza de Vaca declined the opportunity to return but Estávanico did not. Remaining in safety could not compare to the importance of guiding the exploratory expedition or returning to where his ethnicity was not a negative factor among the Indians.

Estavánico served as guide for Fray Marcos de Niza, a clergyman who not only sought gold but also the opportunity to save the Indians' souls. Estavánico led the way, sending back messages to de Niza that lured him northward until they were within eyesight of a pueblo that glistened in the sun. Close enough, de Niza decided, for he could report that the famed Cíbola *appeared* to be golden, and such a report would afford him the opportunity to return as a proper missionary.

So the Viceroy launched a much more ambitious *entrata* in 1540 led by Francisco Vásquez de Coronado, then thirty years of age and the governor of Nueva Galicia. Coronado commanded a mixed group of adventurers, soldiers, priests, pacified Indians, and women. For two years Coronado explored New Mexico, Arizona, and the plains of Texas and Oklahoma and Kansas. His men discovered the Grand Canyon, the smaller but still spectacular Palo Duro Canyon in Texas, and thousands of buffalo that proved the area suitable for cattle raising, but no gold. Their

encounter with de Niza's Cíbola, which turned out to be an ordinary pueblo, taught them how to conquer one but did not yield the precious gold.

De Niza, who had accompanied Coronado that far, returned to Mexico in disgrace. Coronado then followed an Indian named El Turco by the Spaniards, who promised to lead them to Gran Quivira, the true cities of gold. They traversed the Llano Estacado—plains so like the sea that the Spaniards left stakes to mark the way back—before discovering El Turco's deception. El Turco was a captured Pawnee who used Spaniards as a way to get home. He paid with his life.

While Coronado sought gold in the southwest, Hernando de Soto wandered the southeastern portion of North America on the same quest. Starting in Florida, De Soto's expedition moved across Alabama, Mississippi, Arkansas, and after his death led by Moscoso, eastern Texas, but they found no more gold than had Coronado. These two simultaneous failures fixed Spanish policy in the north for as long as they claimed it: thereafter the value of the northern provinces was negative. They kept it as a political and cultural shock absorber against French and English activities in North America, but they refused to fund expensive developments there until rival empires threatened their claims.

Of the other Spanish *entratas* into Texas, that of Juan de Oñate in 1598 to 1601 must be mentioned. Oñate duplicated much of Coronado's route, verified his predecessor's conclusion about the absence of gold, and thus confirmed the soundness of Spanish policy regarding Texas. But Oñate did something more: at each stream crossing he left male and female cattle as an experiment to see if the animals would thrive, and, if they did, as a resource for any subsequent explorations or settlers. Thrive they did, and provided the nexus for the subsequent cattle-horse culture so associated with Texas in the future.

One more Spanish "visitor" came to Texas during the early years of Spanish control. She was María Jesús de Agreda, the Lady In Blue. Father Alonso de Benevides, a priest in New Mexico, reported that Indians from Texas asked for baptism because they had been told to do so by a Lady In Blue who mysteriously appeared among them, instructed them in Christianity, and, because she was female and lacked the authority to celebrate the sacraments, sent them to find priests to perform the ceremony. Later Benevides learned of María, who, though she never physically left Spain, became comatose, and when revived reported "visiting" strange peoples whose description identified them as Indians. Later, other Indians in Texas also testified to visits from the Lady In Blue whose "miracle of transportation" had brought their first hearing of Christianity.

THE FRENCH CHALLENGE

French activity in Texas late in the seventeenth century brought about a change in Spanish policy in the area. Spain remained reluctant to invest sums necessary to protect their northern provinces with soldiers or to subsidize the settlement of civilians who would represent real substance in their territorial claims, but two threats from the French forced them to provide such a presence, a warning even, that Texas belonged to Spain. This "presence" took the form of religious missions and small *presidios*, or minor garrisons of troops, dual representations of the church and the state in frontier Texas.

René Robert Cavelier, Sieur de la Salle provided the first threat to Spanish control of Texas. La Salle previously had covered himself and France in glory by leading the first expedition down the Mississippi River to the Gulf of Mexico, where he claimed all land drained by the continent's greatest river for his sovereign, Louis, for whom the territory was then named. This extraordinary claim included all the territory between the Appalachian and Rocky Mountains. It blocked the English on the Atlantic Coast and encroached on Spain's claims to the south and west. Neither nation paid attention to La Salle then, for mere claims did not threaten. But in 1684 La Salle came again, and this time he represented a hazard that the Spaniards took seriously.

La Salle received permission from the French government to return to the Gulf of Mexico to establish a colony at the mouth of the Mississippi River to anchor New France in the south as did Quebec and other settlements in the north. La Salle recruited his company badly, but perhaps unavoidably, since the effort promised more hardship than financial reward. So the company included several "gentlemen" who knew no work and had no desire to make its acquaintance, but who were full of arguments and objections. La Salle, solitary and reclusive, also quarreled with the naval commander of his ships. The entire company was at odds and remained so for the remainder of their unlucky adventure.

For whatever reason, La Salle overshot the Mississippi River by 400 miles, landing instead in Texas at Matagorda Bay far to the west. Poor navigation may have been to blame, but it is just as likely that La Salle did this deliberately to expand French claims westward. After all, other Frenchmen soon pushed their nation's claims eastward by founding not just New Orleans but also Biloxi, Mississippi, and Mobile, Alabama.

La Salle certainly knew that he had trespassed, for he moved inland to erect Fort St. Louis, the headquarters of his colony. Fort St. Louis was doomed from the first. The vessels that had brought the colonists departed without specific plans to return, and the company continued to argue among themselves and with La Salle. Game in the area was sparse, the Karankawa posed a threat, and topping all was the inevitability of Spanish intolerance of their presence. In the end, Spanish soldiers had nothing to do with the failure of the French colony, though they surely would have if they had found it. And they did try to find it. Alonso de León, governor of Coahuila, launched several expeditions to eliminate the French before finding the ruins of Fort St. Louis and a few French survivors. From them was learned the unhappy fate of the colonists.

La Salle explored central Texas for a time and is credited with discovering the stream later called the Brazos River. But the quarreling and obvious failure of the colony caused him to try to make contact with French settlements on the Mississippi River. The detail of men he selected to accompany him continued to argue, and somewhere northeast of the fort

Viceroy of New Spain, D. Bernardo de Gálvez. As Count of Gálvez in the mid-1780s, he took active steps to strengthen the defenses of the Interior Provinces, particularly those in Texas. From an illustration in "Gálvez. D. Bernardo de Gálvez, Count of Gálvez," in Early Texas Album, 1929, by C. E. Castañeda and Frederick C. Chabot.

COURTESY, ARCHIVES DIVISION - TEXAS STATE LIBRARY.

one of them killed another in a dispute over food. Realizing that La Salle would punish them, or at least report the murder if they reached the French settlements, they murdered him as well. Just where this event occurred has produced controversy, but the citizens of Navasota have erected a statue of La Salle that tips the scales, for tourists at least, that the deed was done in or near their community.

Some of La Salle's men continued to Illinois and their report on the plight of Fort St. Louis brought forth a French relief expedition that never found the lost Frenchmen. But de León did find them in 1689, or at least he found their remains. The fort was burned; books printed in French lay scattered around; and unburied corpses testified to the violent end of the French colony. de León also rescued, or captured, really, several survivors among the Indians, and from them learned that contrary to orders from La Salle—which could be expected from people who had never agreed with anything he said or did—they had admitted the Indians to their fort and unwittingly invited a massacre.

The end of La Salle and Fort St. Louis delayed the French problem but did not end the potential of additional threats to Spanish claims. So de León decided to erect a signpost to the French that would mark a line past which their presence would not be tolerated. With Father Damián Massanet, two other clergy, and sufficient soldiers to make his point, de León returned and founded the first Spanish mission in what was then defined as Texas. It was located 300 miles northeast of the failed French colony, in a Caddo village. De León and Massanet erected Mission San Francisco de los Tejas in three days and commissioned it to commence its dual role of bringing Christianity to the Caddo and a warning to the French. More about this mission will appear later; for now, suffice it to say that it failed in both functions and within a few years was abandoned. But since no more French came to Texas for more than two decades, the signpost worked better than did the saving of souls.

Seemingly insignificant events sometimes produce major consequences. Such was the case when a Spanish priest, frustrated that his own empire had discontinued missionary activities in Texas, wrote an unauthorized letter to the Governor of French Louisiana, Sieur de Cadillac, proposing that France and Spain pursue missionary activities jointly. Cadillac's own policy called for renewed efforts to expand French influence and trade with the Indians westward; in fact, efforts to that end already had begun. The French always had been interested in trade expansion and did not blanche from exchanging whiskey and guns for furs, horses, or other goods.

Cadillac selected Louis Juchereau de St. Denis from Quebec as his agent. St. Denis established a trading cache at Natchitoches and erected the first fort in that area. With his trading business functioning, St. Denis traveled across Texas in 1714 in search of Spanish settlements and reached the Río Grande before finding them, a century and a half after Spain had claimed the area and explored it. Military commander Diego Ramón more or less "arrested" St. Denis because it was illegal for him to be in Texas, but his detention was more official than uncomfortable. He was quartered in Ramón's home and enjoyed a status more like that of a guest than a prisoner.

In 1716 St. Denis returned to East Texas and western Louisiana in the company of several priests led by Antonio Margil de Jesús and Domingo Ramón and other military personnel to establish six missions, one of which was in Nacogdoches. The missions constituted a renewed reminder that Spain controlled the area; for the French they also represented an opening market for trade, illegal or not. With the French permanently operating in Natchitoches and the Spanish present and visible in Nacogdoches and even eastward in other missions, the Sabine River, located approximately half way between those now permanent points of occupation, became the unofficial boundary between Spaniards and Frenchmen.

The second attempt to locate missions in East Texas succeeded in the sense that they operated most of the time until all were closed by a new Spanish policy in 1773. None converted many Indians, most violated Spanish law by trading with the French and all experienced severe difficulties. In 1721 the Marqués de San Miguel de Aguayo visited the area and found the missions and their *presidio* barely

operational with buildings in disrepair, gardens and stock untended, even cannon lying on the ground and unusable. Supplies and strict orders provided a stimulant for the spirits of the priests, but as time passed the East Texas missions reverted to inefficiency.

THE MISSION-PRESIDIO SYSTEM

Spain never lacked for clergy willing to devote their lives, or to sacrifice those lives if necessary, to fulfill the Great Commission. De Niza, Massanet, Margil, and dozens of other

Above: El Paso Plaza and Church.

Below, left: Comanche Village, Women Dressing Robes and Drying Meat *by George Catlin (1786-1872). Catlin spent many years traveling in North and South America, preserving the culture of the indigenous peoples. He made hundreds of sketches and paintings and recorded the ways the Indians lived, worked, played, and worshiped. His works stimulated interest in Indian culture.*

priests prayed and schemed for the chance to carry the Gospel to the Indians of Texas and to the rest of America. In Texas, most of the time the force of their efforts ran into several immovable objects, among them isolation from sources of supply of material needs not produced on site and from the society of their own kind. And mission priests often did not get along well with the soldiers, whom the priests considered, with cause, lazy and poor examples of Christianity for the Indians. These factors, plus the difficulty or reluctance of primitive Indians to grasp such fundamental Christian concepts as the deity of Jesus Christ through Immaculate Conception and Death and Resurrection as symbolized by baptism left many missionaries unsatisfied with their work: the modern term "burn out" would not be inappropriate to characterize their malaise.

Once the Spanish adopted the mission-*presidio* system, which represented perfectly the church-state partnership of Catholicism and Spain's government in Europe and in the empire, it became the primary tool in their policy in Texas. Fundamentally, the Spanish wanted to maintain a society that was as homogeneous as possible, one that was unpolluted by other European population, political institutions, or religious concepts. They did not want to invest money or effort in such a place as Texas that promised so little profit, yet they did not want any other nation to occupied it. So, as a barrier to the French and a concession to the clergy, the mission-*presidio* system was established.

When hearing the word "mission," the mind's eye envisions physical structures such as Mission San José or Mission San Antonio de Valero, with walls, a chapel, a granary, and dwelling places for the priests and Indians. This is not inaccurate, but a more conceptual definition needs to be added: think of a "mission" in the same way it could be said that a diplomat has been sent on a mission to convey his government's policy to another government. This, then, defines a mission as a function, not a place, except that it is also the place where the function is performed. That function was to include several aspects: establish Spanish authority; Christianize as many Indians as possible; in the process of making them Christians, teach the Indians work- and wealth-producing skills that will make the mission as self-supporting as possible; and if the teaching is successful and the area in which the mission is located becomes productive, to use this to attract a civilian population that will develop the area to the profit and glory of the empire.

As far as Texas was concerned, this policy evolved between 1690—when the primary assignment for San Francisco de los Tejas in East Texas was to warn the French to stay away—and the middle of the next century with the founding of the San Sabá mission for the Apaches in southwestern Texas.

The stories of San Francisco de los Tejas, San Antonio de Valero, and the San Sabá mission explain why historian Odie Faulk called the entire period of Spanish activity in Texas a "successful failure." None of the missions fulfilled the policy that produced them.

San Francisco de los Tejas served the Caddo in eastern Texas. The Caddo lived where food abounded in forests, streams, and gardens; by Texas standards, they were wealthy in food, shelter, and peace, since they did not fight often with other Indians. When the priests arrived, hundreds came to watch the dedication of the mission, for it was, after all, a strange, new, and curious thing to them. The colorful vestments of the clergy, the bells and the incense, the chanting of the Latin—or the vernacular Spanish—spoken by the priests and soldiers, captured their attention. But not for long. While some professed Christianity, sincerely or not, most did not; the concepts were so alien and required so much instruction and acceptance on faith that most simply could not make the necessary leap.

And there was trouble. The soldiers wanted the Indians to do their work and the priests wanted them to learn about their new religion, each jealous of the time the Indians spent with the other. Soldiers quarreled with priests, priests with Indians who refused to be confined in the mission, and Indians with soldiers who wanted them to do unaccustomed labor and who sometimes violated their homes. The Spaniards unwittingly brought diseases and illnesses unknown before, causing sickness and death. Eventually, the majority of the

Indians would not go near the mission, the missionaries grew despondent, and after 1692 there was no San Francisco de los Tejas.

San Antonio de Valero fared better. Founded in 1718 and named in honor of the saint on whose feast day the Spanish first arrived at the river where the mission eventually was founded, this mission enjoyed several advantages: the sponsorship of the Marqués de Valero, who ensured that his namesake mission received what it needed; a mild climate that favored both agriculture and stock raising; closer proximity to the sources of supply, so when provisions arrived all that was needed was obtained before the leavings traveled on to the frontier missions; and the fact that their Coahuiltecan Indians, among the poorer of Texas Indians, came to depend on the mission for victuals to a degree unimaginable to the Caddo.

In 1721, de Valero built a fort, San Antonio de Béjar, across the river from the mission, and its protection drew civilian settlers to the area who made beginnings on a real town. Frontier conditions kept the population small as long as Spain controlled Texas, but forevermore San Antonio, the name for the town drawn from both mission and *presidio,* existed. When the East Texas missions were closed in 1773, several were relocated in San Antonio, so eventually five missions operated there, none more than a few miles apart, each supporting the other by their presence, all attracting more civilian settlers as the area assumed a developed atmosphere.

A major stimulus to that atmosphere occurred in 1731 when the government relocated several families from the Canary Islands to San Antonio. This experiment in government-planned development did not prosper but neither did it fail completely. The Canary Islanders anticipated aristocratic status and leisure and found instead that much work needed to be done to develop the area. In their disappointment, many did not provide the labor required to produce the leisure. But the town endured and eventually became the political and economic nerve center of Texas, such as it was.

The San Sabá experience produced a sadder conclusion. By 1730, virtually every Indian group in eastern or southern Texas had one or more missions established to serve them except the Apaches. Between Apaches and Spaniards, relations were not good; attacks and reprisals were common. Then, after a severe attack on a Lipan village by Bustillo y Cevallos, the Apaches asked for a mission and they knew just where they wanted it located. Honoring the Apaches' wishes, the San Sabá mission was located many miles from the soldiers in San Antonio and in Comanche country. Colonel Diego Ortiz de Parilla was forced by the priests to build his *presidio* well away from the mission, so when the attacks came, neither mission nor fort could help the other, and both were felled by Indians who did not want them.

In the 1760s, the consequences of a war in Europe reached thousands of miles westward and changed Spain's policy in Texas once more. Spaniards had sought gold in Texas, but finding none, were content to allow the area to lie fallow so long as no other nation manifested an interest there When another nation did so, they established missions and *presidios* as evidence of claim. Eventually they attempted to use church-state institutions to convert the Indians into Christians and workers; but after more than two hundred years, Texas was nearer the natural state the Spaniards had first encountered in the 1520s than the developed and productive province they desired. With the end of the French menace as a result of a European war, many were ready to give Texas back to the Indians.

Interior of Longhorn Cavern State Park, northwest of Austin near the LBJ Ranch. Its walls could tell of a variety of animals involved in the history of the cave, some who have left fossil remains; other, large beasts, the remains of the prey they devoured there. Human artifacts suggest man used the cavern to some extent. In more recent history, Confederates manufactured gunpowder there, using it as a stronghold, and desperadoes are said to have used it as a hideout. In this century, its use has included a dance hall, nightclub, and restaurant, and currently, a tourist site.

PHOTO BY J. GRIFFIS SMITH.
COURTESY, TEXAS DEPARTMENT OF TRANSPORTATION.

THE NEW REGULATION, NACOGDOCHES AND THE RÍO GRANDE SETTLEMENTS, FILIBUSTERS

THE NEW REGULATION OF THE *PRESIDIOS*

At the beginning of a class, the scribbled notes from previous lessons have been erased from the blackboard; it is therefore "free" of any previous writing or ideas. That is the circumstance of Texas when Spaniards first encountered it in 1519, but such was no longer the case in 1763 when they changed policy toward the area for the final time. At first examination, this might not appear to be so. Several missions and *presidios* had been established and most survived; a few, especially those closest to Mexico, thrived. In San Antonio and in eastern Texas near Nacogdoches, communities of civilian settlers lived and in some cases prospered, and especially along the Río Grande where large riparian grants had been awarded in the 1740s the beginnings of significant economic development had begun. But on the whole, Spain's efforts remained what historian Odie Faulk termed a "successful failure," hardly removed from the wilderness state in which the Spaniards had found it two and a half centuries previously.

Spain's enterprises in Texas could be called a success in land claims, in defense of the area from French intrusion, and in the institutions of Christianity, law, and learning they had introduced to the part of the Indian population who would listen. But those enterprises could be called a failure as well, for after Spaniards did not discover the precious gold, they committed too few resources to develop the area adequately in other ways. Also, until the 1740s every policy regarding Texas had been imposed on the area's vacant blackboard without regard for its environment, human or natural. Spaniards attempted to force-feed the indigenous human population with religious, military, and governmental concepts that their culture was unable to accommodate, and expected economic results that the land could not provide. Only when government and church got out of the way could individuals begin the activities that eventually proved successful along the Río Grande and in Nacogdoches. This is not stated as a modern political tenet: it is a comparison with what the neglectful English allowed to occur at the same time on the East Coast of North America. Because of England's preoccupation with problems at home, the English government could not micromanage their colonies. The colonists therefore remained free to develop as the environment permitted and the market—with some governmental assistance, such as the tobacco monopoly—required.

Let us fill in the details of the final Spanish policy toward Texas and see how individual development, with government toleration, had begun to work there before Spain's control of the area ended in 1821. The story begins in Europe. France and England fought a series of wars from the end of the seventeenth century until the conclusion of the eighteenth century. The most significant of these wars is known in American history as the French and Indian War, in Europe as the Seven Years' War, and sometimes in England as the Great War for Empire, for such was its consequence. It might just as well be called the First World War because it began in North America, then extended to the high seas and to Europe or wherever Frenchmen and Englishmen encountered one another. And in this war Spain sided with England, the winner, and so enjoyed the spoils.

The French and Indian War erupted in North America in 1754 over control of the Ohio Country, the area south of the Great Lakes and west of Virginia. The clash was inevitable because of the westward push of English-based traders into interior areas claimed by France. Things went badly at first for their colonists, so England weighed in with soldiers from Europe and the conflict spread. The tide turned, and with the fall of Quebec to the English, negotiations began in Paris to

Mid-eighteenth century Spanish document registering brands of private ranchers in the San Antonio River Valley. The branding of livestock, along with other charro practices, was brought from Spain to the Americas by the conquistadors.

end the war. The Peace of Paris, 1763, simply eliminated France colonialism from North America. Thereafter, English claims extended westward to the Mississippi River where they joined those of Spain that now extended eastward without dispute from France.

The absence of France as a rival in Texas caused Spanish officials to rethink their policy toward Texas. Since they had been convinced that gold could not be found there, the founding of missions and *presidios* had occurred only in direct response to French penetration. With the French gone, Spaniards wondered about the necessity to continue the operation of these institutional outposts, especially since their new neighbors, the English, were so far away. After all, the English had required over a century and a half to move as far as the Ohio Country, so no one could imagine that within only fifty years they would be knocking at the door of Texas. But Spain did not rush to a new policy. Instead, The Marqués de Rubí received a commission to investigate Spain's northern provinces and make recommendations based on what he found.

De Rubí, with a cartographer, visited Spanish outposts from eastern Louisiana to California to determine the condition of the missions, *presidios*, and villas. Few, if any, could be called a success when measured by the expectations of the government and the church that had founded them. The missions were in disrepair, had recorded few baptisms, and had not been able to convince many Indians to live within the compounds or accept Spanish cultural and economic principles. Those nearest Mexico, such as San Antonio de Valero, compared better than those on the true frontier, but none fulfilled the hopes of its founders.

Presidios were no better. Corrupt officers stole pay and provisions when they were available—which was not often—from their soldiers, who appeared lazy and demoralized. None, found De Rubí, could have defended the missions against hostile Indians or foreign invaders. Further, the Indians were not a real threat except in the west, for many had died from European-introduced diseases or had chosen to move rather than deal with the missionaries or the soldiers. And, of course,

French claims had been eliminated and the English were far away.

De Rubí's report recommended an entirely different approach to Texas. First, he said, close the frontier missions—especially pertinent to our story those located in East Texas—and relocate some of them to San Antonio, which would move from the status of being the hub of the wheel of missions to one of a "frontier" outpost. This would save money spent without profit for church or state on the unproductive missions and *presidios* that would be recalled.

Second, De Rubí advised that civilian settlers who had established farms and ranches near the East Texas missions be required to relocate, to eliminate the necessity of protecting them or providing other services. Third, he recommended making active war on the westerns Indians, especially the Apaches and Comanches, whose raids into Mexico itself cost lives and property. His final recommendation was construction of a line of *presidios* (forts) from the Río Grande to Baja and defense of that line against any penetration by Indians or other Europeans.

NACOGDOCHES AND THE RÍO GRANDE SETTLEMENTS

De Rubí's recommendations were proclaimed in the New Regulation of the Presidios in 1772, and to Governor de Ripperdá fell the duty of enforcement. Removing the missions and the presidios proved easy enough; most were willing to abandon the misery and isolation of their far-flung corner of the Spanish empire. But the civilian settlers who lived in the same area were another story. They did not want to desert homes, fields, and herds established by their individual enterprise. De Ripperdá sympathized with them but followed orders, nonetheless. Soldiers provided the incentive that overcame the reluctance of those who would not leave voluntarily. Some escaped into the wild to return later, but approximately 500 unhappy settlers packed up and trudged southwest to San Antonio.

Antonio Gil Y'Barbo, a rancher-trader who headquartered on the Sabine River southeast of Nacogdoches, and Vital Flores emerged as leaders of these displaced migrants. As soon as they reached San Antonio, petitions were made to be allowed to return toward, if not to, East Texas, because they claimed that they found the good lands occupied and that the territory required different skills and knowledge from those developed in East Texas. Fundamentally, they just wanted to go home.

Ripperdá endorsed their petition, and aided them in preparing for their return. The settlers were warned to remain law abiding and to travel no farther than within 100 leagues of Natchitoches, Louisiana. Y'Barbo led them back to the west bank of the Trinity River and there they founded the community of Bucareli. The settlement lasted but four years, during which they endured floods and sufficient difficulties with Comanche raids to force them to move farther eastward despite the governor's orders. In the spring of 1779, Y'Barbo led the majority of Bucareli's residents to the site of the mission that had served the Nacogdoche Indians of the Caddo Confederacy, and there he founded the villa, or town, of Nacogdoches. Later that summer his actions received approval from authorities in Mexico, as well as their official sanctioning of the town, the first in East Texas.

Y'Barbo's resemblance to Moses as the leader of migrants ended at this point, for he was allowed to enter their "promised land." Armed with natural leadership now reinforced by his official recognition as leader of the militia as well as civic government, he supervised the laying out of the town around central plazas for the church and civil government. On the northeast corner of Plaza Principal he erected a Stone House, in time called the Stone Fort, that served as headquarters for both public and private business. Because official business was conducted there, the Stone House assumed a public character which it retained until it was razed in 1902. Although it was always privately owned, it remained the community's gathering place for such events as several declarations of independence from Spain, meetings of the Committee of Public Safety during the Texas Revolution, and the mustering area for soldiers going away to Civil War.

Y'Barbo assigned lands, supervised construction, lent tools and advice to farmers and tradesmen—and developed an illicit trade with Louisiana that eventually caused his exile to San Antonio. But while he remained in Nacogdoches he provided the kind of proprietary leadership delivered on a grander scale later for Anglo settlers by Stephen F. Austin.

Even before Y'Barbo founded Nacogdoches, José de Escandón had begun the development of the lower Río Grande valley. In 1746 he received a commission from the viceroy to recruit settlers for that area. Escandón awarded large riparian grants, each with guaranteed access to the river as an artery of import-export. Each grant extended from the river front into the wilderness about as far as the awardee, called the *patrón*, had the power to enforce. These land units were known as *mercedes*, for they had been given by "the king's mercy," and were the beginnings of many of the towns and cities along both sides of the Río Grande that remain today. In time, the house of the *patrón* in time became the seat of government, his chapel the town's church, and his storehouses and the dwellings for his workers the community's business enterprises and residences, all laid out around a plaza in the Spanish fashion.

Because the land was too arid for row-crop agriculture, at least without irrigation, the *patrones* developed a cattle-horse economy known as *charro* culture. They introduced the Spanish methods of stock raising, which utilized the open range and horses to work the

The Stone Fort, located on the principal road from the United States, El Camino Real. The structure remained on the Nacogdoches downtown square from 1779 until 1902. The Spaniard Antonio Gil Y'Barbo built the "stone house" when he and former settlers returned to East Texas and the site of an early East Texas mission. He laid out the town, assigned land, supervised construction, and gave his followers a strict code of conduct. Within a decade, Y'Barbo was banished by Spanish authorities for smuggling, but the structure continued in a quasi-official capacity, variously housing everything from land office, post office, Mexican military quarters, and saloons. Filibusters plotted and proclaimed within its walls and from its porches, and Committees of Vigilance and Safety met to help organize the Texas Revolution. In 1936 a replica, now the Stone Fort Museum, was constructed on the campus of Stephen F. Austin State University.

cattle. In time, many of their methods, some modified by the eastern, closed-range concept, spread throughout the western portion of the United States and Canada.

Y'Barbo's Nacogdoches and Escandón's Río Grande grants represent permanent penetrations and development of portions of Texas during and after the failure of government-church planned attempts. This is not to say that government planning in general was wrong, but it is obvious that the specific plan of mission and *presidio* did not work in Texas as it had elsewhere. Perhaps there are many reasons why this was so, but fundamentally it was because they required results that the environment and the indigenous population could not produce. When the planners got out of the way and let the people do what geography tolerated, success followed.

FILIBUSTERS

When Spain and England became neighbors at the Mississippi River in 1763, Spain hoped that the wilderness between their developments in Texas and the English colonies located on the Atlantic Coast would remain a cultural, military, and political shock absorber indefinitely. It lasted only until the end of the eighteenth century, when the "filibusters" began to steal into Texas.

"Filibusters" were products of the mercantile competition in which the modern European states engaged. A good definition would be this: a filibuster is one who does something for private gain, yet his actions yield a reward for his government as well, whether intended or not. Sir Francis Drake is a good example. Drake earned his "Sir" by helping to destroy Spanish shipping, and did so because of the immense profits that came from captured prizes. But his efforts also aided England in its competition with Spain. Such is the case with Philip Nolan, Augustus Magee, James Long, and many other American frontiersman who came to Texas for personal gain and in the process showed the way for thousands of others who eventually followed.

Filibustering began in southeast Missouri, and was known as the Spanish Conspiracy. When the French-occupied land to the west of the Mississippi River was transferred to Spain, the French did not evaporate: they still had to be governed. Spanish policy was to isolate the French, keeping them from commercial activities in Texas. At the same time, policy required the economic development of the area for the benefit of Spain. Since they would no longer admit French settlers and did not want to send Spaniards to the area, the first

principle canceled the second. Francisco Bouligny, governor of Upper Louisiana, and Bernardo de Gálvez, governor of Lower Louisiana, entered a gentle conspiracy: they would make Spaniards out of the Americans they could lure across the Mississippi River with inexpensive land. In return, the Americans agreed to become Spanish subjects and to be or become Roman Catholics. Henry IV said, "Paris is well worth a mass." Many Americans were prepared to judge a league or more of land the same.

To introduce these Americans-become-Spaniards to the land across the river, the empresarial system was established. Colonel William Morgan of New Jersey was the first empresario. With Bouligny's permission and assistance, he recruited Irish settlers—already Catholic—to establish New Madrid in what later would be called Missouri's bootheel. They were but the first, and soon the best known of them, Moses Austin, arrived and established a major lead works at Mine A Burton. Austin expanded into other businesses and founded Potosí. For a time it appeared that this "conspiracy" was a great success for Spain. The settlers behaved themselves with regard to citizenship and religious regulations, and also made a good start on economic development.

On the other side of the river the pressure for westward expansion built up like steam in a boiler, and soon illegal immigrants found their way across. The U.S. Army's commander on the southwestern frontier, James Wilkinson, played a significant role in the development of tension there. Long recognized as a double agent, he evidently profited by assisting Americans to cross into Spanish territory illegally while also receiving money from Spain to stop the flow. Border tensions were good for Wilkinson's profits.

The first provider of that tension was mustanger Philip Nolan, whose name if not his life's story was borrowed by Everett Allen Hale for his short story "The Man Without A Country." Nolan presented a plan to travel to Texas in the 1790s to round up wild horses, known as mustangs, for sale in New Orleans to the Baron de Carondelet, then governor of Louisiana, and received permission to do so.

Nolan also had Wilkinson's approval, and his first trips were successful. However, Nolan's continued association with Wilkinson and other United States government officials on his return trips to the United States aroused the suspicions of Texas Governor Juan Bautista de Elguézabal, who ordered Nolan's arrest. In a fight with Spanish soldiers near the modern city of Waco, Nolan was killed and his men were captured. Survivors spent

Above: John Melish's United States of America *illustrates the extent of the emerging nation when the map was printed in 1818.*

COURTESY, CARTOGRAPHIC COLLECTIONS OF MRS. JENKINS GARRETT, FORT WORTH; HOUSED AT THE SPECIAL COLLECTIONS DIVISION, THE UNIVERSITY OF TEXAS AT ARLINGTON LIBRARIES, ARLINGTON, TEXAS.

Below: Corrida de la Sandía, San Antonio *aka* Día de San Juan, *1848 genre painting by Jean Louis Theodore Gentilz. The competitive watermelon race was a kind of "basketball on horseback" in which riders sought to carry the melon over a designated finish line.*

COURTESY, THE TORCH COLLECTION, HOUSTON, TEXAS

Itinerant eighteenth century French fur trappers operated in southeast Texas, especially valuing the mink, shown here, and beaver found in the region. According to historians Judith Walker Linsley and Ellen Walker Rienstra, their activities are recorded in American Fur Company documents, with Beaumont becoming the most important fur center west of Calcasieu Parish in Louisiana.

PHOTO BY CONNIE THOMPSON.

their first imprisonment in the Stone House in Nacogdoches, then were transferred to Mexico for trial and punishment.

As T. R. Fehrenbach tells their story, one in seven of Nolan's men were to be executed and the rest were to spend the rest of their lives at hard labor. Since only nine remained, one would be the scapegoat, and they determined the identify of this unlucky person by rolling dice. Ephraim Blackburn threw the "snake eyes," or its equivalent. Then emerged the true survivor, Peter Ellis Bean. Mexican republican revolutionaries had broken successively like waves on the wall of Spanish imperialism during the first two decades of the nineteenth century. Bean convinced Spanish authorities to release him for service in the suppression of these republican revolutionaries, then defected, and finally convinced his new friends to send him to New Orleans as a recruiter of men and money for their cause. He sent the help, but did not return, at least not at once. Later he held military rank in the Mexican army following the independence of Mexico from Spain in 1821.

The next episode of border tension came from the curious activities of Aaron Burr, a founder of the Democratic Republican Party in the United States and vice president during the first administration of Thomas Jefferson. At odds with Jefferson over the confused nature of the election of 1800, which could have made Burr president but did not, and rejected by voters for the governorship of New York because of the political opposition of Alexander Hamilton, Burr was either a villain or a victim of history. Concerning Texas, if he thought of it at all, there is speculation and uncertainty. What is known is that he conspired with Wilkinson, that he hired men who could accurately be called mercenaries, and that he stockpiled the kinds of supplies such men would need for conquest.

Before an overt act developed, Wilkinson accused Burr of a conspiracy against the United States, claiming that Burr wanted to detach the Old Southwest—Mississippi, Alabama, and Tennessee—for a personal empire. Since many thought that Burr had tried to steal the Untied States presidency from Jefferson, and that he sought election to

the governorship of New York only as a preliminary to the secession of the northern states into a separate government for Burr to serve as president, the prospect of a personal empire in the southwest sounded reasonable. Burr denied it. He also escaped conviction as a result of the careful definition of treason applied by Chief Justice John Marshall during his trial in Virginia. But Spaniards feared that Burr's goal lay west of the river, not east of it, and that others might pursue it.

Meanwhile, Wilkinson kept the border tense with other activities. Just after William Clark and Meriwether Lewis completed their exploration of the upper Louisiana Purchase, Wilkinson dispatched Zebulon Pike along the Arkansas River into Colorado to examine the lower purchase area. Pike sighted the peak that bears his name before turning south into Spanish territory. He did not resist Spanish military authority when he encountered it in New Mexico, and the Spanish, who did not want a fight either, charitably allowed that Pike had become "lost" instead of invading their land. Pike and his men were escorted as guests, not captives, southward into Mexico and then up El Camino Real through San Antonio and Nacogdoches en route to the United States.

Two significant consequences came from Pike's adventure. First, he observed that Spain appeared strong but in reality was not, with the inference that southwestern lands could be taken by Americans more easily than previously suspected, and, second, that some of the land was not worth taking. He called it a "great desert," and his descriptions of the land's lack of water and other difficulties affected American westward immigration thereafter.

Comes now the more significant problem produced by Augustus Magee and Bernardo Gutiérrez de Lara. Magee's story begins in 1806, when Wilkinson traveled to Natchitoches and General Simón Hererra to Nacogdoches, approximately ninety miles apart, to conduct negotiations on the growing tension between their governments over the imprecise border. It must be noted that neither represented their governments politically, and that the result of their negotiation was a military solution that could have been abrogated by either government at any time.

Wilkinson and Herrera agreed to create a Neutral Ground between the Arroyo Hondo on the east and the Sabine River on the west, a distance of approximately fifty miles. Both pledged to keep military personnel out of the Neutral Ground to prevent the possibility of patrols even encountering one another, much less finding a reason for a fight. The Neutral Ground then attracted a population of the sort who relished the absence of any governmental authority, who began to pillage on both sides of their sanctuary and then beat a retreat to safety when pursued. To deal with this problem, Lieutenant Augustus Magee, with the permission of the Spanish, policed the area effectively, and in the process made the acquaintance of many of the mercenaries and adventurers who later populated his Republican Army of the North.

Several things evidently turned Magee into a filibuster. One explanation was his failure to win the promotion he felt should have resulted from his good work in the Neutral Zone. Another explanation was that he wanted to acquire wealth quickly from those who possessed it in abundance in New Spain. And a third is that he acted as an agent of the United States to expand its territory at Spanish expense and did so as a civilian so that his government could deny culpability. Maybe all three, or even additional explanations, apply.

Magee met Gutiérrez, a Spanish republican in exile in Louisiana following the failed revolt of Father Hidalgo in 1810, through William Shaler, a U.S. government official in New Orleans. Gutiérrez and Magee then formed a partnership to seize Texas from Spain. Magee recruited the Republican Army of the North among acquaintances from the Neutral Ground and other adventurers, and had little trouble doing so at wages of $40 per month (a private in the U.S. Army then drew $11 per month), plus promises of additional riches in land and other rewards later. Gutiérrez, meanwhile, prepared the constitution for the republican government they would establish. At this point, Hispanic and Anglo were to be equal in citizenship under their republic.

The expedition crossed the Sabine River in the summer of 1812, already too powerful for

the Spanish soldiers in Texas to combat, and their numbers increased as they went. They stopped in Nacogdoches to declare the area independent of Spain, and while there the type was set by A. Mower, a printer from Pennsylvania, for the *Gaceta de Tejas* (*Texas Gazette*), since credited with being the first newspaper published in Texas.

Magee led his army southwest to La Bahía, where he encountered military resistance from forces led by Manuel María de Salcedo from whom he captured sufficient stores to support the expedition for months, even through a return engagement when a larger Spanish army tried unsuccessfully to recapture their *presidio*. During the delay at La Bahía, Magee perished. Gutiérrez claimed that he committed suicide, a not altogether improbable explanation, for he had not demonstrated great emotional stability by abandoning his career in the United States Army and becoming involved in the invasion. Others, however, claimed that Magee was killed with the knowledge and/or complicity of Gutiérrez, who planned to assume solitary control of their adventure.

It can be agreed upon in any case that after Magee's death, the promised equality for Anglos and Hispanics tilted toward the latter, and that Magee's passing caused some of the less mercenary among his army to return to the United States. Samuel Kemper replaced

Jane Herbert Wilkinson Long (1798-1880) was called "The Mother of Texas" even during her lifetime. Jane Long was the wife of filibuster Dr. James Long. He was captured at San Antonio and imprisoned September 1821 while on a month-long trip, and went to Mexico City to plead his case. When he failed to return to their camp on Galveston Bay, Fort las Casas on Bolivar Peninsula, Jane insisted on waiting for him there for what proved to be a harsh winter instead of leaving when others left. She spent the winter of 1821-22 virtually alone there with her toddler daughter, Ann, and her young black servant Kian. On December 21, 1821, she gave birth to her third daughter, Mary James. Near starvation, she gave up her vigil early in 1822, and moved to Cedar Bayou, east of what would become the city of Houston, where she lived with a Smith family. It was mid-summer before she learned that James had been shot by a guard in Mexico City. She was awarded a league of land in Fort Bend County and a labor in Waller County by Stephen F. Austin. Jane Long operated a popular boarding house in Richmond and developed a plantation near there, acquiring 2,000 acres of land and nineteen slaves by 1861 by trading land and raising cattle and cotton.

COURTESY, ARCHIVES DIVISION - TEXAS STATE LIBRARY.

Marriage Procession, Mission San Juan Capistrano (n.d.) by Louise Fretéllière. Her father had come to Texas with French Count Henri Castro in 1843. The Spanish brought Christianity to Texas in the 16th century, and their beautiful missions still dot the state.
COURTESY, THE TORCH COLLECTION, HOUSTON, TEXAS.

Franciscan friar outside the sacristy door of Mission San José y San Miguel de Aguayo, founded in 1720. Church construction began in 1768 on the "Queen of the Missions."
COURTESY, TEXAS DEPARTMENT OF TRANSPORTATION.

Magee, and in time Henry Perry replaced Kemper, and each turn of the wheel left a harder core of frontier fighters to carry on. In time, Gutiérrez was replaced by José Álvarez de Toledo, so that neither principal of the original partnership remained at the end.

The expedition moved on to San Antonio, captured that place, and Perry, now with approximately 3000 men, repulsed an army led by General Ignacio Elizondo sent to capture him. Then came north a far more formidable force led by General Joaquín de Arredondo, who had in his command a junior officer named Antonio López de Santa Anna de Lebrón who learned from his chief how to deal with *piratas*. In August 1813, Perry and Arredondo clashed in the Battle of the Medina. Arredondo killed all of the invaders he could in battle, captured the rest for later execution, and temporarily ended the threat

Left: Comanche Feats of Horsemanship, *a painting by George Catlin. The horse dramatically changed Indian life, that of the Comanches more than any other tribe. They became lords of the Plains, and by the mid-eighteenth century were among the greatest horsemen who ever lived.*

COURTESY, NATIONAL MUSEUM OF AMERICAN ART, SMITHSONIAN INSTITUTION, GIFT OF MRS. JOSEPH HARRISON, JR., AND SOUTHWESTERN WRITERS COLLECTION, SAN MARCOS, TEXAS.

Below: Mission San José with riders. This mission features the famous rose window by Spanish sculptor Pedro Huízar.

COURTESY, TEXAS DEPARTMENT OF TRANSPORTATION.

to Spanish authority in Texas.

Finally, Dr. James Long repeated the process, mistakes and all, in 1819 and 1820. Again, the border story was affected by events far away from the territory itself. The Peace of Paris, 1763, had awarded French territory west of the Mississippi River to Spain, but Napoleon Bonaparte made them give it back to France in 1797 while he dominated much of Europe. Then, in 1803, he sold the Louisiana territory to the United States. Its southern and eastern boundaries were fixed by the waters of the Gulf of Mexico and the Mississippi River, but no one knew exactly the western border of the transfer. In 1819, Secretary of State John Quincy Adams, a New England Yankee who cared little for the west and not at all for Texas, agreed to a treaty with Spain establishing the border at the Sabine River to its junction with the nearest longitude, thence north to the Red River and along that

1830 image of the short-lived 1818 French colony Champ D'Asile in Liberty County, by lithographer C. Mott, based on the work of Louis Ambrose Garnerey.

stream to the 100th meridian, then north to the Arkansas and following its course to the continental divide of the Rocky Mountains. Worse, said Southerners, Adams agreed that the Untied States henceforth foreswore claims west of that line for any reason.

An examination of a map of the area shows why Southerners were chagrined. Adams' agreement cut them off at the knees; it stopped the expansion of Southern culture at the western boundary of Louisiana, but Northern culture had a great deal of room for growth. Of course, slavery was what caused the Southerners' concern.

Protest raged throughout the South, but in Natchez, Mississippi, one such meeting produced Dr. James Long, who agreed to lead Southerners into Texas despite the treaty or the objection of United States or Spanish governments. He arrived in Nacogdoches with eighty men in June 1819, and once more proclaimed Texas free of Spain. He traveled on to

Galveston to seek the assistance of Jean Lafitte and the approximately 1,000 real pirates who used the island as a haven, but had no luck.

Long returned to Mississippi for more men and supplies, then returned to Texas with his young wife, Jane. Jane and her servant Kian lived in a fort that Long and his men constructed on Bolívar Peninsula. Leaving his wife and some of his supporters, Long moved on to Goliad, captured it, and then was himself captured by a larger force. Long was taken to Mexico City, where his life ended. Authorities regarded his death as an inevitable consequence of his status as a pirate, but Mrs. Long thought it murder. Before returning to Mississippi, she tried unsuccessfully to have her husband's executioners prosecuted. With the arrival of other Anglos in Texas, Mrs. Long returned and made her final home in Richmond. She is sometimes called the Mother of Texas because of her ordeal in facing a winter without male assistance in the fort on Bolívar Peninsula when Long's men

departed after learning of his death. She could have gone with them, but chose to remain to urge the prosecution of her husband's killers. Perhaps her title is deserved, and in any event, since Stephen F. Austin, who unquestionably may be called the Father of Texas, died a bachelor, it is necessary to look elsewhere for a Mother. Joe Frantz observed that if Mrs. Long is so called, then Kian should be the Black Mother of Texas, because she endured as much hardship with less say in the matter.

In addition to the filibusters who led expeditions that worried Spanish officials and made headlines in the United States, an anonymous but larger number of individuals, singly or in small groups, crossed the Mississippi River while it marked the border between Spain's and England's claims in the New World. They forded the Sabine River when it served as the frontier between Spain and the United States. These really did the damage to Spain.

As stories of Nolan, Magee, and Long circulated in the United States—particularly in the west where the itch to explore and conquer was most likely to strike, where economic consequences of the Panic of 1819 left closed banks and worthless currency circulating,

where land sold for more than $1 per acre and not on credit, and above all, where the horizon would be seen—Americans were ready to go. Nolan, Magee, and Long led the way; and, although all three died in the attempt to gain wealth or fame by appropriating horses or seizing land that seemed to be ripe for the taking, their fates did not deter others.

Coming as individuals or in small groups, these anonymous filibusters moved into Texas unobserved. Some continued to drift while others found streams with good water and good land and began to build houses and establish ferries and produce their living and a little extra for trade. Spain did not have enough soldiers to police the border in order to stop them. The pressure was about to burst the boiler in a flood of American immigration into Texas, overwhelming nature, Indians, governments—anything that stood in the way. But by this time Spain no longer stood in the way. In 1821, the movement for Mexican nationalism completed a two-decade struggle, ending in the creation of the first independent government for Mexico and Texas. So, during the 1820s, westering Americans dealt with a new regime and a new policy that at first welcomed them, then regretted ever having extended the hospitality.

Market Plaza (detail), *genre scene of San Antonio's Military Plaza painted by artist Robert Jenkins Onderdonk circa 1880. San Fernando Cathedral forms the backdrop for this vivid depiction of al fresco diners, cowboys, women and children, charros, and ox wagons. Signage reveals the name "Frank Nagel – " surmounted on a dry goods store, with "DRY GOODS – " painted on the wall."*

COURTESY, THE TORCH COLLECTION, HOUSTON, TEXAS.

EMPRESARIOS, COLONIAL LIFE, CLASH OF CULTURES, AND REVOLUTION

EMPRESARIOS

Prior to the 1820s, all Anglos who entered Texas did so illegally. In later years when the pejorative term "wetback" entered the vernacular of Texans, some enjoyed remembering that the first backs got wet in the Sabine and Red Rivers, not the Río Grande. As we have seen, such well-known filibusters as Philip Nolan, Augustus Magee, and James Long were bellwethers of more numerous and more anonymous Anglos who quietly crossed the rivers and moved into Texas unwanted, uninvited, and unwelcomed. Hardly had the Long episode resolved itself with his capture and death under Spanish authority before the Mexican government, established in 1821, legitimized the migration of Anglos to Texas by granting Moses Austin empresarial rights in their northern province.

Austin's story began in Connecticut, where he was born. Later he moved to Philadelphia and entered a business partnership with his brother. Business ventures led him to Virginia and eventually west of the Mississippi River to Missouri while the territory yet belonged to Spain. Moses Austin followed the mineral frontier, not the normal "pattern" of westering documented by Frederick Jackson Turner. Turner observed that fur trappers led the way west, followed by pioneer farmers. When equipped farmers moved in, the pioneer farmers moved on, and in time the urban frontiersmen—professionals such as lawyers, doctors, clergy, shopkeepers, and educators—joined the equipped farmers, with the entire procession moving ever to the west. In contrast, mineral frontiersmen moved in any direction and at any time in pursuit of the ores that attracted them, out of Turner's order and on the make for the main strike.

Austin experienced success in Missouri. He founded towns, exploited lead mines, helped establish banks and other businesses, and weathered political changes while Missouri passed from the control of Spain to France to the United States. As a subject of the Spanish Crown when Missouri was surrendered, Austin, like all legal residents of the area, retained the privilege of petitioning for admission to other territory controlled by Spain. Probably Austin never thought about doing so until the hard times of the Panic of 1819 drained his wealth.

Austin's son, Stephen Fuller Austin, also seems to have given no thought to leaving Missouri before the economic troubles arrived. Educated at Transylvania University in Kentucky, he had returned to Missouri and worked with his father in the family's various businesses. In time the economic crisis drove both to Texas, the father to his death and the son to his destiny as the Father of Texas.

His wealth gone and in debt, Moses Austin determined to start anew in Texas by duplicating the empresarial venture that William Morgan had begun in New Madrid and others later had pursued elsewhere in Missouri. Stephen Austin was to be a part it, but evidently not immediately, for he secured an appointment as territorial judge in Arkansas and went to New Orleans to study law in the office of Joseph Hawkins.

Moses Austin arrived in San Antonio unannounced and received a cordial if negative reception to his request for land to award to others. Before leaving the city he renewed his request, this time with the endorsement of the Baron de Bastrop, an acquaintance from earlier days along the Mississippi River. This time Austin received the courtesy of having his proposal forwarded to higher authority, and eventually the good fortune of having it accepted. He could settle up to 300 families on lands to be determined in the future in generous amounts and for a price far more affordable than the $1.00 to $1.25 per acre common in the United States.

Austin began the return trip to Natchitoches to begin recruiting his settlers, but mishaps and exposure en route sapped his strength and he developed the pneumonia that caused his death. Stephen F. Austin abandoned his study of law and plans for a judicial post in Arkansas and assumed his father's role as the first legal empresario in Mexican Texas. To this point the younger Austin's involvement appears much like a dutiful son who encourages his father in a dream that has little hope for success, but with the father's death, the fulfillment of the dream becomes a passion for the surviving son.

Austin had a practical as well as an emotional motivation for taking over the Texas venture: the family's legacy from the Panic of 1819 was a large debt, and success in what might be called the first real estate investment in Texas could restore their good fortunes.

First, Austin had to confirm his succession to his father's grant. He traveled to San Antonio, Saltillo, and Mexico City, and for several years spent as much time securing this right and helping Mexican authorities advance the empresarial system to include, eventually, about thirty more such grants, as he did developing his own grant.

Austin located his original grant wisely. He selected an area that was divided into three portions of approximately equal size by the Brazos and Colorado rivers. The streams provided avenues of ingress and egress between interior and the Gulf of Mexico for his settlers. Because they were shallow, crooked, filled with snags, and subject to extreme rising and falling water levels, no river in Texas offered year-round water transport for any distance from the sea, but these two were the best available. And with their tributaries they provided plenty of water for livestock. Furthermore, although later policy would prevent Anglos from owning land closer than within fifty miles from the sea, Austin's grant extended all the way to the coast. His grant was west of the thick eastern forests which would have required much labor to clear for farming, yet east of the twenty-inch precipitation line that would have prevented the row-crop agriculture his first settlers knew. All in all, Austin had a good eye for the land and for the future.

The first settlers arrived in 1821 while Austin was still working to make sure he had the authority to locate them on the land. They arrived aboard the *Lively*, with Andrew Robinson generally accredited as the first of the 297 land awardees now known as the Old Three Hundred.

The process of uniting settler with land to develop was complicated. All were required to present evidence of good citizenship in former homes, an effort to screen out trouble makers; they had to renounce all former citizenship allegiance, usually to the United States, and become naturalized Mexican citizens through an oath not much different from the one used today to naturalize citizens of the United States; and they had to be or become Roman Catholics. Some already had been baptized in the faith; others participated insincerely in such a ceremony because the prize of land was too great to trouble their Protestant or non-believer consciences.

And land was the prize. The colonist who answered to the calling of farmer received 177.7 acres in a unit, called a *labor*; the stockraiser was allotted a league, over 4400 acres. While the *labor* provided plenty of land for any farmer to clear and cultivate, the greater reward turned many who had no stock before acquiring their land into stockraisers.

As far as the government was concerned, the land was provided without charge, but the empresario and the government alienation agent had to be paid, so fees of 12.5 cents per acre were prescribed. The fee was paid to the government agent. In the case of Austin's first colony, this was his father's friend, the Baron de Bastrop, who then was supposed to share it with Austin. In any event, Austin received little money because so much credit was extended to prospective settlers who never paid, either because they lacked the money, or, later, because they resented Austin's possession of more land than any other Anglo in Texas, perhaps 50,000 acres or more.

In *Lone Star*, T. R. Fehrenbach traced the saga of Arthur McCormick in this process. McCormick initiated his petition in San Felipe de Austin, Stephen F. Austin's headquarters community located on the banks of the Brazos River, on August 7, 1824. McCormick declared his intention of settling in the colony, requested the award of land to which he was entitled under the granting system, and pledged that he would be a loyal and law-abiding citizen of Mexico. Austin endorsed McCormick's petition on the same day, specifically stating that he was of good character and well-known for his industry and skill in agricultural practices.

On August 9, the Baron de Bastrop, representing the Mexican government, and Austin, McCormick's presenter, began the processing of his application by outlining the authority that enabled them to alienate land from public to private ownership, in this case a league located on the San Jacinto River. The next day Bastrop, Austin, and McCormick visited this tract of land in the presence of witnesses and neighbors, and, in the language of the document, "put" McCormick in possession of his league. To establish his possession, and perhaps to celebrate, McCormick "shouted aloud, pulled up grass, threw stones, fixed stakes, and performed the other ceremonies fixed by custom." Such ceremonies alerted all present that the land now belonged to McCormick, and that from that moment forward it existed as a specie of private property, not public domain. Its "birth certificate," in the form of an abstract, would follow it in perpetuity no matter how changed by sale, inheritance, or gift to others. Although these ceremonies are rooted in medieval practices, they are reminiscent of animal behavior in the songs of birds or "marking" by canines: each in his way is saying, "This land is mine."

McCormick and several thousand other immigrants came to the empresarial grants now available in Texas. Austin played a role in making this possible for all, not just those who located on his original grant or one of the subsequent grants he received in partnership with Samuel M. Williams. He did so by convincing Mexican authorities of his own sincerity in converting his loyalty from the United States to Mexico and by demonstrating his desire to "get along" with them. He assisted in drafting the Colonization Law under which all other empresarios operated, but it is worth noting that Austin alone received a grant from the central government. All others operated

exclusively under the federalist Constitution of 1824, which turned all land matters over to the states, and under the colonization law adopted by the legislature of the state of Coahuila in 1825.

Within the year approximately twenty-five empresarios engaged in the process of securing grants, attracting settlers, and locating them on land. Among the more significant for positive reasons was Green DeWitt, who laid out the community of Gonzáles on the Guadalupe River to the west of Austin's original grant. Because he operated under the Colonization Law of 1825, his land did not extend to the Gulf of Mexico; instead, land in the lower valley went to Juan de León, who could obtain it because of his Hispanic heritage.

Possibly the most significant empresario for negative reasons was Haden Edwards,

Letter to Moses Austin, March 2, 1821, from Texas immigrant colonizer and legislator, Baron de Bastrop, introducing the bearer as his agent and "a Gentleman of verasity [sic] and my God father." Having assisted Austin in securing Governor Martínez's crucial endorsement for a grant to Austin, Bastrop in the letter pledges further support. After the death of Moses Austin on June 10 of 1821, Bastrop interceded on behalf of his son, Stephen F., and the Austin colonists when the newly independent provisional Mexican government refused to approve the Spanish grant. As representative of Texas to the new state of Coahuila y Tejas in the mid-1820s, Bastrop secured passage of a second colonization act and helped with the establishment of a port at Galveston.

Above: Agarita fruit. This edible fruit develops from bright yellow flowers, which bloom earlier in the season. It has been an important link in the food chain of its region.

COURTESY, TEXAS DEPARTMENT OF TRANSPORTATION.

Right: Prickly pear in the Davis Mountains near McDonald Observatory. This cactus is covered with small clusters of stiff hairs usually surrounding needle-like spines. The flowers, usually yellow, have pear-shaped edible fruit. The prickly pear makes excellent food for deer and cattle. Modern ranchers use flame throwers to burn off the spines and stiff hairs for their cattle, especially during droughts.

IMAGE CRAFTERS, PHOTO BY OUIDA DEAN.

Below: "Private, Texas Hussars, Mexico, 1835," museum exhibit.

COURTESY, PANHANDLE-PLAINS HISTORICAL MUSEUM, CANYON, TEXAS.

although Austin might have nominated Sterling Robertson for that distinction.

Edwards was a Kentuckian who had moved earlier to Jackson, Mississippi, to speculate in land. When he learned of the Austin's plans, he traveled to Mexico City and assisted Stephen F. Austin—especially with money—to secure the approval of the empresarial system. Edwards received land in eastern Texas that encircled the established community of Nacogdoches. All empresarios were required by law to honor previous land grants by the Spanish government, but only in Edwards' grant did this prove to be a problem. Only the areas around Nacogdoches and San Antonio had such grants, and the San Antonio region was never placed in the custody of an empresario.

Edwards arrived in Nacogdoches and posted notice of his authority with the additional information that the burden of proof of previous land grants rested with the grantee and that lands occupied by those who could not prove ownership would be considered available for reassignment. Naturally, this caused concern and anger among the previous settlers. Many had lost their grant documents to fire or flood, and no government registry was available because no government courthouses, land offices, or equivalent facilities existed anywhere in Texas. Only one instance of Edwards' awarding land previously claimed to

a newcomer has been documented, but all reacted to the threat.

The hard feelings that resulted from Edwards' announcement led to the Fredonia Rebellion, to be discussed presently as a harbinger of the Texas Revolution. But a more immediate consequence was the forfeiture of Edwards' empresarial status by order of the political chief in San Antonio and the awarding of the same lands to three other empresarios, David G. Burnet, Joseph Vehlein, and Lorenzo de Zavala.

Robertson's problem was Austin. Robert Leftwich, a representative of the Tennessee Land Company, received a grant to land that lay to the northwest of Austin's original grant, and, in time, between Austin's grant and an additional one that he shared with Samuel M. Williams. Leftwich had accepted the land as an individual, as the law required, but surrendered its disposition to his company, which sent Sterling Robertson to manage its development. Austin wanted to consolidate his grants, but could only do so if the Tennessee Land Company grant was forfeited, a jeopardy it faced if Robertson failed to locate a minimum number of families within a prescribed period of time. Robertson claimed that Austin convinced settlers he had recruited to locate elsewhere to prevent him from fulfilling his contract, and even accused Austin of hiring an

assassin to kill him. Whatever the merit of such charges, some of Robertson's descendants continued to have negative feelings toward Austin well over a century after both had passed from the scene.

Notice should be taken of grants located to the southwest of Austin's colony awarded to James Power and James Hewetson and to John McMullen and James McGloin, because both contained a majority of settlers who came directly from Europe and from Ireland, not from the United States. All other empresarial grants predominately attracted settlers from the United States, who came with the cultural baggage of the constitution of that country; their concepts of citizens' "rights" was radical-

ly different from Mexican and European attitudes about "subjectship" to government. Trouble for Mexico lay in the distinction.

Stephen F. Austin remained the natural leader of all Texas immigrants. Although some empresarios resented or even opposed his pre-eminence, their fortunes were hitched to his success. Austin made the most complete effort at hispanicization. He signed documents as "Estévan," and while he approached his work with practicality, he was always the visionary.

His oft-quoted statement that he hoped "to redeem Texas from its wilderness state by means of the plow alone, in spreading over it North American population, enterprise, and intelligence" is a wonderful window into his mind. Austin looked at a prairie and saw farms, at natural crossroads and saw towns, and in a modern setting, he would view a snow-covered mountain as a development site for ski runs and condos. Although he lived in a wilderness, he longed for civilization. And he gave himself to it completely, vowing never to marry until the family was free of debt and he had established himself. Sadly, neither day ever came, but he achieved much. T.R. Fehrenbach said it best in *Lone Star*: "He began in Missouri as a businessman, but he became something immensely more important: he was a visionary, capitalist, developer, and Father of his People, all in one."

LIFE IN THE TEXAS COLONIES

The westering impulse of Anglo-Americans led them to Texas only two centuries after the original English plantations were established on the Atlantic Coast. Through trial-and-error, they had found the way to adapt and to survive in each new frontier setting in the west from the Tidewater to the Piedmont to the Appalachian Mountains, thence across the Old Southwest and the Mississippi Delta. Some were sons of the Gulf Coast bayous and rivers. They had learned to grow corn and sugar cane and cotton, to hunt for meat in the forests and to fish the streams, to build shelter from whatever materials were available, and to survive contests with Indians. Out of the struggle and the constantly westward progression, they became Americans. Most were fiercely democratic but operated within a pecking order based on skill; they believed in work and honored those who did it well. They believed in limited government and individual "rights," and had lived their lives where self-help and perhaps that of their extended family dealt with most problems. They cherished individual freedom, and they wanted land, for in their time and place the freeholder was a somebody. And in Texas, the land was "free," at least if they ignored the fees owed to the land alien-

Old Fort Parker State Historic Site, replica of a typical colonial Texas cabin, built from materials available locally. Windows and doors were often just shutters, hinged with rawhide, to keep out the elements and marauding wild animals and Indians. Furnishings were often hand made; cooking was done outdoors on an open fire in warm weather and indoors in a fireplace in winter. Luxuries such as glass pane windows and paint did not come to many frontier homes.
COURTESY, TEXAS DEPARTMENT OF TRANSPORTATION.

ation agent and the empresario and lived in sufficient isolation to keep even governmental institutions from intruding.

Their methods of migration had a good deal to do with resources. The least expensive method was walking and carrying a firearm for hunting, with perhaps a bag of salt for seasoning and extra ammunition. The greatest drawback to this method was the paucity of tools and other necessities that could be brought along for use later. Some walked beside a pack horse and so could bring more of those tools, or perhaps they rode one horse and led another. Later, quite a few just rode west with saddlebags full. A wagon was a convenience, for it allowed the bringing of more tools or seeds to be used later, but few would have displaced such necessities with their own weight unless they were ill so they walked beside the wagon. Jared Groce claimed fifty wagons for his move, and he seemed to bring everything from his former home except the buildings and the land. And some, including the first legal settlers as well as many who came thereafter, arrived by coastal boat from New Orleans or other Gulf ports.

Reasons for coming varied, although the "running from" or "running to" formula applied. Some, such as the Austins, escaped debt, or like Sam Houston and William B. Travis, bad memories. "GTT" on cabin doors or tax rolls in Alabama or Tennessee communicated only that the previous occupant or taxpayer had departed and did not plan to return. Others did not flee from established homes so much as they *wanted* to move on. Attracted by fresh land, not just free land, they wanted the chance to start over, whether the road they previously had trod was a dead end or not. Texas represented renewal for all of them.

Texas immigrants, no less that those of any other American frontier, faced some of the same problems, among them food supply, clothing, shelter, providing furnishings, health, religion—and Indians. Texas had plenty of food for those with the skills to obtain it. A wealth of food was available in the forests in the meat of bear, deer, squirrel, and other animals, and swam in its streams in a variety of fishes. Nuts, berries, and edible roots of plants grew wild and could be gathered in season. To harvest food, one must be skilled in hunting and fishing and possess knowledge about when and what to gather and how to prepare it, for some items required boiling or other processing to remove toxic substances. The preservation of food also required skills of dehydration to prevent spoilage. And the land itself, at least where the first waves of settlers located, could produce any kind of edible crop the immigrant knew how to cultivate.

Of course, freezing or pressure canning of food was not possible, so the term "in season" has an important meaning. The diet of Texas colonists was long on meat from the hunt and eventually from the slaughter of livestock, and once fields were cultivated, from corn eaten off the cob or prepared from ground meal. But during the winter months few fresh vegetables were available, so most endured, and eventually suffered from, an unbalanced diet. Inevitably, this had an effect on health and life expectancy.

By the time of the migration to Texas, most if not all frontiersmen had learned the value of making their garments from the skins of animals, especially deer, which could be worked into a soft and pliable condition and sewn into a suit of "buckskins." Such garments were airtight and warm in winter or summer, and after a while they bore the grease and soils of meals and the hunt and work. Of course, wool and other natural fabrics could be acquired by tedious labor in harvesting, carding, spinning, and weaving—or just buying, if money was available. In the 1830s, William B. Travis wrote in his diary of purchasing shirts and other garments by the dozen from others who had made them. And in time, such items could be imported from the United States.

Shelter might be in or under the wagon that was used to get to Texas, but eventually a one-room cabin, made of logs mostly, but of rock or sod as well when logs were not present, became the norm. The one-room or log cabin had long since been the common abode of frontiering Americans. English colonists acquired the skills necessary to build such structures from the Finns, and long before Americans even thought of moving to Texas most knew how to build a log cabin.

The focus of the cabin was the fireplace, the site of cooking and the source of heat and light. Of course, the cook fire makes heat in the summer, too, so in warmer months this function probably was transferred to an open fire outdoors. As for light, or illumination, providing the fuel for the fire was labor intensive, so mostly life was lived by daylight and the dark was spent in rest. Few cabins in the early phases of colonization had glass windows, but animal skins scraped to translucence did admit some light and repelled unwanted insects when stretched over windows.

Prosperity or a growing family might prompt the construction of an additional cabin a few feet away from the original one and joining the buildings under a common roof. The connection between them created a breeze-way, so that name was applied to such buildings, although many people called them dog-runs or dog-trots because of the penchant of those animals to congregate in the cool of the breeze that could be found there when absent elsewhere. And before the Texas colo-

nial period ended some Texans lived in houses constructed from sawed lumber available from the earliest sawmills in the area.

Functional is the word for the furnishings in colonial homes. "Functional" means that something could be used for a chair or table or other items that worked well enough, although they were "home made" and not finished with the craftsman's skills. In *The Saga of Texas Series: The Revolutionary Decades, 1810-1836*, David Vigness quoted a traveler who visited a home in the wilderness and was served dinner at a home-made table. Vessels for liquids were dried gourds with holes cut in them, and some of the forks were made of cane joints carved to create prongs. Every kind of knife, from pocket knife to butcher knife, was used at table. And the meal was mostly milk and corn meal prepared in various ways, but the traveler testified that it was served with generosity, prepared with skill, and tasted good to a hungry man.

The bare ground provided the floor for such homes, and at least until sawed lumber was available, beds were sometimes on the ground as well. Some had beds elevated on frames of lumber with tickings stuffed with tree moss, corn husks, or the feathers of such birds as geese and duck. These materials are organic and therefore subject to mildew and pest infestation; the remedy for both was "sunning" out of doors on warm, bright days.

The health of colonial Texans was both hearty and impaired: the former because they lived a vigorous life, and the latter because of hardships and dangers and an imbalanced diet. If colonists survived Indian troubles, snake bites, and falling trees, the hard work required for survival strengthened muscles and spirit. But if injury or illness occurred, few medical practitioners were available, and, in truth, the unhealthy party might be better off without their help because of their poor skills. Virtually all Texans became knowledgeable with folk remedies which often worked well enough, although few could have explained why.

Travelers often commented about Texas pioneer women, all of whom appeared to be older than they actually were. With no moisturizers to protect their skin from drying, with babies on the way or in the way permitting scant time for rest, and without an adequate diet—and in the gestation process those babies sapping minerals and vitamins whether the host had them to spare or not—women aged quickly and showed it in calcium-robbed teeth and leathery skin. And the babies came and came, partly because they were considered the Lord's blessing and even-

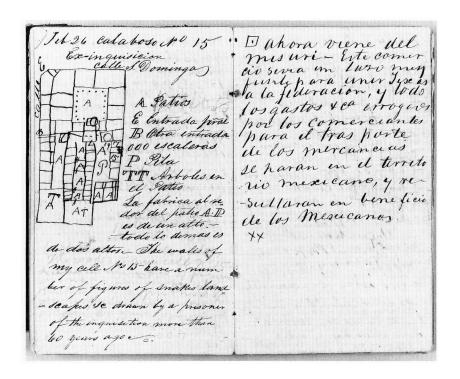

tually a labor resource, and partly because contraception was unavailable or undesirable.

Religion in early Texas was not a "problem," but it was a factor. Since all were required to become Roman Catholics—some were Catholics already and some took to the faith genuinely—obviously quite a few insincere "conversions" occurred. These came to be known as "Muldoon" Catholics after a Father Muldoon who was said to have performed such ceremonies in full knowledge that the convert was more interested in Texas real estate than a title in Heaven. It is sometimes charged that the good Father did so out of an addiction to alcohol that made him vulnerable to such a service; just as likely was that he understood the charade and did not think it worth stopping.

Despite the Established Church requirement, in reality there were few Roman Catholic churches in Texas and therefore few enforcers of the establishment rules. In any event, Methodist and Baptist believers, even if nominal Catholics, continued to worship as they wished and even to meet in societies and Sunday schools. Methodists did so at McMahon's Chapel and the Baptists did so in various places, including Nacogdoches, without interference.

Still, it would be fair to say that life in early Texas was more secular than it would ever be

again. This was true because the institutions of organized religion, including church edifices and clergy, were few, and people found that they could go through the stations of life—birth, pairing, death, etc.—without formal religious ceremony. This would have been unimaginable in such settled places as Nashville or New Orleans, but on the frontier, life went on.

Indian opposition was not as much of a problem in the 1820s as it became when Texans pushed further west into Comanche and Kiowa country after Texas had established independence from Mexico. This resulted from the fact that most of the earliest Texans occupied areas where Spaniards had interacted with the Indians to some degree for a long time, and that the Indians in those areas were less hostile to the coming of the Anglos. But there was enough danger for Austin to hire men to "range" over the countryside to deflect raids, giving birth to the fabled Texas Rangers. Isolated settlers had to remain vigilant to avoid the loss of livestock or other property, and often lives, to the Indians.

Life in the Texas colonies was primitive, harsh, isolated, and sometimes fatal. In this it differed only in geography from the experience of other American frontiersmen who had occupied wilderness areas before them, or those who came afterward, to other frontiers. Life here required hard work and perseverance, but it also promised much in the future when the crops were in, the land developed and yielding, and civilization established once more.

CLASH OF CULTURES

Eugene C. Barker's *Mexico and Texas, 1821-1835*, published in 1928, presented the thesis that the Texas Revolution was inevitable because the Anglos and the Mexicans were products of such different cultural backgrounds that sufficient accommodation to avoid conflict was not possible by either group. While many causes contributed to the conflict, Barker's empirical evidence is difficult to ignore.

Spain's legacy remained a major part of Mexico's culture despite the establishment of an independent Mexican republic in 1821. For three hundred years of Spanish colonialism, residents of Mexico and other Spanish colonies, no less than residents of Spain itself, were subjects of their government, not citizens in the Anglo-American sense. They did not vote for king, viceroy, governor, or political chief; biology determined who would be king and the king determined the rest. The source and application of governmental power, then, was deductive: it resided at the top and was applied downward until the entire structure rested like an inverted pyramid upon the individual, who was "subject" to it.

When an independent state was created in Mexico, its residents lacked sufficient experience in participatory democracy and self-government to make a quick and orderly transition to a stable government focused the other way around, with the pyramid sitting at its base, or citizenry, who delegated power to leaders at the higher various levels. The result of this inexperience was rapid changes from a republic to an empire and back to a federative republic in as many years, and each change came because of force, not as the orderly consequence of elections. Mexico had embraced the *caudillo*, or military strongman, who ran government as long as he had the most guns.

Anglo-Americans were products of a system that involved citizenship; in their tradition, governmental power was "inducted" from the people, who elected representatives to various levels of pubic administration and who had the means to hold them accountable at the next election. And by the 1820s, Americans had come to expect their leaders to accept the consequences of elections with finality if not with grace.

The Mexican Constitution of 1824 established a completely federative government similar to the Articles of Confederation adopted by Americans even during their revolution from England. In both, fundamental power remained with the people, who delegated only such power to state governments as was necessary to provide needed services and precious little of it to their Congress, which became more of a debating society that a true legislature. Americans abandoned the Articles after a decade because the major-

ity quickly understood that more bound them together than separated them and that the state-level adminstration of power was an arrangement which did not serve them well. Still, many Americans, especially Southerners, favored the decentralization of the federation and ensured at least the promise of its survival in the Ninth and Tenth Amendments to the new Constitution of the United States. And when many like-minded immigrants came to Texas during the 1820s, they regarded the federative, "state's rights" Mexican government as just about the right mix of shared powers between the central and state governments. This, after all, was the generation that shortly would be involved in the Nullification Crisis of 1832 in the United States, which also was a dispute between central government and state government powers.

Too, Mexico's established church differed significantly from the plural Christian traditions that had developed during America's colonial period. So, while other factors may qualify as causes for the dissatisfaction that had developed by 1830 between host Mexicans and newcomer Texans, Barker's thesis cannot be dismissed.

Three episodes testify to the unease between host and newcomer: the activities of Joel Poinsett, the first minister to Mexico from

CHAPTER THREE

the United States; the Fredonia Rebellion; and the Law of April 6, 1830.

The outcome of the presidential election in the United States in 1824 and prospects for the next election provided the background for Poinsett's activities in Mexico. John Quincy Adams of Massachusetts won the race for the presidency over his opponents, Andrew Jackson of Tennessee, Henry Clay of Kentucky and William Crawford of Georgia, in what Jackson regarded as a stolen election. Jackson had finished first in both popular and electoral votes but lacked the necessary majority because of the wide field of candidates. But the House of Representatives, exercising its constitutional power to decide such issues, was led by Clay, and when the House selected Adams and then Adams appointed Clay as his secretary of state, Jackson and his supporters believed that a "Corrupt Bargain" had cheated them out of the election. Immediately Jackson began scheming for revenge and vindication by defeating Adams in the next election, and Adams knew he would have to have western votes to survive a two-man race. Since Southwesterners blamed Adams for the Adams-Onís Treaty of 1819 that had deprived them of the opportunity to move westward, he had little chance to gain their votes unless he could give the appearance of changing his position on westward expansion. Enter Joel Poinsett.

Adams sent Poinsett to Mexico with an offer to buy portions of Mexico, including Texas, but Poinsett never seemed to understand that he did not have to succeed in Mexico for Adams to do so among southwestern voters in the United States. Once there, he pursued his mission zealously—and disastrously. Even before he officially informed his host government of his intentions, Poinsett allowed news of his mission to become public knowledge. Mexican officials probably would not have given serious consideration to the proposal under any circumstances, but as long as it remained confidential they could ignore it quietly. Now, however, they had to react negatively and publicly to this insult to national dignity.

Poinsett persevered. He discovered that the Scottish Rite Masonic Lodge operated in Mexico, and, since Masons take vows to keep each other's secrets, had become a quasi-political organization for government officials and other influential leaders. All Masonry began in the Old Testament days of Solomon, when a few who knew geometry and other building "secrets" kept each other's counsel. This is "operative" Masonry; "speculative" Masonry began in Britain in the seventeenth century, and bifurcated into Scottish and York Rite bodies. Scottish Rite Masonry crossed the English Channel through a Scottish-French alliance, thence migrated to Spain, and on to Spain's colonies. York Rite Masonry, meanwhile, came with English colonists to their New World homes and traveled west in their frontiering. Finding no York Rite bodies in Mexico, Poinsett organized one, partially because it was his brand of Masonry and partially to create an alternate "party" that would help him in his mission to purchase Texas.

Mexican Scottish Rite Masons resented his interference and Poinsett became *persona non grata*. He returned home after irritating Mexican government officials and alarming them over the potential of United States interest in Mexican territory. His one positive contribution was in bringing home the plant with bright green and red leaves and tiny yellow blossoms that became so much a part of Christmas decoration in the United States, and now bears his name—the Poinsettia.

Haden Edwards' Fredonia Rebellion intensified Mexican concern about the significant number of Americans who arrived daily in Texas and the ultimate goal of the United States toward this northern province. Edwards' grant in East Texas hosted the only significant number of land grantees approved under the previous Spanish system, and as we have seen, the rules for empresarios required

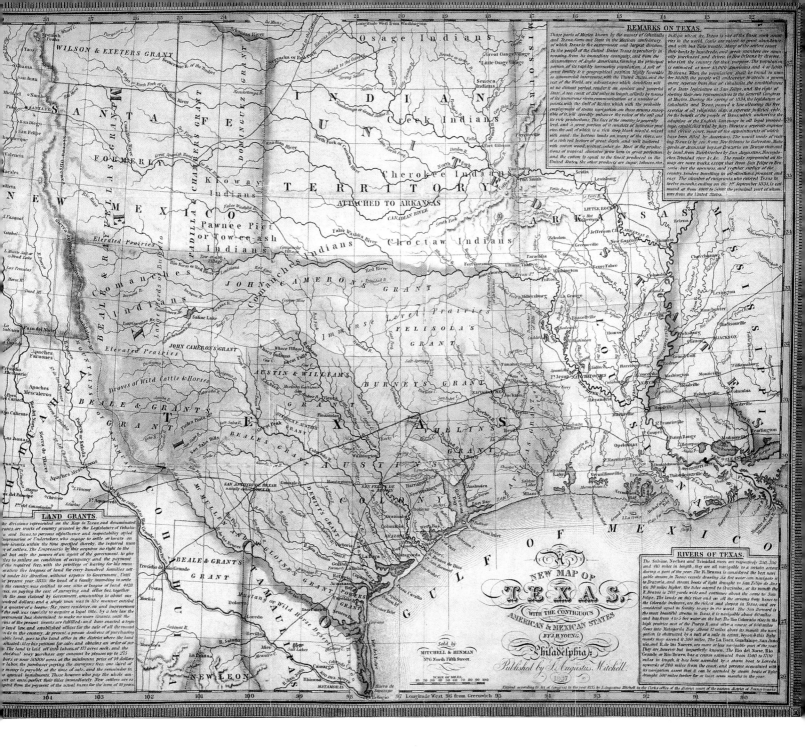

him to honor such grants. But few could produce hard evidence of their grants, although everyone in the Nacogdoches area knew what they owned and generally who owned the rest of the land there.

Edwards posted notice on the Stone House of Y'Barbo, by now the traditional headquarters of official business in Nacogdoches. He warned land holders to come forward with proof of ownership or risk forfeiture, which naturally alarmed them. A second notice produced even greater fear. Protests were sent to the political chief in San Antonio, with whom Edwards already had poor relations, partially because of the abrasive personality of his

brother Benjamin, who ran empresarial affairs in Nacogdoches while Edwards recruited settlers in the United States so he could meet his quota on time.

Tensions in the Edwards colony intensified over an election for *alcalde*, or mayor-judge for the civil community. Older settlers supported Samuel Norris and newcomers backed Chichester Chaplin, Edwards' son-in-law. Following the balloting, Edwards certified the election of Chaplin, but Norris' supporters claimed fraud and protested to the political chief. This was one too many complaints for that officer, who already bristled from undiplomatic correspondence he had received

CHAPTER THREE

51

Sterling Clack Robertson (1785-1842), empresario of Robertson's colony 1834-35, eventually settled 600 families in Texas. He was one of 70 members of The Texas Association asking permission in 1822 to settle in Texas. Among the many difficulties in securing a grant, he was caught by the Law of April 6, 1830. This original painting by William Henry Huddle hangs in the state Capitol.

from Benjamin Edwards, so he voided Edwards' empresarial grant.

Edwards estimated that he had invested $50,000 in the venture and was unwilling to give it up without a fight. His supporters rode into town, "arrested" Edwards along with his critics, and in a mock trail acquitted Edwards of wrong-doing. They then declared the area of his grant free of Mexican rule and its rebirth as the Fredonia Republic. Their flag was a rectangle with a white bar over a red bar to symbolize the union of the Anglos and Cherokees who lived in the area, and many of them signed the flag as a pledge of loyalty.

Word of this action reached Mexican officials, who responded with military force. Lt. Col. Mateo Ahumada brought infantry and cavalry northward, and when they passed through San Felipe de Austin, Stephen F. Austin and some of his colonists joined them in a demonstration of loyalty to the government. The Fredonia Rebellion fizzled without a fight. Edwards and many of his supporters retreated to Louisiana, and others disappeared into the wilderness until the crisis passed. Edwards eventually returned to Nacogdoches as a private citizen, and members of his family continued to live in the area thereafter without interference.

The real consequence of the Fredonia Rebellion was the overreaction to it in Mexican circles already alarmed by what they perceived Poinsett's mission to mean. The *la raza* concept, a strong nationalism that featured xenophobia toward North Americans, flourished amid fears that Poinsett and Edwards represented a Yankee Plot to seize Texas for the United States.

Among the *la raza* leaders were General Manuel Mier y Terán, military commander of the Northern Provinces, and Mexican Foreign Affairs Minister Don Lucas Alamán. Terán ordered an investigation of Texas in the wake of the Fredonia Rebellion, and his report to his colleagues alarmed them. He reported that Americans predominated in the area sur-

rounded by the Gulf of Mexico and the Sabine, Red, and Colorado rivers with a ten to one majority, and the one Mexican in the ratio he found more likely to be a hired worker than a land owner. Although Spanish was the official language and required in all official business, it was scarcely used in daily communication. And although most Anglo colonists had not supported Edwards, Terán distrusted their loyalty anyway.

Terán recommended that the government send as many Mexican colonists to Texas as it could and recruit more direct European colonists to break down Anglo solidarity; that they more vigorously restrict trade between Texas and the United States; and that they station troops in Texas even if they must be recruited from prisons. Mexican President Vicente Guerrero decreed in 1829 that henceforth slavery was abolished throughout Mexico; since only the Texans had the kind of slavery he intended, "all of Mexico" meant Texas exclusively. Not every Texan owned slaves, but most believed in the system, so the majority took offense at the decree. But not as much as they did to the Law of April 6, 1830, the drastic measure by *la raza* to get a firmer grip on Texas.

The Law of April 6, 1830 followed Terán's recommendations closely. The statute forbade further colonization in Texas by United States citizens, and those already in Texas who had not yet received land grants would not be permitted to receive them; Mexican convicts would be sent to Texas as colonists and European colonization could continue—indeed, was encouraged. Customs collectors were to be stationed in Texas to direct trade toward Mexico, and, finally, "investigators" would remain there permanently to monitor affairs.

Such severe measures were rooted in the government leaders' conviction that a crisis of authority had developed in Texas. Although this had previously not been true, the decree created one. Cloture of immigration caught many in the midst of the process and divided families. Americans, without cognitively actualizing the law of physics involved, nonetheless reacted to the cloture thusly: a ball rolling up hill (immigration) will continue until the energy that propels it dissipates; when it stops, it does not remain stationary but begins to roll downhill, meaning that continued population growth for economic development was essential to the success of the immigrants, and without it, their "ball" would roll downhill to failure.

Texans also resented the threat of having convicts located among them since so far they had had to prove their own good citizenship in order to acquire land. They also resented the imposition of customs collection, although they were on less firm ground in this objection since it was within the power of the government to impose and because they knew already that customs collections would commence seven years after colonization began. Still, being Americans, they resented taxes.

So the Law of April 6, 1830, intended to deal with a crisis that did not exist since the overwhelming majority of Texans continued to make genuine efforts toward accommodating the conditions of their admittance and land grants, instead was the precipitant of a crisis.

Texas remained a part of Mexico until the spring of 1836, but after 1830 relations between the colonists and Mexican government officials became increasingly strained. Until 1830, few if any of the colonists wanted or expected Texas to be detached from Mexico and added to the United States, although most retained affection for and affiliation with the citizens and institutions of the United States. Bonds of language, a common history, familiar trade connections, and their general Anglo-Celtic heritage could not be surrendered easily, even if a league of land had looked like sufficient motivation to attempt to do so. Probably the clash of cultures would have erupted into an independence movement eventually. The Law of April 6, 1830 hastened the process.

Left: Samuel Augustus Maverick (1803-1870), He helped Ben Milam successfully enter San Antonio during the siege of December 1835. Maverick opposed secession, but when it became inevitable he vigorously supported the Confederacy. Maverick County was named for him, and the term maverick, which applies to an unbranded calf, was coined when he allowed a small herd to wander freely and virtually untended on Matagorda Peninsula. Samuel Maverick, Jr., and C. Maury Maverick are among his many descendants.
FROM ALBUMEN PRINT FOR THE TEXAS ALBUM OF THE EIGHTH LEGISLATURE, 1860. COURTESY, ARCHIVES DIVISION - TEXAS STATE LIBRARY.

Bottom, left: Daguerreotype of Edward Burleson (1798-1851), made in San Marcos the year before his death. During the siege of Béjar (San Antonio) in November of 1835, Stephen F. Austin relinquished command of the Texan forces to Colonel Burleson to take on critical diplomatic duties. On December 10, Mexican General Martín Perfecto de Cós surrendered the Alamo fortress to Burleson, who allowed Cós the honors of war and sent him and his forces to re-cross the Río Grande. Having arrived in Texas in 1830, Burleson was among the established colonists who on December 20 disbanded and returned to their homes and farms, expecting no further armed conflict until the following summer. However, on April 21, 1836, he found himself among the victors at the Battle of San Jacinto. Later, Burleson, the experienced military leader, served in various official capacities, including the vice presidency of the Republic of Texas.
COURTESY, ARCHIVES DIVISION - TEXAS STATE LIBRARY.

Revolutionary War
& First Attempt
at Independent Government

Disturbances of 1832

Trouble came to Texas in 1830. Americans and *tejanos* reacted to the Law of April 6, 1830 as a violation of state's rights: they believed that the central government had exceeded its powers delegated in the Constitution of 1824 by taking over immigration and land alienation within the states. They also were insulted by the provisions for convict settlement and military garrisons.

Beginning in 1830, Manuel Mier y Terán's soldiers began arriving and were quartered among the Texans, not to protect them but to police them. Colonel John (Juan) Davis Bradburn headquartered at Anahuac with approximately 150 men, Colonel Domingo de Ugartechea had another 100 or so men at Velasco, and Colonel José de las Pietras commanded a similarly sized garrison in Nacogdoches. Like the arrival of Redcoats in Boston in the 1770s, the mere presence of troops in Texas was provocative even before an offensive act occurred.

More trouble developed in 1831. The governor of Coahuila challenged the central government's ban on immigration by asserting the constitutional power of the state in such matters and directing local officials to resume granting land to bonafide applicants. General Terán ordered his commanders to prohibit state officials from performing these actions, and the first incident occurred when Bradburn marched to the new community of Liberty, abolished it, and arrested the state's land commissioner. When settlers complained, Bradburn closed all the coastal ports except Anahuac, which he could watch closely from his headquarters.

Bradburn's actions drew more earnest protests, particularly from a meeting in Brazoria, so he reopened the ports, but tension remained and was re-ignited by his arrest of William Barret Travis and Travis' law partner, Patrick Jack. Travis' arrest resulted from activities in behalf of a client who had come to Texas in search of runaway slaves. Bradburn first refused to surrender the slaves because Mexican law forbade slavery; later he said that he could not hand them over without legal proof of ownership. Before leaving to obtain it, the slave owner threatened to return with sufficient strength to make the legal documents superfluous.

Bradburn evidently worried about the threat because when Travis passed a spurious note to a sentry that armed men were approaching Anahuac in the middle of the night, Bradburn alerted his garrison and began a needless search. In retaliation, he ordered Travis' arrest; Jack so protested that he, too was arrested. Lacking a jail, Bradburn confined his prisoners in a kiln used to fire brick for the construction of Fort Anahuac, and intended to hold them for military trial.

Jack's brother William hurried to San Felipe to obtain help, and history turned on the absence of Austin from his headquarters. Had Austin been present, he probably would have gone alone to Anahuac to reason with Bradburn; instead, armed men made the journey and were joined by others at an encampment on the upper end of Galveston Bay at Turtle Bayou as word spread of the arrest of the Americans. They adopted the Turtle Bayou Resolutions, a statement of their continued loyalty to the legal government of Mexico under its constitution and a denouncement of the use of central government military power in excess of delegated authority. And they wanted Travis and Jack released immediately.

When negotiation failed to produce results, events escalated feelings. The Texans captured one of Bradburn's patrols and proposed an exchange, only to lose their advantage when they released their prisoners and Bradburn did not. Next, John Austin led a group to Velasco to seize a cannon left there

Opposite: Portrait of soldier and statesman Thomas Jefferson Rusk (1803-1857), which hangs in the Senate Chamber of the State Capitol. After his heroic role during the San Jacinto campaign, Rusk served the Republic of Texas in numerous capacities that ranged from Chief Justice to Major General of the Army during Indian troubles. At an 1837 session of the Nacogdoches district court where he practiced law, he delivered an eloquent address in which he stated in unequivocal terms the value he placed on representative government. "We have battled against the damages and difficulties of the wilderness, the savage and of our common enemy," he said, "but all this a savage might do… It is in vain we fight, it is in vain we conquer if we do not establish on this soil a government of equal and just law... I have seen [the enemy] met in their mad career by a handful of freemen and I have seen the tide of war roll back to its source and the bloody tyrant go in chains, an humble supplicant. That, gentleman of the Grand Jury, was a proud day, but the feelings I then had do not compare with those I now feel." In 1845 he presided at the assembly which wrote the state constitution, and in 1846 represented the state in Washington as one of the first U.S. Senators.

COURTESY, THE INSTITUTE OF TEXAN CULTURES, SAN ANTONIO, TEXAS.

by the crew of a departing ship to lighten its load so it could pass over the bar into the sea. Presumably, Austin wanted the cannon to fire into the Mexican camp at Anahuac. Most importantly, Colonel Piedras, who had received word of the trouble from Terán, arrived from Nacogdoches to investigate.

Piedras stopped by the insurgents' camp on his way to Anahuac and from them learned their side of the argument. Not persuaded, he nevertheless realized that firepower was on their side. Once in Anahuac, Piedras relieved Bradburn of command and gave him a day's start out of town. Then he released Travis and Jack to civil authorities for a trial that he and they knew would never occur. It was simply a way to defuse the situation.

John Austin made it to Velasco, captured the cannon, and had to shoot his way down the river, thus firing the first shots of the Texas Revolution. And Piedras returned to Nacogdoches, where he precipitated the third and final "Disturbance of 1832" with an order that settlers in his jurisdiction surrender their guns. Obviously, he wanted to prevent a repetition of the trouble at Anahuac; instead his order produced it. The firearms he rightly perceived could be used as tools of war were also tools of the hunt for the Texans who depended on game for food. And, although they had knowingly left the constitutional right to bear arms back in the United States when they became Mexican citizens to obtain land, obviously this was one right they had not intended to surrender. So, when they brought their guns to Nacogdoches, it was to use them rather than to surrender them.

Most of the participants in the Battle of Nacogdoches lived in the Ayish Bayou area. They arrived at the home of Adolphus Sterne, located on the eastern edge of Nacogdoches, and Sterne showed them how to move north along Lanana Bayou and then cut to the west behind the Stone House and the Red House, both occupied by Piedras' garrison. A few residents of Nacogdoches joined in the fight, which lasted until evening. Covered by darkness, Piedras attempted to lead his men to safety but they were caught at the Angelina River and a second battle developed. Piedras surrendered and was conducted under guard to San Antonio.

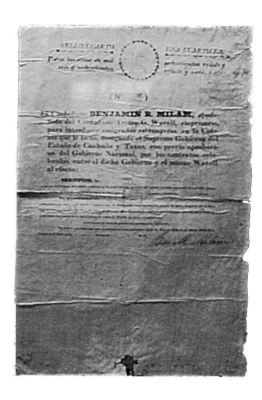

The Disturbances of 1832 at Anahuac, Velasco, and Nacogdoches launched the movement for an independent Texas, although few Texans thought so at the time. To them, these clashes represented support for the state's rights Constitution of 1824 and were in opposition only to centralist usurpers of power. To the centralists, who now regarded themselves the lawfully established power, however, the disturbances represented a serious threat to their authority. Since the Fredonia Rebellion, the *la raza* group had regarded any opposition in Texas as a plot to seize control of the area for eventual transfer to the United States. The cultural clash continued, and the disturbances led inevitably to the conventions of 1832 and 1833 and additional misunderstanding.

THE CONVENTIONS
OF 1832 AND 1833

Historians have argued that the Texas Revolution was a continuation of the American Revolution, transferred to the Southwest. There are several similarities: both developed in locations far from their central government; both occurred after a period of "salutary neglect"—admittedly brief in Texas; and both resulted from attempts of the central government to reassert control. T. R. Fehrenbach points out differences as well: English colonists came to America with their constitutional principles still forming, while Americans arrived in Mexican Texas with them intact and institutionalized in the Constitution of the United States, especially as they perceived it to reflect their state's rights beliefs; and while English colonists came to an undeveloped area, Americans who moved to Texas entered an area with long established religious, legal, and cultural customs. And the Disturbances of 1832 occurred at a time when Mexico itself was in turmoil.

In January 1832, Antonio López de Santa Anna Pérez de Lebrón raised the *grito*, or cry of revolution, in Vera Cruz. Santa Anna called for the restoration of the Constitution of 1824, although subsequent events proved his *grito* to be insincere, for as soon as he had taken over he moved to centralize all power again to himself. Biographer Oakah Jones has called Santa Anna a "political chameleon" who could appear to be a monarchist, republican, empiricist, or state's rights advocate as the situation benefited his ultimate goal of personal power.

When the Texans learned of Santa Anna's call for the restoration of state's rights, many declared their support. Stephen F. Austin was able to convince Colonel José Antonio Mexía, Santa Anna's lieutenant in the north, that advocacy of state's rights and the Constitution of 1824 had been the motivation behind the disturbances, which did not represent an effort to be free of Mexico itself. This was a truthful explanation; the real problem was that Santa Anna was not sincere about state's rights. What is important to understand at this stage is that the Texas Revolution had not yet taken on the ethnic proportions that resulted from events in 1836 at the Alamo and Goliad. So far, a genuine division over centralism versus state's rights was the issue, with many *tejanos* supporting the Americans.

The *ayuntamiento*, or local council, of San Felipe called a convention for October 1, 1832, to draft statements of explanation and petitions for changes in the governance of Texas. They chose Stephen F. Austin as their presiding officer, then petitioned the government to begin to convey land titles again, for more *ayuntamientos* so local governments could be created, for continued exemption from customs, for repeal of the Law of April 6, 1830, and for separate statehood within the Mexican government. Their petition was returned by the political chief of the central government, stationed in San Antonio, who reminded them that they did not enjoy the rights of assembly and petition under Mexican law.

In January 1833, Santa Anna announced his candidacy for the presidency of Mexico, and citizens of San Felipe issued a call for another convention to commence on April 1. Santa Anna won the presidency, with Valentín Gómez Farías elected to the vice presidency, and the Texans held their convention. This time a more militant spirit prevailed than had been present at the convention in October 1832, symbolized by the election of William H. Wharton as presiding officer instead of Austin, who was nonetheless commissioned to convey the convention's petitions to the central government. The petitions were the same, except this time they included a constitution for their proposed state. Once again, the dissimilarity of cultural backgrounds produced a clash. This was the way such was done in the United States when Tennessee or Mississippi was ready for statehood: residents of a territory petitioned Congress and offered a constitution for that body to accept or reject. Unfortunately, in Mexican opinion, as Fehrenbach observed, the first convention looked like the *pronunciamiento*, and the latter the *plan*, the second and final stages of revolution, Mexican style, not like an orderly progression to statehood within the Mexican system.

Austin faithfully traveled to Mexico City to present the petition, but made no progress. Santa Anna had retired to his *hacienda* near Vera Cruz and left the administration in the hands of acting President Gómez Farías, who busied himself with reforms in the church-state relationship, the army, and in land-owning patterns, simultaneously offending the three most conservative institutions in Mexico and giving Santa Anna the opportunity to return and lead what amounted to a revolution against his own government that resulted in dispensing with the Constitution of 1824 altogether. Now he ruled

Chief Bowles (1756-1839), or "The Bowl," as sketched by William A. Berry. The Cherokee chief migrated to East Texas in the 1820s, but had difficulty securing the Mexican land titles he sought. In February of 1836, he signed the Houston-Forbes treaty, agreeing to remain neutral during the Texas Revolution. Afterwards, the Texas congress invalidated the treaty. President Lamar's policies led to the Battle of the Neches, during which the "The Bowl" was killed and the survivors were forced north of the Red River into Indian Territory. William Goyens, "the free Black on the frontier," who helped negotiate the treaty that saved the Texans from a two-front war, was denied his league and labor of land for aiding the revolution because of his color.

COURTESY, ARCHIVES DIVISION - TEXAS STATE LIBRARY.

with a puppet congress and support of the army.

Austin persevered in Mexico City while these events occurred, but his patience played out. In desperation, he wrote an ill-advised letter to the governing body in San Antonio urging them to implement the proposed state government, perhaps to show that it was harmless. Instead his letter was returned to the capital to incriminate Austin in a plot.

Austin met with Santa Anna before departing for Texas. The visit was cordial. Santa Anna accurately explained that Texas was not ready for separate statehood because of insufficient population and development, something the American mind could understand. He also told Austin that he intended to send more troops to Texas for defense—presumably against Indian attack.

Austin started north, but when he reach Saltillo, the capital of *Coahuila y Texas*, he was arrested, returned to Mexico City, and lodged in the Prison of the Inquisition, where conditions of his confinement indicated that he was considered a dangerous person indeed. He was denied reading or writing materials and kept under constant observation.

In Texas, quiet descended. It was like the quiet that developed after the Boston Massacre in 1770, or on American college campuses after the tragedy at Kent State University in Ohio in 1970—uneasy, apprehensive, fearful. No one wanted to be the cause of harm to Austin while he was a captive. By Austin's testimony, things were so quiet that he felt abandoned. But back in Texas, Peter Grayson and Spencer Jack raised money and traveled to Mexico City where they spent it wisely to secure Austin's release from prison, though he had to remain in the city under "house" arrest. In the summer of 1835, he was allowed to return to Texas under general amnesty, having

never been charged formally with anything, or tried, or cleared.

THE BATTLES OF THE TEXAS REVOLUTION

The events of the Texas Revolution, known far beyond the present State of Texas, began in 1835. In January, customs officers and soldiers returned to Anahuac. General Martín Perfecto de Cós now commanded the northern territory for Mexico, and he stationed Captain Antonio Tenorio and a garrison in Anahuac to support the customs collectors and give military evidence of the central government's authority.

The mere presence of Tenorio and his men caused trouble before they had an opportunity to provoke it. A group led by J. B. Miller met in San Felipe and asked William B. Travis to lead a force to expel Tenorio from Texas. This was an *ad hoc* venture, one not countenanced by any local government, although Travis then served as secretary to the *ayuntamiento* of San Felipe. Following the difficulties in Anahuac in 1832, Travis had moved there, and despite his age, had prospered and risen in politics and society as a leader. In July 1835, Travis was only twenty-five years of age, about to become twenty-six in August.

The presence of Tenorio and the reaction of Miller, Travis, and the others, helped define groups known as the Peace Party and the War Party. The former favored conciliation and did not want to anger the government; the latter, although far less numerous, did not much care who they irritated. Travis and twenty-five or so men traveled to Harrisburg, where he delayed long enough to consult with David G. Burnet, then moved by barge to Anahuac. They fired a shot upon their approach, which brought the townspeople and the soldiers out to learn the cause of the shot. The townsmen were disappointed to learn that Travis had returned, for they associated him with trouble.

Tenorio's men could not defend the still uncompleted Fort Anahuac so they retreated into the brush. With his men ashore, Travis called for Tenorio to meet him in a clearing, where he demanded the immediate surrender of the Mexican forces. Tenorio complied, and the next day Travis started them on the road

to San Antonio and followed somewhat later. Travis caught up with the advance party in Brazoria and found them attending a Fourth of July party as guests while his own "soldiers" suffered condemnation: Brazoria, at the moment, was in the hands of Peace Party advocates who tried to minimize the damage. Condemnation of Travis was so severe that he published a card in the *Texas Telegraph & Register* asking people to suspend judgment until he could explain his motives and actions.

Travis never got the chance to present his explanation because events moved too swiftly. When Cós learned of the fate of Tenorio, he demanded the surrender of the "outlaws" led by Travis for military trial and decided to move his headquarters to San Antonio to direct events. This was too much for the Texans, even those who had condemned Travis themselves. William Wharton presided at a meeting at Columbia on August 15 that called for a Consultation of all citizens to meet in November to decide what course they should take about the military occupation of Texas.

Austin returned to Texas in late summer, and immediately reassumed his position as the natural leader of Texas. What did he think should be done? Austin, who had made the most sincere effort of all to hispanicize, to accommodate, to get along, who had even signed his name "Estéban," was now "Stephen" again. "War is our only resource," he said in a speech on September 19. Cos, meanwhile, arrived in San Antonio and condemned the call for the Consultation. Rumors that he had brought along 800 hobbles to deal with prisoners helped crystallize the Texans for resistance to military occupation, if not yet for complete independence.

Above: "Pioneer Couple." Dancers in frontier homespun costuming perform in Texas, *the outdoor epic musical production at Palo Duro Canyon.*
COURTESY, TEXAS DEPARTMENT OF TRANSPORTATION.

Left: Interior of the Anson Jones house.
COURTESY, TEXAS DEPARTMENT OF TRANSPORTATION.

*William Barret Travis (1809-1836), Texas
commander at the Battle of the Alamo.
Travis' involvement in the 1832
disturbances at Anahuac, occurring the
same year the Mexican military was
expelled from Nacogdoches, alarmed the
central government. Both towns were
significant ports of entry, where immigrants
were granted Certificates of Entry upon
accepting the Catholic religion and
presenting character references. Travis,
finding minimal religious institutions,
requested the churches in the United States
to send missionaries to Texas. He moved his
practice from Anahuac, and in 1834 was
elected secretary to the* ayuntamiento. *His
decision to stand at the Alamo gave the
Texans invaluable time to organize, and his
letter appealing for assistance motivated
many to support the Texans' cause.*

PAINTING OF WILLIAM BARRET TRAVIS
BY CHARLES B. NORMANN.
COURTESY, CORPUS CHRISTI PUBLIC LIBRARY.

Cós precipitated the next "event" of the revolution by sending cavalry to Gonzáles late in September to seize a brass cannon previously allowed to remain there for Indian defense. Upon arriving, the troops were stalled by *alcalde* Andrew Ponton while riders hastened about recruiting help. Ponton refused to surrender the cannon unless presented with written orders, and when the troops returned to San Antonio for them, he buried the cannon. When reinforcements arrived, the cannon was resurrected and readied for action. The men elected John Moore as their leader and fashioned a flag, a white cloth with a drawing of a cannon and the words "Come And Take It" lettered upon it. When Mexican troops returned early in October, the Battle of Gonzáles, which some have called "The Lexington of the Texas Revolution," resulted with the cannon secured.

Word went forth that bloodshed had begun, and now many more men came to Gonzáles to defend a cannon that no longer needed defending. Primed for action, they were easily persuaded to go on to San Antonio to chase Cós out of Texas. The Army of the People, as they called themselves—as yet there was no Texas government—proceeded to San Antonio and settled into a siege of the place after preliminary skirmishing at Mission

Concepción. Austin was the citizen general of the force, and with him were Edward Burleson and even William B. Travis, serving as a scout.

While these men gathered at San Antonio, too few did so at San Felipe to commence the Consultation. Austin finally took a formal vote to allow those men who should go to the Consultation to quit the siege with the pledge that they would not be regarded as cowards. But of all who should have gone, Austin did not; this natural political leader instead remained in an unnatural military command assignment.

The siege of San Antonio was never complete, but it was effective since Cos, despite having superior numbers, declined to come out on the prairie and do battle. A "grass fight" occurred on November 26 when scouts attacked a pack train south of San Antonio in the hope that it carried gold; instead they garnered only hay intended for Mexican artillery and cavalry horses.

As the days dragged on without real action, these civilian soldiers of the Army of the North began to drift away to neglected chores on farms and ranches. Even Austin finally left for a diplomatic assignment, to be discussed presently, surrendering command to Burleson. When Burleson began to prepare for winter quarters, the force began to disintegrate. Just then, a Mexican courier was captured and interrogated in the presence of the men. He disclosed that Cos' men were disheartened and that their commander was preparing to surrender. This illustrates the danger of interrogating prisoners in public; what they say, whether true or not, can either worry or encourage soldiers falsely.

Believing that San Antonio was on the verge of collapse, Ben Milam shouted, "Who will go into San Antonio with old Ben Milam?" and received enthusiastic acceptance to his proposition. Siege became battle on December 5, but far from being ready to capitulate, Cos' men fought bravely and well for five days before surrendering on December 10. Milam fell early in the assault, and thus became the first martyred hero of the Texas Revolution. The fighting was fierce, and house-to-house, and featured tragedies such as one group of Texans firing at another group of Texans for most of a day until identities were established.

When Cós surrendered, Burleson paroled him and his men on condition that they leave Texas and never again take up arms against the Texans. Whether or not Cós would have kept this pledge, when he met Santa Anna coming north, he had no choice but to return and try to help remove the shame of loss.

THE CONSULTATION AND THE CONCLUDING BATTLES OF THE TEXAS REVOLUTION

While these events unfolded in San Antonio, the Texans met in consultation to make sense of them and to decide if additional action would be necessary. In a meeting in San Felipe in October, Richard Royall had already attempted to organize a government behind a Permanent Council. Royall served briefly as its president, arranged to commission privateers to prey on Mexican ships in the Gulf of Mexico, authorized postal routes, sent agents to the United States to recruit men and raise money for the Texas cause, and otherwise behaved as if he was the president of a real government—until the Consultation finally began on November 3. Afterwards, few ever thought of the Permanent Council again.

The options considered at the Consultation were simple: continued war within the Mexican system for the restoration of the Constitution of 1824, or independence from Mexico and the creation of an independent country. Even if some already thought of joining Texas to the United States, none articulated it now.

Discussions failed to produce a decision. Some wanted to affiliate with other revolutionaries in Mexico, such as General José Antonio Mexía, a state's righter, who had broken with Santa Anna after he had centralized power. Others wanted to declare independence and be done with Mexico's evident inability to govern itself democratically. In any event, their Declaration of Purpose split the difference and reflected as many policies as possible. They attacked Santa Anna for violating the Constitution of 1824, called for its restoration and affirmed their belief in indi-

Christ Episcopal Church, San Augustine, established in 1848. Although not the oldest, this 1869 building is the longest continuously standing Episcopal church in Texas.
COURTESY, TEXAS DEPARTMENT OF TRANSPORTATION.

vidual rights inviolate from government usurpation, but pledged to fight for independence if Mexico did not restore the state's rights constitution. And they agreed to meet again on March 1 to reexamine the situation before making a decision.

To see after affairs until they met again, the delegates created a provisional government under Governor Henry Smith of Brazoria, Lieutenant Governor James Robinson of Nacogdoches, and a council. They also commissioned William Wharton, Branch T. Archer, and Stephen F. Austin to travel to the United States to seek support in men and money for their ultimate course of action. This explains Austin's absence from San Antonio when the battle was fought there in December—he already had left on this diplomatic mission. The Consultation also named Sam Houston, former U.S. military officer, congressman, governor of Tennessee, Indian trader, well-known inebriate, and a delegate to the Consultation, as commander of an army that did not really exist when he accepted the job. All this required less than two weeks; the first meeting of the Consultation adjourned on November 14, 1835.

In San Antonio, Burleson relinquished command to Francis Johnson and went home, as did most of the men who had been in Texas long enough to have farms or ranches to tend.

The few volunteers who replaced them or joined James Fannin in Goliad were the more adventurous, less rooted with responsibility, or were recent arrivals from the United States who had ridden to the sound of the guns of Gonzáles or San Antonio.

Then Dr. James Grant arrived from Matamoros. Grant had lost land to Santa Anna's government and wanted it back, but he lacked the firepower to obtain it. That is where the Texans came in; Grant persuaded Johnson to lead some of the men who remained in San Antonio on a raid of Matamoros. Their reward would be plunder, his the restoration of his land. Sam Houston, titular commander of a scattered army that paid scant attention to his wishes, opposed the venture, but when the provisional council approved it, he could not stop Johnson. Houston left for East Texas, where, with the assistance of Adolphus Sterne, William Goyens, and others, he negotiated with The Bowl, a Cherokee chief, for the Indians to remain peaceful while the Texans faced danger from the southwest in return for generous land titles from the Texas government when it was established.

The various schemes to raid Matamoros with men led by Johnson, or later by James Fannin, never developed, but the departure of the men from San Antonio seriously weakened the Texans' ability to defend the place. James C. Neill commanded there after the departure of Johnson, and he implored Smith to send reinforcements. Smith did what he could, which was little enough because by then he was involved in a quarrel with the provisional council. The council eventually impeached Smith and recognized Robinson as governor, but Smith refused to acknowledge their authority, so the result was impasse.

Before the civilian government reached this sorry state, Smith had ordered William B. Travis to recruit 100 men and report to Neill. Travis tried but could rouse fewer that thirty men. This failure produced Travis' only loss of composure in the Alamo story; he asked Smith to relieve him of the assignment because he had failed to secure the full company requested. In the end he complied with the order, and soon after arriving in San Antonio in January 1836 found himself in

Above: The mythic scope of Texas history is graphically captured in this mural painted by Peter Rogers. The flames of the Alamo and the piercing gaze of revolutionary Sam Houston dramatically claim the center of interest. Flanking Houston on the left is colonizer Stephen F. Austin; on the right, Mirabeau B. Lamar and Anson Jones, from the period of statehood. Houston himself is surrounded by the remembered heroes of the Alamo, James Bowie, David Crockett, and William Barret Travis. The mural, designed by Peter Hurd, was commissioned in 1964 for the entrance to the Lorenzo de Zavala Texas State Archives and Library Building near the east end of the Capitol.

COURTESY, ARCHIVES DIVISION, TEXAS STATE LIBRARY.

Left: "The Battle of San Jacinto," Senate Chamber.

PAINTING BY HENRY A. MCARDLE.
COURTESY, STATE PRESERVATION BOARD

Right: Johanna Troutman, sewing the "Liberty or Death" flag for the Georgia Volunteers in 1835. She was honored as "The Betsy Ross of the Texas Revolution," and recognized in 1913 as the maker of the first Lone Star Flag, an "exquisite" silk banner which flew over Fort Defiance at Goliad. The painting, by Marie Cronin, hung in the State Senate until renovations in the early 1980s.

COURTESY, ARCHIVES DIVISION - TEXAS STATE LIBRARY.

Above: A tough frontiersman, James Bowie grew up on the Louisiana bayous. He gained fame riding alligators, wielding the awesome Bowie knife, dueling with pistols, and ultimately fighting to defend the Alamo. He gained his fortune in slave-smuggling and land speculation.

ORIGINAL PAINTING BY CHARLES B. NORMANN.
COURTESY, ARCHIVES DIVISION - TEXAS STATE LIBRARY.

command of the garrison when Neill departed on leave.

Travis' and Neill's regular troops combined numbered less than fifty; approximately 100 other men occupied San Antonio but they followed only Jim Bowie, a wild frontiersman debauched by drink and dispirited over the loss of his family to cholera two years earlier. Travis' youth clashed with Bowie's maturity, as did virtually every other aspect of their personalities. Eventually they worked out an uneasy truce in the form of a joint command, with all written and oral orders to have force only if both agreed, until Bowie's failing health—he was confined to a sick bed during the assault on the Alamo—left Travis in sole command by default.

With the assistance of engineer Green B. Jamison, Travis readied the abandoned Mission San Antonio de Valero compound, now known as the Alamo, for battle. They shored walls, built a palisade from the chapel to connect to a wall, and mounted cannon. David Crockett showed up with approximately twelve men who had joined him en route from Tennessee, and though he was the only genuine officer present with that peculiar kind of frontier military experience, he agreed to serve under Travis and Bowie as a "high private." Even in this capacity, his fiddle and tall tales and—when the battle came—his

marksmanship established for him an undeniable leadership role.

Santa Anna came north to avenge the insult caused of the loss of San Antonio in December, and whether consciously or not, vowed to follow the example of Joaquín de Arredondo, who had killed as many of the Magee Expedition participants as possible twenty years earlier. Santa Anna had been a member of Arredondo's army, and remembered the lesson well: he would deal these new *piratas* a similar fate.

The Mexican army reached the Río Grande, where Santa Anna divided his force. General José Urrea led one group on a southerly route to Goliad, while General Ramírez y Sesma led the other to San Antonio. Santa Anna remained with the latter group, and they reached San Antonio on February 22 to begin a siege that ended on March 6 with the fall of the Alamo and the death of every defender who remained within the compound. Some who had been there, such as Juan Seguin, were away serving as couriers when the assault came, and so survived; one, James Butler Bonham, had returned and did not survive.

Travis wrote many letters immediately before and during the siege pleading for reinforcements. About thirty men from Gonzáles answered his call; Fannin started out from Goliad to join him but turned back and found his fate at the hands of Urrea two weeks later. Travis' most famous letter, written on February 24 and addressed not just to Texans but to all the Americans in the world, spoke of his intention to "die like a soldier who never forgets what is due to his own honor and that of his country" whether help arrived or not. It did not come.

It would be appropriate to ask why Santa Anna chose to fight at the Alamo, an insignificant outpost, instead of hastening on with superior numbers to chase the rest of the Americans from Texas, or to wonder why Travis and the others remained when the outcome seemed so obvious. The answers are complicated.

Santa Anna fought at the Alamo for political, not military reasons; he could have bypassed the Alamo and cordoned it with several hundred men while he went about his

business elsewhere. But this would have been faithless to his promise to "sweep all before" him. And the loss of the Alamo may not have seemed so obvious to the approximately 180 men within the compound. Travis had all those letters out, and already the Gonzáles men had responded. Surely Fannin was on his way, and others as well. His second most famous letter, written on March 2 to David Ayers, who had custody of Travis' son, Charles Edward, began, "Take Care of my little boy. If the country should be saved, I may make him a splendid fortune; but if the country should perish, he will have nothing but the proud recollection that he is the son of "a man who died for his country." We emphasize "a man who died for his country" because we know that is what happened, and forget "If the country should be saved," which seems to be more the point of the statement. Probably Travis did not expect to die in the Alamo; instead, he thought help would come.

The siege lasted for thirteen days, the final assault only a few hours, and Travis was among the first to die after taking a bullet in the head while encouraging his defenders along the Alamo's north wall. Bowie died on his cot, and, of course, Crockett also met his death. For decades the story that he had died fighting remained an article of faith. Lately some have suggested that he and a few others surrendered when resistance was futile and were executed soon afterwards. It is a distinction without much of a difference; Crockett died at the same place, by the same hands, at

nearly the same time. And all the other defenders died as well, including the *tejanos.* Only a few women survived, including Mrs. Susanna Dickinson, wife of Alamo defender Almeron Dickinson, and their daughter, who were sent east with news of the Alamo's fall to frighten others in Texas.

While these events occurred, the Consultation met on March 1 in Washington-on-the-Brazos. The fifty-nine delegates knew that the Alamo was under siege and that the circumstance was grim. The next day George Childress produced a Declaration of Independence that resembled in form and substance the model provided in 1776 by Thomas Jefferson. The first section explained and invoked the theory of natural rights; the middle section indicted the Mexican nation for violating these rights, for putting up with Santa Anna and centralism, and pronounced Mexicans unfit for self-government; and the concluding section pledged their mutual efforts to make their independence a fact.

The Consultation asked Houston once more to lead their army, and continued in session until March 17 to write and adopt a constitution for the Republic of Texas should they have the luxury of establishing an independent government after the war. An interim president, David G. Burnet, was selected, along with Lorenzo de Zavala as vice president, and Thomas Jefferson Rusk was appointed secretary of war. Richard Ellis presided at these proceedings, so some regard him as the "first" president of an independent Texas; others give that honor to Burnet, but most would say that Sam Houston, elected by popular ballot in September long after the fighting ended, deserves it.

Houston had little time to worry about such matters. He left immediately for San Antonio and arrived in Gonzáles on March 11, where he found 374 men who had answered Travis' call. Leaderless, and failing to hear a signal cannon fired each morning in the Alamo since March 6, they had not advanced. Soon after Houston arrived Erastus "Deaf" Smith brought in Mrs. Dickenson and with her the story of the Alamo. The despair of a community that had just learned of the deaths of almost all of its male population was communicated to the men who had gathered there, and Houston realized that his "army" was in no condition to fight such a superior force as Santa Anna commanded.

Houston ordered the abandonment of Gonzáles and the town burned. Promising to fight later, he led his men east to the Colorado, then to the Brazos, where he stopped for rest and drill. The men grew restless with the retreat and mutiny was a possibility. Still Houston delayed, but by now he had learned the fate of Fannin at Goliad. When Urrea drew near, Fannin had tried to escape but his men were caught in the open and forced to surrender to superior numbers. Later, most were massacred. Now news of so many deaths at Goliad joined that of the Alamo and produced a panic known as the Runaway Scrape in which civilian dependents and prospective soldiers fled eastward, some all the way across the Sabine River.

Houston continued eastward, too, despite the grumbling, and Santa Anna came after him. Despairing at his slow-moving train and thinking that Houston would cross the Sabine as well, Santa Anna moved ahead with only 500 men to capture Burnet and his pretender government at Harrisburg, but arrived there after Texas officials had departed for the coast. Still in pursuit, Santa Anna's outriders arrived in time to watch Burnet, aboard a ship, sail for the safety of Galveston island. When he turned back to the north, Houston was waiting on the San Jacinto plain.

There is much controversy over Houston's leadership during the forty-three-day San Jacinto campaign. Branded a coward by many, including Burnet, who exhibited even less courage by his own flight, Houston plodded on, biding his time. Evidently he felt that his army had only one good fight in it, and he wanted as much advantage for that one as possible. There is even disagreement over how he came to be at San Jacinto, since he had given no order to go there when his line of march reached a literal and figurative "fork in the road." Some believe that the army took over and led Houston to battle; others think he let them do so to confirm their commitment. The latter option seems improbable; these men had wanted to fight since March 11.

The armies clashed first on the afternoon of April 20, 1836, before settling down for the night. Mirabeau B. Lamar, a private in the cavalry, so distinguished himself by saving the life of Secretary of War Rusk that he began the next day as a colonel. While Houston's men rested, still with a majority, reinforcements arrived for Santa Anna which gave him a few hundred more men on the field. The day dawned without battle; at noon Houston held a council of war—the first of the campaign—and was heard to exclaim, "Then fight and be damned," lending weight to the argument that he still did not want to fight. But fight he did.

The Texans moved across the plain, hidden by a swell in the land, at approximately 4:30 in the afternoon of April 21. Paced with a fife and drum playing "Will You Come To The Bower I Have Shaded For You," perhaps appropriately a song about seduction, the Texans reached the Mexican lines nearly undetected until their artillery, two pieces known as the Twin Sisters, blew a hole in the Mexican line. The battle lasted minutes, the slaughter for hours. Shouting "Remember The Alamo!" and "Remember Goliad!" they swarmed the Mexican camp, at first taking no prisoners. Eventually the Texans killed approximately 600 Mexicans and captured about 700 more, while losing two and suffering thirty wounded, seven of whom later died from their wounds. Among the wounded was Houston, who sustained a grievous wound in the leg, but Santa Anna was not among the killed or captured until the next day. He had escaped during the battle but was apprehended later.

At the time, the Texans' victory at San Jacinto and the capture of Santa Anna did not necessarily mean that the Texas Revolution had ended. Several thousand Mexican troops remained in Texas under General Vicente Filísola and the Mexican nation remained undefeated, if leaderless. Filísola's men or another vigorous invasion with better leadership probably could have reversed the outcome. But, Filísola obeyed Santa Anna's order to leave Texas and no more invasions came. While much remained for the Texans to worry about, they could now begin the process of implementing the government of the Republic of Texas envisioned at Washington-on-the-Brazos, and some could dream of making Texas the twenty-eighth star on the flag of the United States.

Mirabeau Buonaparte Lamar (1798-1859), successor of Houston as president of Texas in 1838. Lamar volunteered for the Texas army after the Alamo fell and was a cavalry colonel at San Jacinto. His harsh position on the Indian question helped defeat ratification of the Houston-Forbes treaty with the Cherokees. These memorable words epitomize the Georgian's attitude toward education: "The cultivated mind is the guardian genius of democracy." ✦

THE REPUBLIC & THE STATE, IN PEACE AND IN WAR

FROM INTERIM GOVERNMENT TO REPUBLIC

While the battles of the revolution raged, Stephen F. Austin, William Wharton, and Branch T. Archer prowled the United States seeking support for the Texans' cause. They secured approximately $100,000 in pledges, much of it never paid. Adolphus Sterne recruited two companies of New Orleans Greys at a personal expense of $990.00, which he later billed to the Republic of Texas. Unfortunately most of his recruits perished either in the Alamo or in the Goliad massacre. Units came from many places in the South, but unlike the New Orleans Greys most arrived too late to take part in the actual fighting. So many came in search of adventure or because of the promise of generous land grants for those who served in the Army that they became a problem when there was nothing for them to do after the Battle of San Jacinto.

Austin continued his quest for support. He even wrote to U.S. President Andrew Jackson for money, hoping to obtain part of the surplus in the national treasury during the one and only time in American history when the government had no debt and took in revenue faster than it could spend it. Austin knew of Jackson's attitude on westward expansion and regard for Texas as a potential accession for the U.S., but Jackson refused the request because the U.S. was bound by the Adams-Onís Treaty of 1819 in which interest in Texas was specifically disclaimed.

Treaties cannot alter feelings, and Jackson was interested in Texas. But he did not allow his personal feelings to become policy because he did not want war with Mexico. Instead he bided his time, assured by investigators that Texas faced no immediate danger because Mexico was in a disorganized state and not likely to mount another invasion soon. But he did post General Edmund Gaines with a force at the Sabine River, ostensibly in case Santa Anna decided to cross it, but actually to render aid and comfort to the Texans. Quite a few of Gaines' militia mustered out, crossed the river, and joined up with the Texans.

After Santa Anna's capture following the Battle of San Jacinto, he began negotiation for a settlement with Interim President David G. Burnet. The result was the Treaty of Velasco, signed on May 14, 1836. Santa Anna agreed to cease hostilities in Texas, to order his troops to return to Mexico and to release any Texan prisoners of war; and he acknowledged Texas independence. About all Santa Anna received was a promise that he would live—something Burnet had difficulty ensuring. It was also agreed that henceforth the boundary between Mexico and Texas would be the Río Grande. This river had not served as a boundary, even of internal Mexican political entities, and what had been regarded as Texas did not extend beyond San Antonio or the Colorado River. The Treaty of Velasco recognized Texas as a much larger portion of North America than anyone had thought previously. The Río Grande does not stop at El Paso; it continues northward to headwaters in the San Juan Mountains of southwestern Colorado. If the provisions of this treaty prevailed, Texas would include over half of New Mexico and Colorado and portions of Oklahoma, Kansas, and even Wyoming when the treaty line was projected northward from the Río Grande to the Louisiana Purchase line in the Rockies.

Burnet—and Santa Anna—had a scary moment when it came to living up to the Texan's bargain. Burnet put Santa Anna aboard the *Invincible* early in June 1836 to ship him home to Mexico, but armed men prevented the ship from sailing because they still wanted to punish the Mexican leader for excesses at the Alamo and Goliad. Burnet maintained custody, however, and like other problems, prepared to turn Santa Anna over to his successor following elections for permanent officers.

The continuing flood of Americans into Texas was, in the summer of 1836, perhaps the chief of those problems. Men who came to fight at Gonzáles twice before then had been easy to lead to a siege of San Antonio and later to a battle on the San Jacinto River. Only a spark was lacking to ignite another Matamoros expedition or some other potentially disastrous scheme that would solidify support behind some Mexican *caudillo* who promised to reclaim Texas. These men came in response to the promise of land for military service. A case in point was James McMahon, who arrived in the summer and entered the Texas army. Eventually McMahon claimed a 640-acre headright, his for merely coming to Texas, and three 320-acre bounty grants, one for each three month's service. The army posed a delicate problem for Burnet and the Republic's permanent presidents: they needed men in case of Mexican attack, but they did not need for the attack to occur in the first place.

Burnet lacked real authority to deal with such problems, so he hastened the election for permanent officers by calling an election early in September. Henry Smith announced for the presidency immediately, and Austin followed, although more reluctantly. Just before the election Sam Houston threw his hat into the ring and in doing so secured the election: Houston received 5,119 and Austin but 587 of the 6,640 votes cast while Smith received

the remainder. Mirabeau B. Lamar was elected vice-president. On the same day about half as many voted in a referendum regarding U.S. statehood for Texas, and the vote was 3,277 to only ninety-one who favored Texas' continued status as a republic.

How might one explain this rejection of Austin, who had led Texans ably since 1821? Houston's military reputation, denounced while the campaign occurred, soared in the aftermath of victory, and this is one obvious answer. Equally, the turnout was small considering the population. Most of those who remembered Austin's leadership from colonial days were home tending their farms and ranches, while the newcomers, who were still earning land by military service, knew little about Austin and much about Houston.

Judging by the vote on seeking admission to the United States, few expected the Republic to remain in business for long. Southerners especially expected Texas to become the next territorial acquisition for the U.S., for although the term "manifest destiny" had not been coined, the spirit it identified was strong. Even the Republic's president, Sam Houston, was an advocate of admission. His policy reflected his examination of his country: virtually without money, recognition from a single established nation, and facing a potential enemy in the south that now renounced the Treaty of Velasco, he thought

admission to the Union the best course for Texas so he could turn these monumental problems over to an established government.

The Republic began with a population of approximately 40,000 people—too few for admission to the U.S. It hosted mainly subsistence farmers with little to export besides cotton, sugar cane, and beef, and none of these exports were sufficiently developed to produce much trade or revenue for individuals or for the government. Still, Houston's sense of the inevitability of admission caused him to press for it immediately. He ran into the objections of northeasterners, led by John Quincy Adams, and abolitionists everywhere who did not want additional slavery territory added to the American union. President Jackson, who privately favored the admission of Texas, was near the end of his second term and did not want to interfere with the election of his hand-picked successor, Martin Van Buren of New York, who also opposed slavery. So Texas' request languished. The best Jackson could do before his term ended in March 1837 was to signal that, if Congress would back him, he would recognize Texas' independence from Mexico in order to prevent England or France from gaining influence there. His move succeeded, and Texas

received official U.S. recognition. One of Jackson's last official acts was to appoint Alcee LaBranche of Louisiana as the first U.S. diplomat posted to the Republic of Texas.

Texans celebrated even this achievement, but the Republic's problems remained: lack of money, a restless army, potential Indian problems, and the threat of a new Mexican Invasion—all issues of potential high expense. Secretary of the Treasury Henry Smith reported to Houston that he had no money and few prospects for obtaining any, and that he faced a debt of over $1 million from the revolution. Houston's policy was to spend as little as possible, not provoke the Indians or Mexico, and continue efforts to join the Union.

Money problems increased. Texans might have gained some revenue from land sales, but instead continued to give land away as an attraction for settlement and development. Taxes produced little money because the population had none to give. Borrowing from financial institutions in the U.S. yielded perhaps $500,000 while the public debt increased to over $2 million despite Houston's parsimonious administration. And a bitter political rivalry developed between Houston and Vice President Lamar.

Lamar's views differed from Houston's in every detail. Whereas Houston wanted to join the U.S., Lamar dreamed of an independent empire; Houston spent little, but Lamar did not fear deficit spending in the least, evidently believing that future growth of the Republic

would provide the means to pay off the expenses that encouraged such growth; and Houston's well-known affection and respect for Indians was reversed by Lamar, who wanted them gone from Texas. Regarding Mexico, Lamar did not much care if that nation renewed the war or not. So Houston, whose first term was limited to only two years by a constitutional provision that also prevented him from serving successive terms, hoped that someone, anyone, besides Lamar would succeed him. He first supported Peter Grayson, and later James Collingsworth, but both died during the campaign. It probably would not have mattered; at this point Lamar reflected the spirit of the majority much better than did Houston.

Lamar, who served a three-year term, stepped out boldly. He spent money—money he had printed, not real, secured, gold-backed money—to create the image of success. He authorized campaigns against Indians, blocked the fulfillment of the treaty Houston had negotiated with the Cherokees during the revolution, and "rented" Commodore Edwin Moore to secure Yucatán rebels whether Mexico appreciated it or not. He sent an expedition to Santa Fe, partially to convince that area that it really had become part of Texas and partly to tap into the lucrative Santa Fe Trail trade. Most of this produced negative rather than positive results.

Lamar did achieve some diplomatic recognition among European countries and he succeeded in relocating the Republic's capital. Sam Houston had assumed office in Columbia,

which was the Republic's capital only because that was Burnet's location when the transfer of power occurred. He soon moved to the new city of Houston, partly because the city's founders had named the place for him and partly because they offered a building for the government. Lamar would not serve there, even as Houston later refused to serve his second term in Austin, Lamar's capital. Lamar secured congressional approval to relocate the capital, then selected a site on the Colorado River near the village of Waterloo. He wisely named the new city Austin, instead of Lamar, to honor the Father of Texas and Houston's secretary of state until his death in December 1836. It is ironic that the image of the bold Texan is owed more to Lamar than to Houston despite the differences in physique and historical image of the men. In historical image Houston, tall and robust, overshadows the diminutive and often ill Lamar, but it was the latter who pursued the vision of an independent and growing Republic and Houston who worked always to merge Texas with the United States.

Lamar's term ended in 1841 when Houston won re-election. Houston cut expenses every way possible, although the money question was out of control; the printing presses continued to roll and the value of their products continued to decline. He faced down such domestic problems as the "Regulator-Moderator War," an election dispute that developed into a full-scale feud with lethal qualities. And he faced additional trouble with Mexico.

In the spring of 1842 Mexican raiders ranged as far into Texas as Goliad and produced another Runaway Scrape hysteria. Troops were raised but the raiders retreated into Mexico before an engagement developed. They came again in September, this time led by General Adrian Woll. Woll temporarily captured San Antonio and left with hostages when he retreated. Houston raised 750 men to deal with the invasion and placed Arthur Somervell in command with orders to pursue the raiders to the Río Grande but not to cross it. When he reached Laredo, Somervell refused to cross the river but the men deposed their leader and elected William S. Fisher to command them.

Fisher led the Texans to the villa of Mier and placed it under siege. They asked for tribute to prevent a sacking of the town, but while they waited for response, General Pedro Ampudia quietly reinforced the area, and surprised the Texans when they attacked. He captured those who remained alive and marched them under guard to Mexico City. Some found freedom in an abortive escape attempt, but the majority eventually participated in one of the most famous episodes in Texas history that contributed the idiom

"drawing the black bean" to the language. The men were sentenced in this way—one in ten would be executed, the remaining nine to a life in prison. Black and white beans were drawn, black meaning death and white life. One legendary figure, "Bigfoot" Wallace, claimed that he noticed that the black beans were smaller, so he searched until he found the smallest bean remaining when it was his turn to draw. Those not executed were released later through diplomatic efforts by the United States. Fortunately, the incident did not lead to renewed "hot" war between Mexico and Texas, although the Mexicans continued to claim that Texas was not an independent nation.

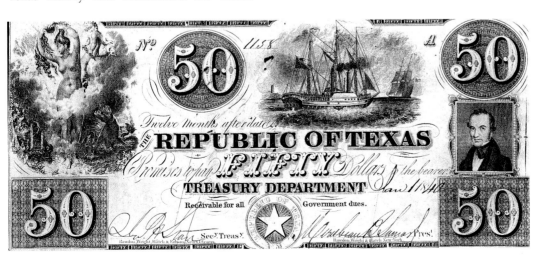

CHAPTER FIVE

A first cousin of Queen Victoria, "Karl, Prinz zu Solms-Braunfels." Prince Carl was one of the Prussian nobles forming the Adelsverein in 1842. Their group, the Society for the Protection of German Immigrants in Texas, sent Prince Carl to Texas in 1844 as executive head of its immigration project. The prince resigned the following year amid many difficulties, and the Adelsverein appointed Von Meusebach to replace him. The first permanent settlements in the area above the Balcones fault were German ones.

ANNEXATION AND STATEHOOD IN THE AMERICAN UNION

Faced with the potential of renewed war and continuing financial and other domestic problems, Houston renewed efforts to gain admission to the United States. His ministers, Isaac Van Zandt and James Pinckney Henderson, pressed the U.S. government on grounds of Texas' need for assistance, but also emphasized that if admission was not forthcoming that the influence of England and France in Texas would increase. Early in the 1840s, a more sympathetic administration prevailed in Washington after the succession to the presidency of Vice President John Tyler following the death of President William Henry Harrison. John C. Calhoun, Tyler's secretary of state and a Southerner, concluded a treaty of annexation providing for territorial status for Texas with Van Zandt and Henderson. The Southern way of life, including slavery, already had expanded to Texas, and Calhoun wanted to attach the area to the United States formally. Unfortunately, a two-thirds majority of the U.S. Senate did not agree and failed to ratify the treaty. Texans were disappointed, but in truth some Texans still agreed with Lamar's preference for independence and others thought that Texas deserved full statehood.

When Houston's second term ended in 1844, Anson Jones defeated Edward Burleson for the presidency of Texas. Although he resented the reference, Jones was considered a "Houston man," and he did agree with Old Sam on most issues, especially on annexation, and this was an issue in the campaign. Equally important, westward expansion became the principal issue in the presidential election in the U.S. held that same year. Whig and third party candidates opposed to annexation tried to ignore "the Texas Question," but the Democratic platform boldly embraced it by calling for the "re-annexation of Texas and the re-occupation of Oregon;" and the campaign for their candidate, James Knox Polk of Tennessee, a protégé of Jackson, emphasized this issue strongly. The "re-occupation" referred to the long-standing joint occupation of Oregon by the U.S. and England, and the

American attitude that it was time for the U.S. to have sole authority there. The "re-annexation of Texas" meant to some the re-affiliation of Americans in Texas with the country of their birth and to others that the U.S. really had purchased the territory from France in 1803 and lost it by the Adams-Onís Treaty. Both gave definition to the naming and spirit of Manifest Destiny, the term for westward expansion coined by John O'Sullivan in the midst of the campaign.

Polk's victory prompted lame-duck President Tyler to commence the process for the annexation of Texas even before his term ended by asking Congress for a joint resolution on the issue rather than reviving the treaty process. A two-thirds majority still would have trouble in the Senate, but a simple majority in both houses was easier. The joint resolution passed on February 26, 1845, called for the admission of Texas as a slave state, allowed Texas to retain control of its public land as well as responsibility for its debt, and provided for its potential division into other states in the future.

Texans generally supported the offer of statehood, but England and France attempted to prevent the loss of a potential client state that blocked U.S. expansion. They first obtained an agreement from Jones for a ninety-day delay in Texas' response, and used the time to convince Mexico at last to acknowledge the independence of Texas if it would agree not to join the U.S. Mexican officials knew that if Texas did join the U.S. that their long-standing threat of war with that country would have to be fulfilled or they would look foolish and weak. Jones presented both offers to the Texas Congress, which made the inevitable choice for statehood.

A convention gathered in July 1845 to write a new constitution for the state of Texas. Thomas J. Rusk presided at the convention and was the dominant influence in drafting the document that was accepted on October 13. The constitution established the familiar pattern for state governments that reflected the example of the national government: executive affairs under a governor and lieutenant governor; legislative matters the business of a bicameral legislature; and a judiciary. President

Polk signed the resolution making Texas the twenty-eighth of the United States on December 29, although the full surrender of authority from Republic to state officials was not completed until February 16, 1846. Texans selected James Pinckney Henderson of San Augustine as their first governor, and the legislature elected Rusk and Houston as the first two U.S. Senators from Texas.

The life of citizens in the new state differed little from that of colonial or republican days. It is easy to think of such watermark shifts in political allegiance from Mexico to independence to statehood as taking place over a long period of time, but such was not the case in Texas—early 1830s as a colony to statehood in 1845 or 1846 was but fifteen years. Food, shelter, clothing, health, and advocacy of state's rights and slavery, remained the same. So did efforts to attract new residents, and the legislature continued the Texas Congress' program of generous land grants and even resurrected the empresarial system for the Peters Company and others. The state of Texas was Southern in most respects, save two: it had a frontier line where confrontations with Indians continued, and an international border with a still hostile neighbor.

The admission of Texas to the Union provoked Mexican hostility and led to war. Polk sent John Slidell to Mexico on a mission to avoid the conflict, but the diplomat could not even gain a hearing with Mexican officials. Polk also sent General Zachary Taylor to the Nueces River to guard against military penetration from the south. When Mexico manned the Río Grande, the impression was created that what the two nations disputed was the territory between the rivers. Such was not the case. Texas was not the cause of the Mexican-American War (1846-1848) so much as it was the excuse for it. To secure Texas from Mexico, Taylor need never have left the Nueces River line. Instead, after a clash between American and Mexican patrols in the area between the rivers, each commander could communicate to his political headquarters in Washington or Mexico City that his troops had been fired upon on their own soil. A declaration of war and an invasion of Mexico led by Taylor followed, and eventually Mexico was invaded at Vera Cruz by forces

led by General Winfield Scott. Eventually a truce and the Treaty of Guadalupe Hidalgo officially ended the war in 1848. The treaty confirmed Texas as part of the U.S. Mexico ceded approximately one half of her territory to the U.S., including land that became the states of New Mexico, Arizona, part of Colorado, Utah, Nevada, and above all, California—likely Polk's principal goal of the war.

Texas served as the staging area for the war against Mexico. Both Taylor's and Scott's expeditions were launched from bases in Texas, and more Texans served during the conflict that did citizens of any other state. The Texas Rangers fought so fiercely, and behaved so badly in the view of their commanders, that for both Mexicans and American generals they well earned the name "los diablos tejanos"— The Devil Texans.

In 1850, Texas surrendered claims to western and northwestern lands and assumed its present boundaries as a result of the Compromise of 1850, enacted by the Congress. The compromise was made necessary by the desire of Californians to enter the Union as a free state, which would have upset the sectional balance between free and slave states in the Senate, probably permanently. Henry Clay, the Great Compromiser, pulled one last card out of his hat. The compromise admitted California as a free state, organized New Mexico and Utah as territories without reference to slavery, eliminated the slave trade but not slavery from the District of Columbia,

"Texians Paving the Streets at the Archbishop's Palace," aftermath of the Mier Expedition. In a counter demonstration of force to Mexican General Woll's temporary recapturing of San Antonio in September of 1842, a large Texan force left San Antonio on November 8, 1842 under General Alexander Somervell (1796-1854). After Somervell's successful capture of Laredo, the largely ragtag-recruited army plundered the town without orders. Somervell declared the demonstration aborted and marched home, but about 300 men stayed and marched to the adobe town of Mier, Mexico, where, after being surrounded by a large Mexican force, they voted to surrender. The prisoners were marched into the interior of Mexico and participated in the "black bean" decree. Survivors, including "Big Foot" Wallace, were eventually returned to Texas through the efforts of American and British diplomacy.

COURTESY, ARCHIVES DIVISION - TEXAS STATE LIBRARY.

Above: Treaty of Peace, depicting negotiations for the Meusebach-Comanche Nation Treaty one week before its ratification in Fredericksburg on May 9, 1847. The treaty enabled the immigrants to claim their land from the state of Texas. Copied from an original painting by Mrs. Ernest Marschall, daughter of John O. Meusebach.

COURTESY GILLESPIE COUNTY HISTORICAL SOCIETY, AND THE ARCHIVES DIVISION - TEXAS STATE LIBRARY.

Below, right: Texas, 1846 map drawn by David H. Burr.

COURTESY, CARTOGRAPHIC COLLECTIONS OF MRS. JENKINS GARRETT, FORT WORTH; HOUSED AT THE SPECIAL COLLECTIONS DIVISION, THE UNIVERSITY OF TEXAS AT ARLINGTON LIBRARIES, ARLINGTON, TEXAS.

contained a stringent fugitive slave law making federal law enforcement available to return runaway slaves to their owners, and whittled away from Texas those lands whose citizens did not think they were in Texas anyway. For this, the state received a grant of $10 million to deal with its public debt. The sum was adequate to this purpose and also enabled the legislature to remand most state taxes for a decade.

The principal political issue in Texas during the first half of the 1850s concerned transportation and whether the state should concentrate on subsidizing the construction of railroads or dredging its rivers to improve water transportation. Governor Elisha M. Pease led the fight to do something, but little was done in either area, and by the end of the decade Texas hosted only 400 or so miles of railroad track, most of it a spider-web of short lines that served Houston and Galveston but connected little else in a railroad network.

During Texas' first experience of statehood, notable changes and advancements occurred. Baylor University, supported by the Baptists, was founded in 1846. Prince Carl von Solm-Braunfels and the *Adelsverein*, a society that aided Germans emigrating to the New World, and other agencies assisted a large group of Europeans to resettle in Texas, mostly in the area northwest of Indianola, where they established Fredericksburg, New Braunfels, and other communities. And of course immigrants continued from the U.S. as well, particularly from the South.

SECESSION AND CIVIL WAR IN TEXAS

The end of the first decade of statehood found many Texans in doubt about their continued affiliation with the Union. As a slave

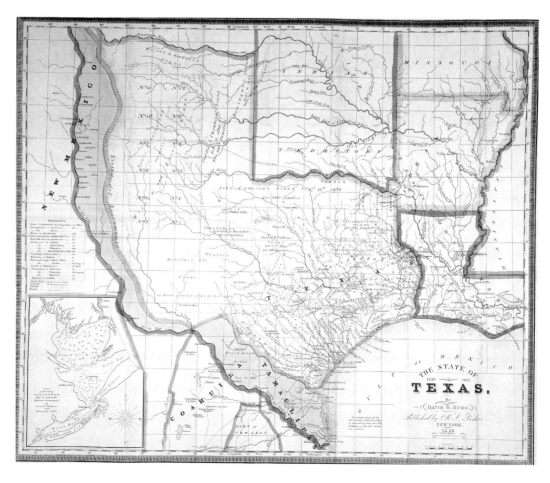

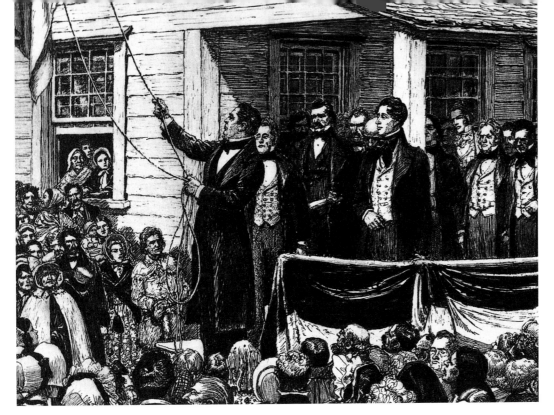

holding state, they resented the activities of abolitionists and anti-slave groups to interfere with their internal institutions. The passage of the Kansas-Nebraska Act in 1854 pleased many Texans because it opened for the expansion of slavery territory closed since the Missouri Compromise of 1820. But Senator Sam Houston voted against the law, losing favor with many in his home state. Criticism of his vote included a promise that the legislature would not return him to the Senate at the completion of his second term. He returned to Texas , ran for governor in 1857, and lost to Hardin R. Runnels, a state's righter and advocate of slavery. Houston's loss was owed partially to his long absence from the state while serving in the Senate. When he ran for the office again two years later, he unseat-

ed Runnels. This should not be regarded as a change of attitude by Texas voters on the issues of slavery and state's rights; instead, Houston was able to remind old timers and inform newcomers of his previous military and governmental service during the Revolution and the Republic, and their vote represented gratitude more than endorsement of his love for the Union.

Houston assumed the governor's office in time to preside over secession, however reluctantly. When the Democratic Party split in 1860, giving the new Republican Party a solid chance to elect Abraham Lincoln to the presidency, Houston attempted to be the nominee of a new Constitutional-Union Party, whose goal was to deny Republican or Democratic "extremists" a victory and force the House of Representatives to select a compromise candidate who might hold the Union together. None of this happened. Houston did not run; and Lincoln was elected, prompting the secession of South Carolina, Georgia, Florida, Alabama, Mississippi, and Louisiana, and causing many Texans to want to follow suit.

Because he loved the Union, Houston impeded secession as long as possible. He refused to call a

secession convention or to convene the legislature, two secession methods that had been used in other states. The secessionists, however, persuaded county judges to call an election for delegates to a secession convention that would meet in Austin in January 1861. Houston then called the legislature into session. But, since many legislators had also been elected as delegates to the secession convention, they took no action to prevent the convention. Oran M. Roberts presided over the convention that enacted an ordinance of secession, subject to a popular vote, and dispatched delegates to meet with representatives of the other seceded states in Montgomery, Alabama, where the Confederate States of America was organized. The Texans participated only unofficially, if effectively, awaiting the outcome of the popular vote at home. Texans voted three to one in favor of secession, and March 2, the anniversary of the Texas Declaration of Independence from Mexico, was selected as the date when Texas officially became a Confederate state. At the secession convention, delegate James Throckmorton displayed uncommon courage in the face of abuse from other delegates when he voted against secession. He responded, "Mr. Chairman, when the rabble hiss, well may patriots tremble!"

Amendments were adopted to the Texas constitution to accommodate the Confederate affiliation, and the convention demanded that all elected officials take a new oath of office to confirm their loyalty to the new national government. On the designated day Houston sat quietly and heard his name

called three times to take the oath; when he did not do so, Lieutenant Governor Edward Clark took the oath to complete Houston's term of office until new officials were elected.

Texas then hosted approximately twenty-five percent of the entire U.S. Army, and most were posted along the frontier for Indian defense. Their commander, General David E. Twiggs, sympathized with the South but had a long career of loyalty to the U.S. as well. He attempted to retire before he had to surrender troops he had no intention of sending into battle against the Texans, but issues forced him to surrender before his retirement was approved. These troops had been offered to Houston to prevent secession, but he, too, refused to use them, claiming that he had fought for Texas in the past and would not fight against her now. He lived as a pri-

vate citizen in Galveston for a time, then moved to Huntsville, where he died in July 1863. Houston remained a Unionist, but the old soldier could not resist criticism of some Confederate military leaders, seeming to indicate more support for their cause than might be expected from one who had opposed secession so vigorously. Too, his son Temple fought in the grey, and neither could Houston restrain pride in his son's accomplishments. In 1861 Texans elected Francis R. Lubbock as their first Confederate governor, and in 1863, he was succeeded by the state's second and last Confederate governor, Pendleton Murrah. Texas sent Louis T. Wigfall and W.S. Oldham to represent the state in the Confederate senate, and Texan John H. Reagan served as the Confederacy's only postmaster general. Lubbock readied his state for war and supported the central Confederate government under President Jefferson Davis so enthusiastically that he resigned to join the Confederate army and to serve with Davis in Richmond, Virginia. Murrah was also a sincere supporter of the Confederacy, but was more of a state's righter than Lubbock in dealing with the central government.

Texans served enthusiastically in the Confederate military. Estimates based on the census of 1860 indicated approximately 90,000 males of eligible age for military service; approximately 65,000 Texans did serve. Albert Sidney Johnston, who held the post of Secretary of War during the Republic but who served in the U.S. army in 1861, resigned and joined the Confederacy. Lubbock formed volunteer companies into the Texas Brigade, better known as Hood's Texas Brigade after its first commander, John Bell Hood, who had served in Texas in the U.S. army before the war. Robert E. Lee called them "my Texans"—Lee, too, had served long in Texas during the 1840s and 1850s—and they learned that his confidence in their fighting ability led them into the thick of most battles and a high casualty rate. Other famous units from Texas included Terry's Texas Rangers, commanded by General B. F. Terry until his death, and the brigade commanded by Lawrence Sullivan Ross, later a governor of Texas. Most Texans

who served in combat during the Civil War did so outside Texas, but a few battles were fought in close proximity to their state. General Henry Hopkins Sibley led many Texans on an expedition into New Mexico to make it Confederate territory, but they were driven back by the desert and by Union forces commanded by General E. R. Canby. After the Union blockaders captured Galveston, the island was retaken by Texans commanded by General John Bankhead Magruder on January 1, 1863. On September 8, 1863, Lieutenant Dick Dowling and an artillery battery successfully prevented nearly 5,000 Union troops from disembarking from vessels by disabling two ships in the channel at Sabine Pass. In 1864, Confederate forces commanded by Richard

Top: Confederate Evacuation of Brownsville.
COURTESY, ARCHIVES DIVISION, TEXAS STATE LIBRARY.

Above: Home of Captain John Anderson, who arrived in Corpus Christi in 1852. Note the stack of hides, lower left. The photograph can be dated after the Civil War, since that was when he built the "Dutch windmill." The mill was used to saw wood, grind corn, gin cotton, and grind salt – fine for the table, coarse for preserving hides and curing meat.
COURTESY, CORPUS CHRISTI PUBLIC LIBRARY, CORPUS CHRISTI, TEXAS.

Taylor, including many Texans, repulsed
Union General N. P. Banks' Red River
Campaign at the Battle of Mansfield in
Louisiana. And the last land battle of the
Civil War was fought at Palmito Ranch in
southern Texas after most other Confeder-
ates had surrendered.

Lubbock's and Murrah's efforts forced some
industrialization on an otherwise wholly agricultural state. Powder mills were established
in Austin and elsewhere, and even the state
penitentiary in Huntsville was turned into a
textile mill. The state government wrestled
with the problem of exporting its cotton

despite the Union blockade, and found that
hauling it to Mexico and passing it through
the port of Baghdad was their most efficient
solution. They also sold bonds to support the
Confederacy financially.

Civil War produced internal problems for
Texas. Unionism within the state remained,
and such prominent Texans as Throckmorton
refused to serve in either the Confederate
civilian or military posts, but he did consent
in 1864 to lead Texans against hostile Indians.
Others, such as financier S. M. Swensen, left
the state and contributed their considerable
talents to the Union. Edmund J. Davis, later
Texas' Reconstruction governor, left but
returned as commander of a Union military
unit. Texans were suspicious of all who did
not support their cause, including Germans,
and some persecution of this group occurred;
in north Texas, fears of unionist fifth-column
activities prompted the hanging of over forty
persons.

Texan civilians suffered hardships from
shortages that resulted from the blockade,
military priority for commodities, and lack of
production since so much of the work force
was away. Women and children had to shoul-
der the load when their men left for military
service, and often had to do without sugar,
salt, coffee, writing paper, and other things, or
find substitutes for them. Refugees from
threatened areas of Arkansas, Louisiana, and
other states sought haven in Texas, and, like

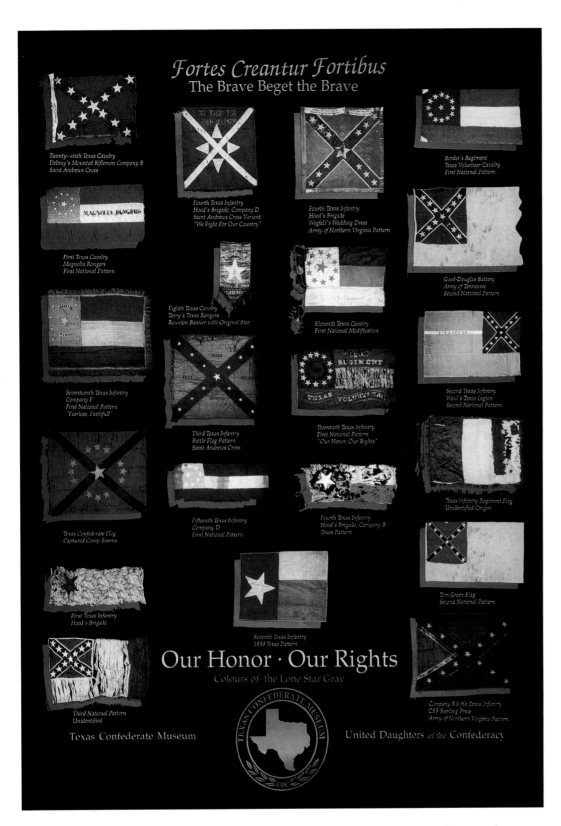

Fortes Creantur Fortibus
The Brave Beget the Brave

Twenty–sixth Texas Cavalry
Debray's Mounted Rifleman Company B
Saint Andrews Cross

First Texas Cavalry
Magnolia Rangers
First National Pattern

Seventeenth Texas Infantry
Company F
First National Pattern
"Fearless, Faithfull"

Texas Confederate Flag
Captured Camp Simms

First Texas Infantry
Hood's Brigade

Third National Pattern
Unidentified

Fourth Texas Infantry
Hood's Brigade, Company D
Saint Andrews Cross Variant
"We Fight For Our Country"

Eighth Texas Cavalry
Terry's Texas Rangers
Reunion Banner with Original Star

Third Texas Infantry
Battle Flag Pattern
Saint Andrews Cross

Fifteenth Texas Infantry
Company D
First National Pattern

Seventh Texas Infantry
1839 Texas Pattern

Fourth Texas Infantry
Hood's Brigade
Wigfall's Wedding Dress
Army of Northern Virginia Pattern

Eleventh Texas Cavalry
First National Modification

Twentieth Texas Infantry
First National Pattern
"Our Honor, Our Rights"

Fourth Texas Infantry
Hood's Brigade, Company B
Texas Pattern

Border's Regiment
Texas Volunteer Cavalry
First National Pattern

Good-Douglas Battery
Army of Tennessee
Second National Pattern

Second Texas Infantry
Waul's Texas Legion
Second National Pattern

Texas Infantry Regiment Flag
Unidentified Origin

Tom Green Flag
Second National Pattern

Company B Fifth Texas Infantry
CSS Sterling Price
Army of Northern Virginia Pattern

Our Honor · Our Rights
Colours of the Lone Star Gray

Texas Confederate Museum

United Daughters of the Confederacy

TEXAS CONFEDERATE MUSEUM
UDC

Kate Stone, who described Texas as the "dark corner of the Confederacy," were sometimes unwelcomed guests, as were the 200,000 slaves brought to Texas to prevent their confiscation.

The war ended at different times for Confederates because each army was surrendered independently. Many never surrendered so much as they just quit because they were tired of fighting, were needed at home, or were disheartened. Some, such as Governor Murrah, fled to Mexico; most trudged home to whatever was left and awaited the definition of Reconstruction by those who had defeated them.

The poster print "Our Honor - Our Rights" features the patriotic slogan "Fortes Creantur Fortibus, The Brave Beget the Brave" and illustrates twenty-one of the thirty-three Confederate flags owned by the Texas Division of the United Daughters of the Confederacy. The Albert Sidney Johnston chapter of the UDC began collecting material relating to the South and the Civil War in 1903. Its collection was first located in the northwest corner of the first floor of the Capitol; then from 1917 to 1989, in the Old Land Office building; and, since 1989 it has been in storage. In 1997 the collection will open at its new site at Hill College in Hillsboro, Texas. Among miscellaneous memorabilia in the collection are the Dick Dowling Collection and items of Terry's Texas Rangers (Eighth Texas Cavalry). Research since the printing of the poster reveals the need for the following corrections: the second flag from the top in column one should be labeled "Nineteenth [instead of First] Texas Cavalry"; the fourth flag from the top in column one should be labeled "Captured at Fort Semmes at Matagorda" instead of "Captured at Camp Simms"; the top flag in column two should be labeled "Thirty-Sixth Texas Cavalry" instead of "Fourth Texas Infantry"; the flag at the top of column three originally had a yellow border; and the third flag from the top in column three bears the inscription "Our Homes - Our Rights" instead of "Our Honor - Our Rights."

PHOTOGRAPHY BY DAN HATZENBUEHLER. COURTESY, TEXAS CONFEDERATE MUSEUM, UNITED DAUGHTERS OF THE CONFEDERACY.

Opposite, bottom: Civil War POW "Camp Ford, Texas," sketched by G.W. Simmons and published in the March 4, 1865 issue of Harper's Weekly. *Beginning in the summer of 1863, when John S. "Rip" Ford's training camp in East Texas near Tyler was converted for prisoners of war, Camp Ford operated as the largest such facility west of the Mississippi River, with 4,700 federals—from nearly one hundred regiments, plus sailors from transports and gunboats, as well as some Union sympathizers, spies and Confederate deserters—essentially housing themselves within the ten-acre, sixteen-foot high stockade enclosure. They built log huts, burrows called "shebangs," and brush arbors, and made tents from blankets. The overcrowding was somewhat lessened by prisoner of war exchanges; but the frequent escape efforts were usually thwarted by the guards' tracking dogs and the distance to Union lines.*

COURTESY, ARCHIVES DIVISION - TEXAS STATE LIBRARY.

RECONSTRUCTION
& ECONOMIC RECOVERY

Opposite: Joseph F. Glidden (1813-1907) received the first patent on barbed wire in 1867. In 1873, he perfected it in Illinois and the same year, together with a partner, formed the Isaac L Ellwood Manufacturing Company to produce a two-strand, twisted barbed wire in a back room of his hardware store. The wire permitted a technological revolution in ranching, especially on the western plains where other fencing materials were prohibitive in price. With windmills and enclosed pastures, both herds and pastures could be upgraded and improved. The company expanded and reorganized in 1881 as the Superior Barbed Wire Company, and in 1898 merged into the American Steel and Wire Company, which became United States Steel. Ellwood began ranching in Texas, and while his home remained in DeKalb, Illinois, he focused on his ranches until he eventually had total holdings of 395,000 acres in Texas.

COURTESY, PANHANDLE-PLAINS HISTORICAL MUSEUM, CANYON, TEXAS.

REJOINING THE UNION

The story of Reconstruction in Texas may be understood better if we agree on what the term means, because it has plural uses. Political Reconstruction could mean simply the process of Texas being regarded as a part of the American Union once more, but Texans would never accept this as adequate because at the time Radical Republicans continued to control the state. Texans generally regarded to be Reconstruction over only when their state had been "Redeemed," meaning that local white Democrats once more controlled state government and business affairs. Texas was recognized as a member of the Union a second time on March 30, 1870, but most Texans insisted that they continued to endure Reconstruction until the adoption of the Redeemer constitution of 1876.

Economic Reconstruction lasted longer. By the end of the Civil War, Texans and other former Confederates had suffered enormous economic loss, including investment in slave property that now was, in the words of Margaret Mitchell, "gone with the wind;" the former slaves were still there but they no longer represented investment or wealth. Land values plummeted because few had the means to purchase it except "Carpetbaggers"—Northerners who came south in war's aftermath to take advantage of political and economic opportunities created by the outcome of the war—or "Scalawags"—local whites who cooperated with the Carpetbaggers, and perhaps a few local whites who had managed to salvage enough money to survive. Confederate money and bonds were worthless and the people disheartened by loss. The result was an economic recession that persisted until World War II except in areas where successful cattle ranches or oil bonanzas yielded sudden and substantial wealth.

Social Reconstruction refers to new arrangements for former slaves, whose status as a specie of property formally ended with the passage of the Thirteenth Amendment in 1865. Although the Fourteenth Amendment (1868) recognized the U.S. citizenship of all persons "born or naturalized" within its boundaries, the actual status of blacks in relation to whites in political, economic, and every other relationship could not be solved easily by the Constitution or other federal law. Indeed, if we define the goal of Social Reconstruction as establishing a society in which race consciousness was absent and all citizens interacted without "place" assignments, then it must be concluded that this definition of Reconstruction has never been achieved.

Disappointment from military loss in the Civil War merged into bitterness over Reconstruction experiences for many white Texans. Redeemers and early twentieth-century historians have pointed out the high taxes and political corruption prevailing in the defeated Confederate states under Radical rule and consider the era of Reconstruction only negatively. Most later historians view the end of slavery and at least the goal of a non-discriminatory society positively, and also point out that Reconstruction—high taxes, corruption and all—prevailed throughout the nation and was not something confined only to the South. They also argue that for the first time states such as Texas used some of those taxes for the support of public education and transportation and other services long established elsewhere.

We should briefly review the five plans of Reconstruction to learn how each affected Texas. There were two "executive" plans, based on the presidential power to pardon: one each from Presidents Abraham Lincoln and Andrew Johnson. The three "congressional" plans, based on the power of the Congress to determine qualifications for statehood and for recognizing its own members, included

the Wade-Davis Bill, the Fourteenth
Amendment, and the Reconstruction Acts of
1867. The presidential plans were termed
"conservative" by the definition of the times
but would be called "liberal" at a later date
because they called for an easier path for the
seceded states. Congressional plans were called
"radical" after the faction of the Republican
Party and congressional leadership which
offered them, and this definition does not necessarily change with the passage of time.
Suffice it to say all three demanded significant

changes in Southern life and Southerners
regarded them as unnecessarily harsh.

All wars end with the victor determining
the nature of the peace that follows, and
always there are good reasons for a "hard" or
a "soft" peace. In this case, Northerners
resented secession, had suffered deaths and
mental and physical wounds, and generally
wanted to guarantee the continued freedom of
former slaves—justifications for a "hard"
peace. Others wanted to "bind up the nation's
wounds and care for him who has borne the

battle, and for his widow and his orphan," and, most importantly, prevent the reccurrence of conflict. Generally, the two presidents wanted a "soft" peace and congressional Radicals wanted a "hard" one.

Lincoln began the process in 1863, using his plan as a tool of the war itself—to show Confederates how easy it would be to resume their place in the Union if they would stop fighting. He asked for only ten percent of the number of voters in 1860 to sign a oath of future loyalty, write a new constitution renouncing secession, and accept war-time proclamations. Not so fast, responded the Radicals; instead, their Wade-Davis Bill (1864) required fifty percent of the voters in 1860 to sign an "Iron Clad" loyalty oath asserting past as well as future loyalty, an impossible requirement under the circumstances. Lincoln "pocket vetoed" the bill, but said he would accept any state that qualified under it.

Lincoln appointed Andrew Jackson Hamilton to begin the process of reconstruction in Texas, but because of the war Hamilton did not reach the state until the summer of 1865; Texans ignored the Wade-Davis Bill plan, but did attempt the Johnson Plan, only to be rebuffed by Congress. They rejected the Fourteenth Amendment plan, and so had to reenter the Union under the more stringent Reconstruction Acts.

Military occupation began with the arrival of General Gordon Granger in Galveston on June 19, 1865. He proclaimed the war ended and all war-time proclamations in effect, and black Texans have celebrated the day—long since known as "Juneteenth"—as the anniversary of their freedom from slavery. Texas eventually hosted more Army occupiers than any other former Confederate state, because its size required more, because of its frontier-Indian problem, and finally, to serve as a threat to France to surrender the control that nation had established over Mexico in violation of the Monroe Doctrine during our preoccupation with Civil War.

General Wesley Merritt commanded the army in Texas, but also noteworthy was the stationing of General George Armstrong Custer in Austin. Custer established his headquarters in the state asylum for the deaf.

Hamilton arrived in July and began the process of registering voters so delegates could be elected to a constitutional convention, which began deliberations in January 1866 by electing James W. Throckmorton as its chairman. The convention devised amendments to the Confederate constitution taking it back to the constitution of 1845, but did not renounce secession because they considered the outcome of the war sufficient. They did outlaw slavery, but adopted a Black Code prescribing political, economic, and social rules for blacks that Radicals regarded as only a substitute for chattel slavery. The code represented a sincere effort to make sense out of the chaos, but the Radical view had validity, and in any event prevailed. Finally, the election of Oran Roberts, who had presided at the secession convention in 1861, to the U.S. Senate convinced congressional Radicals Texas had learned nothing from the war and was not sorry for secession or disrupting the Union. Voters accepted the constitution and elected Throckmorton governor. Despite Congress' refusal to accept Texas back into the Union, Throckmorton provided Texans with their only civilian government for nearly two years, and for what it was worth, President Johnson proclaimed Texas a member of the Union.

Texans rejected the Fourteenth Amendment, delaying the recognition of statehood by Congress until after the Reconstruction Acts of 1867. Military District Five was commanded

"Stag Dance."

successively by Generals Phillip Sheridan, George Thomas, Winfield Scott Hancock, and E.R. Canby, and the "subprovince" of Texas by Generals Charles Griffin and J.J. Reynolds. Early in the process the military commander replaced Throckmorton with former Governor E.M. Pease when Throckmorton refused to release black prisoners from the state penitentiary in Huntsville.

Throckmorton thought they were there because they were criminals, but Griffin thought they were in prison because they were black. Each was partially correct. Some blacks had been convicted of serious crimes, but others were in prison for actions that would not have been unlawful if they were white, and, in most cases, blacks received stiffer sentences than did whites.

A new convention met in 1868 in two sessions and produced a constitution acceptable to Congress. It was also a superior constitution for Texas, reposing more power in the governor than had been the case

before or since and providing generously for public services such as education. Possibly the most significant issue at the convention was a proposal by Edmund J. Davis and others to divide Texas into two states. A.J. Hamilton and others blocked the proposal, thus preserving a single state.

Davis and Hamilton each sought the governorship of the state under the new constitution with "dirty" politics a campaign feature of each. General Reynolds had all ballots sent to Austin for his review, and then he certified

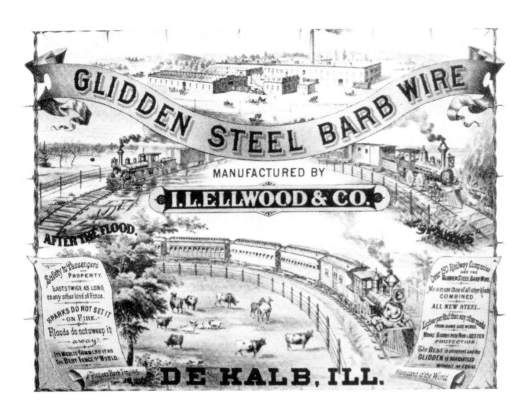

Davis the victor by a margin of 809 votes out of 78,903 votes cast. Morgan Hamilton and J.W. Flanagan were selected by the legislature as U.S. Senators. When the legislature convened, they ratified the Thirteenth and Fourteen Amendments, and Congress certified Texas' readmission to the Union on March 30, 1870. But this did not end Reconstruction for most Texans, who chafed under Davis and Radical rule for four more years.

Davis often is regarded as Texas' most disrespected governor. The majority of white Texans had not voted for him or his party because they had not been enrolled by military registrars. They resented efforts of the Radicals to enforce the citizenship rights of blacks, and they opposed centralization of power in the governor by the constitution and his legislative program, which they termed the "Obnoxious Acts." These laws created a state police force and a militia answerable only to the governor, and many Texans feared these would be used for political purposes. Another law permitted the governor to fill all vacancies in public office, which would enable him to control all state positions. A fourth law allowed the governor to select newspapers for the printing of public notices, and Texans expected him to award such business only to those newspapers whose editorial policy favored his administration. Historians now generally agree that the police and militia were necessary because of lawlessness among the Texans and Indian hostilities, and that Davis did not abuse his power beyond normal partisanship in filling state vacancies and selecting newspapers for state printing contracts.

Texans expressed their opposition to Davis and the Radicals early. In 1871, a "taxpayer's convention" in Austin denounced Davis' government for increasing taxes, an action made more onerous because the state had remanded most taxes during the 1850s and because most people had little revenue to share. In 1872, with more white Texans registered, the state gave a majority to the Democratic presidential nominee, Horace Greeley, whose personality and previous role as an advocate of abolitionism would not have endeared him to them save for the fact that he was not running as a

14 tons Broom Corn raised by one man
on 60 acres, sold for $160.00 per ton.
Canadian, Tex.

Top: *Laying ties to bridge a cut for the Santa Fe Railroad construction into Lubbock, 1909.*
COURTESY, SOUTHWEST COLLECTION, TEXAS TECH UNIVERSITY, LUBBOCK, TEXAS.

Middle: *"14 tons Broom Corn raised by one man on 60 acres, sold for $160.00 per ton. Canadian, Tex."*
COURTESY, SOUTHWEST COLLECTION, TEXAS TECH UNIVERSITY, LUBBOCK, TEXAS.

Bottom: *Early mechanical cotton picker.*
COURTESY, SOUTHWEST COLLECTION, TEXAS TECH UNIVERSITY, LUBBOCK, TEXAS.

Republican. The election produced a Democratic majority in the legislature, which repealed the Obnoxious Acts. And when Davis ran for reelection in 1873, they turned him out as well in favor of the Redeemer and Democratic candidate, Richard Coke. Richard Hubbard was elected lieutenant governor on the Redeemer ticket.

Davis at first refused to relinquish the governor's office, as if physical possession of the place where the governor worked represented the job itself. He asked President U.S. Grant for troops to maintain his office, but Grant had grown tired of what he called "autumnal disturbances"—election disputes in the fall of the year across the South to sustain obviously unwanted Republican governments—so federal troops were not allowed. Davis sought relief in the court, and thought he had found it, when justices he had appointed ruled that the election had been illegal, although it had been conducted under enabling legislation Davis had signed. Their ruling was based on punctuation in the state constitution, and they became known as the "Semi-Colon" court.

Coke's supporters gained access to the second floor of the capitol and inaugurated their man a few minutes past midnight on January 15, 1874. When even the state militia failed to support him after Coke's inauguration, Davis relinquished the office.

Coke gave white Texans the kind of government they wanted: he cut state expenses in half and asked for no more taxes. The legislature increased the size of the state Supreme Court so Davis could appoint a majority, including the new chief justice, Oran Roberts. Governor Davis advocated a new constitutional convention to rid the state of the one written by the Radicals after deciding that the amending process would be unable to produce a truly Redeemer document.

The constitutional convention met in 1875 with ninety delegates present, seventy-five of them Democrats. Republicans managed to achieve fifteen seats, six of them filled by blacks, so redemption was not total, but that time neared. The convention was dominated by farmers who were members of a new advocacy group called the Patrons of Husbandry,

better known as the Grange. In reaction to Davis, They wanted to reduce the size and power of government as much as possible, particularly in the governor's office. And they did not want to pay taxes. A good way to view the result is that they stripped the governor of as much power as possible, gave the legislature only the minimum power necessary to operate the state and then allowed legislators to meet only 120 days every other year, a provision enforced by reducing legislator's pay if they extended beyond the limit in special sessions.

The constitution written in 1875, adopted in February 1876, and still in use in the 1990s, is long and so restrictive that it has been amended over 400 times, which represents less than one percent of all amendments proposed during 125 years. Most proposed amendments have not survived the legislative process, and, of those that have, few have passed. Still, Texas voters face a lengthy ballot filled with amendments every time the legislature meets, and, because the legislature lacks the authority to act in matters not mentioned in the constitution, are asked to vote statewide on such narrow issues as whether or not Fort Bend County should create a hospital district. But several attempts to revise or replace this out-of-date document, the latest in 1975, have been rejected by Texans who fear the revisions more than they feel burdened by the old document, regardless of how many times it must be amended for the state to function.

LAWLESSNESS IN THE AFTERMATH OF THE WAR

Seymour Connor attributed the wave of lawlessness in Texas in the 1860s, 1870s, and 1880s to various causes: the frontier, where self-help was required to solve disputes with Indians or bandits; the general breakdown of government as state administration moved from the Confederacy to the Johnson Plan government to military rule to the detested Radical government and finally to the redeemer movement, with special hostility toward the military occupiers and Radicals; the increasing use of the revolver, so ready to be used riding on the hip; and the boom in the range cattle industry with its land-use disputes.

Top, left: (Probably) the E.B. Penney home.
COURTESY, SOUTHWEST COLLECTION, TEXAS TECH UNIVERSITY, LUBBOCK, TEXAS.

Top, right: "The Western Windmill Co.," patriotic parade float featuring gasoline engines, Eclipse Windmills, and McCormick Harvesters.
COURTESY, SOUTHWEST COLLECTION, TEXAS TECH UNIVERSITY, LUBBOCK, TEXAS.

Below: "Nacogdoches Yellow Pine" logs exhibited downtown in 1900 on the "Courthouse Square," with Henry Millard, Robert "Bob" Lindsey, and Dick Cason posed atop a large pine log on an oxen drawn wagon.
COURTESY STERNE-HOYA MUSEUM, NACOGDOCHES, TEXAS.

The first targets of lawlessness were government warehouses containing supplies that returning Confederate soldiers could easily rationalize as intended for their use anyway. In Austin, former Confederates raided the state treasury in June 1865 to seize the $300,000 reportedly held there, but netted only $2,000. Union soldiers, now posted to the occupation army, had been enemies for four years anyway and robbing from them seemed justified. One could have received a medal for capturing Union supplies in 1864 or l865, yet the same act was defined as theft in 1866. Need and greed spawned such outlaws as Cullen Baker, who operated Robinhood-style in the Sulphur River area, often hidden or aided by people who still regarded his Union pursuers as enemies. Even the head of Davis' state police force was accused of absconding with state funds.

Reconstruction and Redeemed Texas witnessed substantial feuds such as the Sutton-Taylor War which began when a deputy sheriff arrested the scion of a prominent family and spread to the relations and friends of both. The Salt War erupted near El Paso after Samuel Maverick attempted to charge for the extraction of salt from a natural outcrop which had been in the public domain since its discovery. This was the era of the gunfighter and the romantic robber, and native or transplanted Texans John Wesley Hardin, Bill Longley, Ben Thompson, and Sam Bass contributed to the breed. Hardin reportedly killed thirty-two men, one for the offense of snoring too loudly; Longley ended the life of thirty men; Bat Masterson said that Thompson was the mostly likely to survive any gunfight, since he often shot from ambush; and Bass, although he never killed, robbed banks and trains until he reached a bad day at Round Rock. All died violently.

To deal with the violence, Texans turned to their Rangers. In 1874, a new Ranger organi-

zation was created with John B. Jones in command of the Frontier Force while L.H. McNelly led the Special Force. Their specialties focused on Indian defense and law enforcement, but Rangers had to be ready to deal with either. The most accurate things which can be said about the Rangers is that they were ready for anything and that they were lethal.

Indian troubles constituted a great deal of the violence of the era. Plains Indians took advantage of the whites' fratricide during the Civil War to push the frontier line eastward as much as fifty to 100 miles. James Norris organized a frontier force to deal with Comanches, Kiowas, or other hostiles, but his predictable patrols could be avoided by raiding Indians. J.E. McCord replaced Norris and instituted irregular patrols which were more effective, and in 1864 J.W. Throckmorton reorganized the frontier defenders once more. The largest engagement between Texans and Indians occurred at Adobe Walls in 1864, which discouraged raids for a while.

In the post-war period, Texans assumed that federal troops would resume the defense of the frontier, but these troops were busy with voter registration, maintaining order, and serving as agents of diplomacy. Besides, few Union soldiers wanted to risk harm defending former Confederates who would have shot them themselves during the war.

Until 1871, Union soldiers did little to police Indians beyond treaty negotiation and unenthusiastic patrols. The result was the rise of Comancheros, Indians, half-breeds, and whites who stole cattle and other property from Texans and processed their loot through the Santa Fe trade. Ranchers such as John Hittson learned self-help was more productive than depending on soldiers.

In 1868, "Buffalo Soldiers" arrived to garrison western forts to protect trade routes. These were black troops, commanded by white officers, and they proved their race worthy of trust in military assignments. Soon afterwards, the military was limited in its relation with Indians by President Grant's "Quaker Peace Policy." This policy was based on the generally good relations between whites and Indians in colonial Pennsylvania and the assumption that Quaker benevolence was more effective in dealing with Indians than force. The policy was two hundred years too late for Texas: Pennsylvania's Indians in the seventeenth century lacked the guns, horses, and accrued hostility by then abundant among Comanches and Kiowas in Texas. Quaker Laurie Tatum arrived to give the policy a try, and the usual result was that Indians who lived on reservations in Indian Territory by provision of the Treaty of Medicine Lodge Creek would raid and then return to the reservation when pursued; they convinced Tatum

that they were falsely accused—must be some other Indians, they said—and Tatum would forbid the military to arrest them.

Indian raids continued until the Salt Creek Massacre in 1871. This raid was led by the Kiowa Satanta on a military paymaster and supply wagon accompanied by General William T. Sherman, the ranking general officer in the army, and General Randolph Marcy. Sherman and Marcy had ridden on to the next fort and thus escaped the fate of the paymaster, but Sherman realized how narrow his escape had been. He had Satanta arrested—though he was pardoned later by civil authorities—and then committed the army to a vigorous program to end the Indian problem in Texas. This event, plus the continued activity of state forces and civilians, and the near elimination of the buffalo from the plains, eventually ended Indian problems in Texas.

Colonel Ranald S. Mackenzie commanded the roundup of Plains Indians in Texas in 1874. He was joined by forces from Kansas led by Nelson T. Miles, from New Mexico led by William Price, from Fort Sill led by John Davidson, and from Fort Griffin led by George Buel. They drove the majority of Plains Indians into Palo Duro Canyon, where they shot the Indians' horses, the measure of their wealth, and besides their courage and perseverance, their greatest tool for fight or flight. Without horses, and with the buffalo disappearing from the plains, the Indians had little choice but to accept the reservation life.

Plains Indians depended on the buffalo to sustain their life and their culture. They ate its meat, used its bones for tools and its hide for their shelter, and generally operated in ecological balance with the herd by extracting only what they needed (or could) and utilizing all they extracted. Then came the white and black buffalo hunters, who traveled down to Texas after killing most of the buffalo on the upper plains. Some people, including European nobility, hunted buffalo for sport; others did so to provide meat for railroad construction crews; most wanted only the hides for the leather market. Bob and Jim Cator were among the first to arrive. The hunters headquartered at Adobe Walls where John Harralson operated a saloon and Charles Roth maintained a general store. A Second Battle of Adobe Walls occurred in 1874 when the Indians tried to drive the hunters out, but proved no match for their long-range and powerful rifles. According to legend, Billy Dixon shot an Indian off his horse at the range of one mile with his gun, and the Indians accepted the inevitable: they were no match for such weapons.

Buffalo hunters staked out herds and slaughtered all the animals they could. Skinners moved in and removed the hide, which was pegged to the ground for scraping and drying, then stacked on wagons for trailing to market. The hunters harvested the hides and just enough meat for their own use and left the rest to rot on the plains. Two significant developments resulted from such harvest methods: the Indians were deprived of sustenance and forced to live on reservations; and the way was cleared for the expansion of the range-cattle industry.

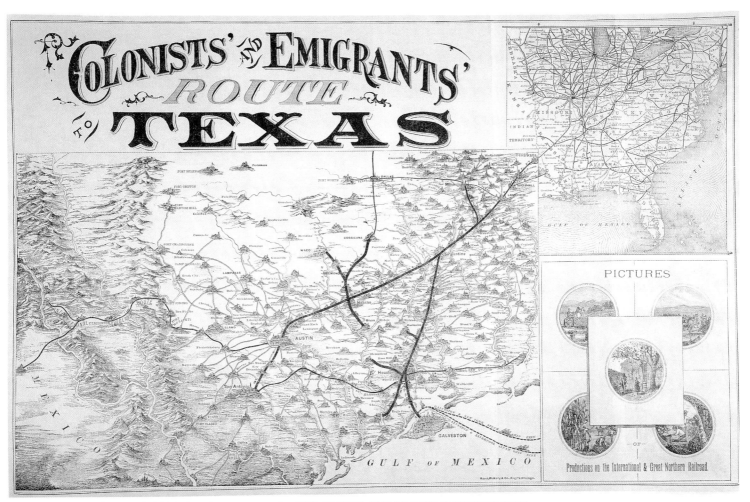

Death of Sam Bass

By LORRAINE BARNES

At 89, Jefferson D. Dillingham of 4501 Duval Street is perhaps the last man alive who saw Sam Bass die at Round Rock that sultry July day in 1878.

Because he witnessed the young outlaw's death and heard his dying words, Dillingham scoffs at the various romantic legends that have grown up around the battle in which Bass was mortally wounded. "Stuff and nonsense" is Dillingham's opinion of these stories.

"He didn't die under an oak tree west of old Round Rock. He was brought into New Town and died in August Glober's tinshop, surrounded by many persons drawn to the scene," Dillingham declares.

"And those stories that he escaped—that another body was buried and Sam was later seen on a train between Fort Worth and Dallas—why, they're far-fetched. There's nothing to them."

Dillingham, who is a retired railroad man, was 12 years old when the Rangers laid their famous trap for Sam Bass. His recollection of the street battle is so keen and accurate that Dillingham's description has been accepted by many researchers, among them Wayne Gard. In his book "Sam Bass," Gard refers to the Austin man in these words: "The afternoon was hot in Round Rock, and everyone who could stayed in the shade. About the only activity in sight was that of a country youth, Jeff Dillingham, who had started to unload some fodder at the livery stable."

This is the way Dillingham describes the scene:

"The battle between officers and Texas Rangers and Sam Bass and his gang took place about 11 a. m. on that July day. I saw it all. Sebe Barnes, Frank Jackson and Bass went into a grocery across the street from the livery stable in front of which, on a bench, sat officers. The latter noticed the strange men carried bulges beneath their shirts. They went over to inquire about their authority for carrying weapons.

"The Bass gang broke for their horses tethered to a fence in the rear of a hotel operated by a woman. In the melee Barnes fell dead of a gunshot wound as he turned into the avenue. Bass and Jackson mounted their horses, came out of the alley with bullets flying after them and sped westward toward old Round Rock."

Bass was seriously wounded, and Jackson hid him in a thicket, then took the horses and tethered them in another thicket.

"Sam Bass lay in the thicket all night, a wound in his left arm and another under his heart," Dillingham says. "The next morning a Negro stopped with a load of wood near the thicket, heard the moans and came on into Round Rock. He said, 'Sam Bass is in that thicket.'

Last Words

Dillingham says his brother-in-law, G. P. Baines, who sold vegetables, took his hack to the thicket

(See BASS, Page 3)

Below: Private, U.S. Tenth Cavalry, United States of America, 1880.

EXHIBIT AT PANHANDLE-PLAINS HISTORICAL MUSEUM. COURTESY, PANHANDLE-PLAINS HISTORICAL MUSEUM, CANYON, TEXAS.

Top: "Colonists' and Emigrants' Route to Texas," 1878 railroad promotion brochure.

COURTESY, CARTOGRAPHIC COLLECTIONS OF MRS. JENKINS GARRETT, FORT WORTH; HOUSED AT THE SPECIAL COLLECTIONS DIVISION, THE UNIVERSITY OF TEXAS AT ARLINGTON LIBRARIES, ARLINGTON, TEXAS.

Above: "Death of Sam Bass," a contemporaneous article and photograph appearing in the Austin American Statesman.

COURTESY, ARCHIVES DIVISION - TEXAS STATE LIBRARY.

THE CATTLE KINGDOM

Cattle outnumbered people in Texas in 1865, and, if taken to market, they represented wealth on the hoof which could help the state recover from the devastation of war. The usual method of raising cattle in Texas evolved from the *charro* culture of the Rio Grande Valley and even earlier, from the cattle culture of Spain, the origin of all Texas bovines prior to the Anglo intervention. Walter P. Webb observed that the Texas, and later Western American, method of cattle raising—essentially working cattle on open range and from horseback—originated in a diamond-shaped area in South Texas bordered by the Rio Grande, the Gulf of Mexico, the Nueces, and imagination in the northwest.

Spanish *entratas* and missions brought along cattle for beef and leather and their progeny had spread over much of Texas by the time Anglos arrived. Stockraising also was an important activity of the South, and many Anglos who arrived in the 1820s and 1830s were experienced in the process. According to Forrest McDonald and Grady McWhinney, their closed-range and working-cattle-dismounted methods merged with the Hispanic customs to produce the Cattle Kingdom. Cattle drives to the Mississippi River began early, but before the war many cattle were driven to the coast, slaughtered, skinned, and rendered for their hides and tallow alone.

Often riverboat captains were reluctant to take live cargo aboard, and even drives which made it to the railroad connection at Sedalia, Missouri, had to cross settled country where farmers resented the herd's consumption of pasturage, brigands stampeded herds to pick off strays or waylaid drovers on the way home, and the "Texas Fever"—a bovine disease communicated by a parasite—infected domestic cattle along the trail.

Texas beef fed Confederate civilians and soldiers until 1863, when they no longer could cross the Mississippi, and for the remainder of the war the herds and wild mavericks accumulated. Entrepreneur Joseph G. McCoy convinced railroad interests to build a line to Abilene, Kansas, and sent word down the Chisholm Trail to Texas ranchers that they could receive $30 to $40 a head for their cattle at the railhead. With Andy Adams, many a cowman "figured up a fortune" awaiting them and began the long drives through Indian Territory to Abilene. By 1869, over 350,000 cattle a year were walking to market over the Chisholm, Dodge City, or some other trail, some as far north as Ogalalla, Nebraska. Since spring arrivals brought the best prices, so some cattlemen began to winter their cattle in Kansas on government range in order to be first to market the next spring. Eventually the Cattle Kingdom spread as far north as Canada and through most of the west. Calves were "dropped" in Texas, trailed north as yearlings, and fed out another year or two on the richer grasses of the upper plains.

Texas cattle were Longhorns, a hybrid produced by random breeding whose characteristics were stamina, survivability, and orneriness, and edible but stringy flesh. Eventually blooded stock from the British Isles was imported to improve the quality and quantity of beef when operations were well established. The British stock, however, would have had difficulty keeping up with the Longhorns on the long drive. Picture a trail herd of a 1000 or so cattle as a human body, prone, head to the north. Out in front is the scout, who picks the route according to the best water and grass and the least danger, and it was not easy to get these necessities lined up advantageously. Beside the "head," or the lead cattle, rode the most skilled drovers who guided the herd along the route. Along the sides rode flankers to keep the herd bunched, and others rode "drag" at the rear to prevent straggling. Drovers did not motivate the herd to move so much as they kept it together and going in the right direction, for once in motion, the herd tended to remain in motion. A wrangler looked after the *remuda*, or additional horses, a cook prepared breakfast and dinner with the aid of a swamper, and overseeing the lot was the trailboss. At first, ranchers trailed their own herds, but later many consigned them to commission agents such as Charles Schreiner, who usually received $1 per head delivered to the railhead.

Major ranches, or "spreads," as Texans called them, developed in Texas to produce the cattle, including the JA, a partnership between James Adair and Charles Goodnight that combined the money of the former and the skills of the latter in a successful operation in Palo Duro Canyon; the Matador, the anchor of a string of ranches that spread northward to Canada; the 4 6s, operated by Samuel Burkburnett on the northcentral Texas plains; the XIT, a three-million acre ranch belonging to a syndicate and located in the Panhandle; and the most famous and enduring of all, the south Texas King Ranch, founded by Richard King and Mifflin Kenedy in 1853 and operated by King until his death and afterwards by his heirs in the Kleberg family.

Above: "Heads of Departments, Texas State Government," 1882 collage.

COURTESY, PANHANDLE-PLAINS HISTORICAL MUSEUM, CANYON, TEXAS.

Bottom, left: Well-stocked general merchandise store interior in Memphis, Texas, December 25, 1883. Memphis is east southeast of Amarillo, the county seat of Hall County.

COURTESY, PANHANDLE-PLAINS HISTORICAL MUSEUM, CANYON, TEXAS.

Bottom, right: The 1886 "Hill City Quartette" photo included W. S. Porter, lower left, better known as the internationally famous short story author, O. Henry.

PHOTO BY H.B. HILLYER
COURTESY, ARCHIVES DIVISION - TEXAS STATE LIBRARY.

Above: Capitol construction in Austin, 1888.
COURTESY, ARCHIVES DIVISION - TEXAS STATE LIBRARY.

Bottom, right: "Funeral cortege moving down Waco St.," Corpus Christi, 1890.
COURTESY, CORPUS CHRISTI PUBLIC LIBRARY, CORPUS CHRISTI, TEXAS.

The rise of the cattle kingdom sometimes produced land use conflicts between cattlemen, farmers, and sheep raisers, but such disagreements have been exaggerated in fiction and in any event were rooted not in innate prejudice but in how to use the land. Frequently arguments between cattlemen and sheep raisers are cited, but in fact some cattlemen also raised sheep to earn an extra payday. The cattle and sheep would graze together amicably, but since the sheep could crop the grass closer to the ground than could cattle, the solution was separate grazing. Farmers provided ranchers with extra labor at roundup and vegetables, and ranchers provided farmers a source of cash from work or sales.

J. F. Glidden's and I. L. Ellwood's barbed wire solved many problems of separation, but also caused other problems, although perhaps fewer than motion pictures would indicate. J. W. "Bet-a-Million" Gates convinced many ranchers of the value of fences to prevent their stock from drifting, and ranchers strung many miles of wire. But some who were accustomed to riding in a straight line sometimes objected when they found no gate, and made one. Often such fence cutting led to violence. Rustling was more of a problem, and possession of a "running iron" to alter brands could be a hanging offense.

Railroads also added wealth to postwar Texas. Prior to the war, the legislature awarded eight sections of land for each mile of track constructed, but generated only approximately 400 miles of track. During Radical Reconstruction the legislature tried to use bond revenues as subsidies, but the unsettled times prevented much construction. Under the constitution of 1876 the state reverted to land subsidies but increased the amount to sixteen sections per mile. By 1904, Texas led the nation with over 10,000 miles of track. In addition to state subvention, many communities also contributed depots, right-of-way, roundhouses, and cash to ensure that their community would be on a railroad. Dallas, with the first east-west and north-south crossing of railroads is perhaps the best example of how a community benefited from rail access. By contrast, the major antebellum port town of Jefferson lost water access when a raft on the Red River was demolished by engineers, and often is cited as what happened when a community missed out on main-line service.

The United States eventually was served by five transcontinental railroads, and two crossed Texas, the Texas & Pacific from Shreveport through Dallas to El Paso and the Southern Pacific that ran from New Orleans via Houston, San Antonio, and El Paso and on to southern California. Grenville Dodge, of

Union Pacific fame, began construction of the Texas & Pacific in 1873 and reached Dallas in 1875 before Jay Cooke took over and completed the line to El Paso. The Southern Pacific featured another race between eastern and western lines that joined near El Paso, but together linked the Mississippi Valley and the Pacific Coast. Scores of smaller lines, such as the H.E.&W.T.—Houston, East & West Texas, or, to wags, "Hell Either Way Taken"—connected smaller cities to the major lines.

Railroads enjoyed a symbiotic relationship with the lumbering industry. Prior to 1890, grist milling was the state's dominant manufacturing or processing industry, but after that date lumber surged to front position. Eight-foot crossties supported the steel rails at intervals measured in inches, and millions were required for railroad construction and maintenance. Once the railroad was in place it could transport millions of board feet of processed lumber to markets around the country or the world. The East Texas lumber industry centered on 68,000 square miles eastward from the Sabine River, north of Orange and Beaumont to Lufkin and Nacogdoches, and as far west as the Trinity River which contained over 300 billion board feet of lumber in pine and hardwood forests.

John Henry Kirby, the "Prince of the Pines," founded Texas' first million-dollar corporation, the Kirby Lumber Company. Later the Kurth family's Angelina County Lumber Company, Lutcher-Moore, and other timber barons moved in to develop this major industry. Thousands of mill sites, however temporary, were established throughout the region to process the virgin pines and hardwood into lumber. For decades the woodsmen followed a "cut and get out" method with little regard for damage to young trees or reforestation. W. Goodrich Jones from Temple, a place with so few natural trees that he seemed to regard them more highly, sounded the alarm that, although trees were a renewable resource, they also required a long time to mature. Unless cutting practices changed and new trees were planted, he warned, this great industry would destroy itself. During the twentieth century significant reforestation occurred on lands owned by large corpora-

tions, small private holdings, and in the four national forests set aside in East Texas.

Farming underwent several significant changes in post-war Texas. As the population moved west beyond the twenty-inch per year rainfall line into arid regions, farmers had to change to crops that required less moisture, and in the marginal areas learn such dry-land techniques as keeping the crust of the soil loose so even the dew could be absorbed. Wheat, oats, and other grains could be germinated with snowmelt and harvested before the intense heat and dryness of summer occurred. Most importantly, new patterns of land ownership appeared.

Before the Civil War, anyone who wanted to farm his own land could do so since Mexico, the Republic, and state governments gave land away for little more than occupancy or military service. After the Civil War, land ownership was concentrated into the hands of fewer owners and up to seventy percent or more of Texas' farmers tilled soil which belonged to someone else as "share croppers" or "share tenants." In the share crop system, the land owner contributed the land, shelter, equipment—including seeds, horses or mules, and implements—and credit, and received three-quarters of the crop; the share cropper received one-quarter but still had to pay for the "credit," or living expenses until the crop was harvested, which usually consumed all of the value of his share and con-

Top: A youthful Douglas MacArthur (1880-1964), is reclining in the foreground of this group photograph taken at West Texas Military Academy in San Antonio, 1896. The academy was founded in San Antonio in 1893 near Fort Sam Houston. General MacArthur commanded the Allied troops in the Pacific during World War II and supervised the post-war occupation of Japan.
COURTESY, ARCHIVES DIVISION - TEXAS STATE LIBRARY.

Above: Group of prospective German settlers on wagon, 1906, in front of Keiser Brothers & Phillips Land Office in the panhandle town of Canyon, fifteen miles south of Amarillo.
COURTESY, PANHANDLE-PLAINS HISTORICAL MUSEUM, CANYON, TEXAS.

Below: 1906 mid-way scene in Dalhart, near the Oklahoma panhandle.
COURTESY, PANHANDLE-PLAINS HISTORICAL MUSEUM, CANYON, TEXAS.

Top: "Corpus Christi's Central Wharf, March 3, 1908."

COURTESY, CORPUS CHRISTI PUBLIC LIBRARY,
CORPUS CHRISTI, TEXAS.

Middle: Cotton houses, seed storage, gin, and other buildings, 1924-25, on the Armstrong ranch, founded by John B. Armstrong, the Texas Ranger known as "McNelly's Bulldog."

GIFT OF CORPUS CHRISTI CALLER-TIMES.
COURTESY, CORPUS CHRISTI PUBLIC LIBRARY.

Above: "Plainview, Texas, 1908." This coach was operated by Ben Gardner and used for bus service between Plainview and Lubbock. Hattie Dailey is nearest the camera in the middle seat; the male passenger is believed to be Carl Rosser.

COURTESY, PANHANDLE-PLAINS HISTORICAL MUSEUM,
CANYON, TEXAS.

demned him to cycle after cycle as the years passed. Under the share tenant system, the landowner contributed the land and probably shelter, but the tenant furnished his own equipment and credit and so the shares were more evenly divided. A third alternative, which might involve the landowner himself if he was short of cash, was the crop lien system. In this case, to make a crop, a farmer obtained a loan, which could be paid in shares of the crop itself, but if hail or disease destroyed the product before harvest, the loan still had to be paid. All of these agricultural methods emphasized the need for a cash crop—usually cotton.

Wealth and political power became concentrated among cattle barons, lumber barons, landowners, and other industrialists, eventually producing protests among labor, blacks, and small farmers. The farmers found voices of protest first. Oliver Kelly's Patrons of Husbandry, or the Grange, was intended to be a fraternal organization for farmers to relieve the tedium of rural lives. The men gathered for "lodge," the women to visit, the young to "court," and the children to play. But getting together at meetings shattered their isolation and they began to share complaints against railroads, lending institutions, or government, and the Grange became a political action group. Essentially still local, their highest focus was control of state government to regulate the industries they felt abused them. But they found the U.S. Supreme Court would not allow state governments to regulate railroad rates and practices, since they operated within a federal jurisdiction of interstate commerce. So farmers moved to the Alliances—the National Farmers Alliance,

also known as the "Northern" Alliance which served the Great Plains, and the Farmer's Alliance and Cooperative Union, founded by C.W. Macune of Burnet, Texas, also known as the "Southern" Alliance, serving the states of the American South. Eventually the Alliance movement proved ineffective in persuading Congress, and the People's (Populist) Party was formed in 1892 in an attempt to influence the government through elective policies. The Populists did not win a national election, but much of their program was adopted by either the Democrats or Republicans and eventually became the law of the land.

Prior to the Civil War there were no labor unions in Texas. Here and there benevolent organizations composed of laborers who cared for their members and their families when they could not work were established, but none led strikes. The first real labor union in Texas was formed in 1866 as the Screwmen's Benevolent Association, a trade union of specialized longshoremen. Four years later a Negro Screwman's Benevolent Association was formed by N.W. Cuney, illustrating the degree of racial segregation in the state. Soon these unions were joined by a typographers' union in Houston and other groups as well. The 1880s witnessed over 100,000 work days of strikes by over 8,000 laborers. These strikes ranged from the "Capitol Boycott," which resulted when, to the disgust of Texas craftsmen, the contractor for the new capitol building imported stonemasons from Scotland, to the quixotic "cowboy strike" of 1883. The cowboy strike illustrates the lack of experience and the discomfort of Texans in labor disputes. Essentially, cowboys from adjacent ranches, in comparing employment conditions and wages, found them wanting, and agreed to strike. But since they were not working at their own jobs, most of them traveled to other ranches to work while the strike lasted, and in the end, everyone was back at work—somewhere else— under the same conditions and wages.

Post-Civil War Texas also witnessed many social changes. The state's population increased from 818,597 in 1870 to 3,048,710 in 1900, and its rank jumped from nineteenth to sixth in the U.S. The ratio of rural Texans dropped from 93.3 percent to 82.9 percent, and, although the state remained largely rural, the pattern toward urbanization so prevalent in the twentieth century had begun.

Education in Texas lagged far behind eastern states. Since the revenues for elementary and secondary education were based exclusively on *ad valorem* property taxes, which most Texans hate, support remained low. Segregation meant black students received even less support. Higher education fared better. The Morrill Act provided funds for the founding in 1876 of Texas Agricultural & Mechanical College, located at College Station, near Bryan. Seymour Conner pointed out that Texas A&M began operations with six faculty members and forty students; near the end of the twentieth century its student body exceeded 40,000. Sam Houston Normal School, located in Huntsville and partially funded by the Peabody Fund in 1879, set the pattern for nearly a dozen teacher preparation colleges founded in Texas in the next five decades. The University of Texas, envisioned during the days of the Republic by Mirabeau B. Lamar, began holding classes in Austin, with a medical branch in Galveston, in 1883. Addison and Randolph Clark established Add-Ran College in 1873, and it eventually became Texas Christian University. Baylor University, founded by the Baptists in 1846, continued to operate in Waco, and Baptists also founded Howard Payne College in 1889 and Hardin—later Hardin-Simmons—in 1891. Methodists founded Southwestern University in 1873, the Presbyterians established Trinity University in 1869, and Catholics supported St. Mary's, located in San Antonio.

In Texas artistic circles, the preeminent figure was a woman sculptor. Elizabet Ney's statues of Sam Houston and Stephen F. Austin stand in the Hall of Statues in the nation's capitol in Washington and in the state capitol in Austin. Mrs. Percy Pennybacker wrote a Texas history text which taught the facts and legends of the state to thousands of scholastics for fifty years. And in the state capitol in 1897, a group, which included three women, met to form the Texas State Historical Association, the state's "oldest learned society."

Civil War, Reconstruction, and economic recovery affected Texas permanently from 1865 to the 1890s. This period confirmed Texas would remain in the American Union, saddled the state with its now archaic constitution, eliminated Indian resistance to the westward march of American civilization, gave birth to railroad, industrial, and agricultural "kingdoms," and established demographic and social trends that extend to the present. On the eve of the twentieth century, some Texans looked forward to more wealth and some longed for more reform.

Above: Water gushes down a sluice into an irrigation ditch for farming in the arid but fertile Amarillo area.

COURTESY, PANHANDLE-PLAINS HISTORICAL MUSEUM, CANYON, TEXAS.

Below: Fifty-ton blast furnace at the Rusk penitentiary.

COURTESY, ARCHIVES DIVISION - TEXAS STATE LIBRARY.

"OLD RED"
(ASHBEL SMITH BUILDING)

FIRST, AND ORIGINALLY THE ONLY
BUILDING OF UNIVERSITY OF TEXAS
MEDICAL BRANCH. MASTER ARCHITECT
NICHOLAS J. CLAYTON DESIGNED THE
MASSIVE ROMANESQUE STRUCTURE. IT
WAS DEDICATED OCTOBER 5, 1891.

ALTHOUGH ROOMS WERE ALMOST
DEVOID OF EQUIPMENT, THE SCHOOL
BOASTED A YOUNG, VIGOROUS STAFF.
ENROLLMENT IN 1891 WAS 23.

THE BUILDING WAS NAMED IN 1949
FOR ASHBEL SMITH (1805-86), PIONEER
SURGEON, DIPLOMAT, AND "FATHER OF
THE UNIVERSITY OF TEXAS"

RECORDED TEXAS HISTORIC LANDMARK - 1967

REFORM, PROGRESSIVISM, AND REGRESSION

THE POLITICS OF RECOVERY AND REFORM

When Texas rejoined the Union, some may have thought that a Texas Redeemed would be similar to antebellum Texas. If so, they were surely disappointed.

Redemption Governor Richard M. Coke ran a tight budget and a lean state government under the Constitution of 1876. When Coke assumed office in January 1874 the state had only $40,000 in its treasury and an estimated revenue of $500,000 with which to satisfy anticipated annual expenses of $1.2 million. Coke advocated the issuance of bonds, tax increases, and land alienation to satisfy the state's obligations. The legislature responded with new business taxes and occupational license fees. Then, in 1877, the legislature elected Coke to replace Samuel Bell Maxey in the U.S. Senate. The administration of state affairs passed to Richard Hubbard, the lieutenant governor, who completed the term of office by generally following Coke's policies.

Hubbard wanted to be elected in his own right in 1878, but the Democratic convention deadlocked among him, former Governor J.W. Throckmorton, and William Lang. The delegates solved their dilemma by opting for Judge Oran M. Roberts, who won a second two-year term in 1880; Seymore Conner observed that Roberts should be regarded as Texas' most significant chief executive between E.M. Pease (1853-1857) and James Stephen Hogg (1891-1895).

Probably it is too much to claim that Roberts introduced the idea that taxes should be low and government small in Texas, but he certainly advanced the concept—and passed it along to most of his successors to the present. Roberts forced the renegotiation of state bonds to achieve lower interest rates by the threat of default. He persuaded the legislature to reduce veterans' pensions, canceled state expenditure for public education for a time, and, because he believed land should be under private rather than public control, released significant amounts of the public domain through the Four Section Settler Act and other legislation. Land owners did pay taxes on their lands, though they paid little to obtain them, so at least some revenue accrued to the state.

Roberts did permit some new taxes to be passed for regulatory purposes and what might be called a "fair share" program. For example, the "Bell Punch" tax on liquor-by-the-drink was intended to produce revenue and to force honesty on the bartender-tax collector. Each establishment had a recording machine which consisted of a wheel turned by gears when a punch penetrated a piece of paper and then struck a bell located behind the plate to which the paper was attached; when the punch was withdrawn, the device rotated so another hole could be punched to record the next sale. Periodically a state agent came to count the holes in the paper to tabulate the tax. Since the device could be rigged to punch the same hole over and over, it yielded little revenue.

The Drummer Tax, although based on logic, was found unconstitutional. Roberts reasoned that in Texas "drummers," or traveling salesmen, operated on railroads in Texas constructed with public subsidies, yet paid no taxes to the state since they merely took orders and sent them—and money—off to St. Louis, Chicago, or some other out-of-state center. This made sense to everyone but the U.S. Supreme Court, which ruled that the tax interfered with the exclusive power of the federal government to regulate interstate commerce.

Roberts' successor, John Ireland (1883-1887) continued much of his predecessor's fiscal policies but did try to retain control of public lands and stem their hasty transfer to private ownership with-

out fair compensation to the state—read the people. Ireland instituted the concepts of "graduation"—establishing a minimum price for land based on its market value, and the "public auction"—or allowing open bidding to take the price as high as the bidders were willing to pay for specific acreage.

The election of 1886 introduced an interesting and successful team into state government. Governor Lawrence Sullivan "Sul" Ross and Attorney General James Stephen Hogg each brought a special strength that enabled the other to succeed. Hogg, the reformer and in many ways the first Progressive in Texas politics who offended conservative interests regularly, was able to accomplish much because he was supported by Ross, a hero of the Civil War and one of Texas' most popular governors.

Hogg began his crusade with the insurance industry, which has had a cyclical history in Texas: state regulatory laws fall behind those of other states and unscrupulous insurance providers proliferate; then the legislature toughens the regulations for these individuals, who move on until the cycle repeats itself. Hogg's powers did not allow him to file suits against individual companies or agents, but he issued a "circular letter" to the state's district attorneys that pledged the full support of his legal team if they did so. Insurance Commissioner L.L. Foster estimated that Hogg's action saved Texas insurance rate payers over $1 million annually.

Hogg also forced the railroads to honor commitments to communities and citizens. After accepting state land and local subsidies for route lines to certain towns, some companies wanted to discontinue service, even as trains continued to roll through, arguing that insufficient business did not justify a stop. Hogg believed that the railroads' acceptance of subsidies constituted a commitment for service which they must continue to provide. Through court action he was able to force restoration of service in some instances and delay its discontinuance in others, and to effect better maintenance by Southern Pacific of its lines.

Hogg was not always successful. He lost the "Drummer Tax" case in federal court. He also lost the "Grass Lease" case, in which the state sought an increase in fees for state lands leased to cattlemen—as a result of the trial's being held in West Texas and Judge Frank Willis' instructions to the cowboy jury, most of whom worked for the cattlemen. But he and Ross were able to secure over $1 million from the federal government for state expenses in frontier defense, and were credited with an amicable solution to an election dispute that became the Jaybird (Democrats) and Woodpecker (Republicans) War in Fort Bend County. (These party names were derived from the symbols used on ballots to denote political parties, a testimony, among other things, about the literacy rate in the state).

COWBOY DANCE – SPUR RANCH. 1918.

At the completion of Ross' second term as governor, Hogg announced his candidacy for the office and made creation of a Railroad Commission to regulate railroads his principal issue. By then Hogg had offended leaders of the insurance, railroad, cattle, and other large industries, but not always their employees, and he remained popular among East Texans, who composed the largest number of voters. Upon his election to the governor's office in 1890, which was taken as a mandate, the legislature created the Railroad Commission, and Hogg appointed John Henninger Reagan, a sitting U. S. Senator from Texas and former Postmaster General of the Confederacy, to lead it. He also appointed Lafayette Lumpkin Foster and W. P. McLean to the commission.

The election of 1892 provided Texans with the first candidacy of the Populist Party, which nominated T. L. Nugent for governor, and it involved divisions among both the Democrats and the Republicans. The Democrats met in Houston's roundhouse, named for its streetcar company. When Hogg's enemies were unable to prevent his renomination, they adjourned to Turner Hall and nominated George Clark for the office, thus creating Car Barn Democrats and Turner Hall Democrats for the election. Among Republicans, the divisions were known as the

Lilly Whites, who refused to follow the Regulars, led by Norris Wright Cuney, because he was black. This incident provides further testimony to the growing grip of racial segregation in Texas. Despite the division among Democrats, Hogg won reelection and led Texas into the Progressive Era. Historian Joe Frantz said that Hogg, who always placed the interests of the public over those of the private, was the governor by whom all his successors have been judged.

The most powerful political figure in Texas from the 1890s until well into the twentieth century never held an elected or appointed office. Edward M. House's inherited cotton

factorage business and considerable business skill created a fortune, enabling him to retire in middle age and devote the remainder of his life to what interested him most, politics, first in Texas and later as President Woodrow Wilson's principal advisor. House decreed that Charles Culbertson would succeed Hogg, followed by Joseph D. Sawyers, S.W.T. Lanham, Thomas M. Campbell, and Oscar B. Colquitt. Beginning with Hogg, these six governors provided Texas with its most progressive leadership and advanced the state as a leader in the Progressive Movement.

Progressive measures that affected the state during the tenure of these governors included the creation of the poll tax in 1901; the Terrell Election Law in 1905, which abolished nomi-

Top, left: Cornerstone dedication for the Texas Technological College Administration Building, November 11, 1923, with a crowd of 20,000. When the school was renamed Texas Tech University in 1969, enrollment was 19,490.
COURTESY, SOUTHWEST COLLECTION, TEXAS TECH UNIVERSITY, LUBBOCK, TEXAS.

Below: "Great Plains Potato Co., Quality Spuds the Year 'round."
COURTESY, SOUTHWEST COLLECTION, TEXAS TECH UNIVERSITY, LUBBOCK, TEXAS.

Bottom, left: Breaking land with cat tractors.
COURTESY, SOUTHWEST COLLECTION, TEXAS TECH UNIVERSITY, LUBBOCK, TEXAS.

nating conventions and established the primary election to select candidates, thus opening the process to everyone; child labor legislation that forbade the employment of anyone under twelve and sixteen years of age—later raised to fifteen and seventeen years—in machine industries and breweries; legislation limiting the number of consecutive hours trainmen could work, in the interest of public safety; the Robertson Insurance Law of 1907, which required reinvestment and deposits of premiums paid to insurance companies in Texas institutions; and prison reform that eliminated convict leasing.

A meaningful progressive reform grew out of the lessons learned from the hurricane that struck Galveston in September 1900, still called the worst natural disaster in U.S. history. The storm paralyzed Galveston. City government was unable to cope with the enormous tasks of disposing of the dead, caring for survivors, and rebuilding the city. The state legislature, with Galveston's approval, provided the town with an appointed city commission. Each commissioner (police, fire, waste disposal, etc.) wielded extensive power over his jurisdiction and coordinated efforts for the common good to get Galveston on its feet. The system worked so well that Galveston and several hundred other cities in the state and nation adopted a modified version of this form of municipal government, with elected city commissions. In 1912, Amarillo introduced the city manager form of municipal government, which was also subsequently adopted widely in the nation.

In 1912, House moved his interest to the national political scene. Impressed by New Jersey Governor Woodrow Wilson, House moved to New York to support Wilson in presidential primaries and in the general election, even bringing Texas Ranger Captain Bill MacDonald to serve as Wilson's body guard and holding the Texas delegation to the National Democratic Convention in line through several ballots until Wilson was nominated. House's efforts made him Wilson's closest advisor until near the end of the president's second term, and resulted in the appointment of Texans Albert S. Burleson as postmaster general and David F. Houston as secretary of agriculture.

In 1914 a new "hurricane" struck Texas politics in the person of James Ferguson, a.k.a. "Farmer Jim." Ferguson, a successful banker in Bell County, had never held any office before his candidacy in the governor's race. Although no longer a farmer, he became "Farmer Jim" by campaigning exclusively in rural areas and by advocating a Farm Tenant Rent Law. This law, which more equitably fixed shares of crops under the share crop system was later passed by the legislature but declared unconstitutional. Ferguson also won support by declaring that he would veto any legislation to change the state liquor law.

Prohibition had been the primary political issue in Texas since 1875; a proposed constitutional amendment on the issue had failed; and Texans were tired of it. Actually, Ferguson's pledge favored the "wets;" however, it also allowed a rest for the "drys," although they returned vigorously with the beginning of World War I.

Ferguson, along with his wife, Miriam Amanda Ferguson, remained important figures in Texas politics until 1934, with one or the other on the ballot during all but two election years during that period. Ferguson's first term (1915-1917) produced legislation enabling rural schools to consolidate to pool funds for a better educational yield; authorized new colleges; and created a state highway department to "get Texas out of the mud"— a goal that the Texas Good Roads Association had advocated since the 1890s. Unfortunately for Ferguson, he lost a battle with the University of Texas, as well as his job before his second term ended. The trouble

began when professors at the university criticized Ferguson, who demanded they be fired. President Robert E. Vinson refused, and Ferguson retaliated by vetoing the university's appropriation bill. his veto offended even those regents whom Ferguson had appointed, especially George W. Littlefield, as well as students, alumni, and many others. The legislature impeached Ferguson on twenty-one counts of malfeasance and eventually convicted and removed him from office. Ferguson called the legislature a "kangaroo court" and said that he "tied a knot in the rope" by resigning one day before the sentence was effective so he could claim it did not apply. He ran unsuccessfully for the U.S. Senate and for president in subsequent elections, but never won again. When Ferguson left office, Lieutenant Governor William P. Hobby completed the term, then won re-election in 1918.

WORLD WAR I AND "NORMALCY"

While "Fergusonism" dominated the agenda in Texas, the western world went to war. In 1914, squabbles in the Balkans, secret interlocking alliances, and territorial acquisitiveness erupted into what later would be called the First World War. At the time it was known as the Great War, or to Americans, who joined in 1917, the War To Make The World Safe For Democracy.

Texans were more concerned with events to the south during the early years of the century. Waves of revolutions led by Flores Magón, Gilberto Guerrero, and Francisco Madero finally overthrew Mexico's longtime leader, Porfirio Díaz, and were then followed by revolts led by

Top, right: Edward M. House (1858-1938), native-born, independently wealthy Texan entered state politics when the 1892 reelection of his friend, James Hogg, was challenged by conservative Democrats and Populists. Protégés of Col. House served as governors of Texas from 1894 to 1906. House met Woodrow Wilson in 1911and became an influential player on the international scene.

Top, middle: "Four Texas governors", c. 1895: James Stephen Hogg, right, served from 1891 to 1895; others, left to right, Lubbock, 1895-1905; Roberts; and Ross (1838-1898).

Top, left: Part-Cherokee humorist Will Rogers (1879-1935), an avid flyer, poses with close friend and newspaper publisher Amon G. Carter at the Fort Worth Airport. After the Alaska plane crash in which Rogers was killed, Carter flew to Seattle to meet the plane carrying Rogers' body and accompanied it to Los Angeles. The Oklahoma-born philosopher-entertainer, true to his iconoclastic leanings, ran away from military school in 1898 to live the western cowboy legend in the Texas Panhandle, even driving herds up the trail to Kansas. In 1903, he broke into show business in South Africa as "The Cherokee Kid, the Man Who Can Lasso the Tail Off a Blowfly" in Texas Jack's Wild West Show.

Bottom, left: Highlights of the fascinating career of John H. Reagan (1818-1905), Tennessee-born and largely self-taught, include: the Battle against the Cherokee Indians in 1839 in East Texas; service as the only postmaster general of the Confederacy; and, resigning a sitting U. S. Senate term to serve as head of Governor James Stephen Hogg's first Railroad Commission in 1891.

Victoriano Huerta and Venustiano Carranza. Most of these revolutions were plotted in Texas by exiles, then transferred to northern Mexico. President Wilson welcomed the rise of Madero as a kindred spirit who believed in democracy, and was shocked when the Mexican president was slain—"butchers" was what Wilson called the assassins. Wilson then adopted a policy of "watchful waiting," supporting no side while Mexico sorted out its affairs.

"Watchful waiting" aloofness did not work. An incident in Tampico involving U.S. sailors produced an American invasion at Vera Cruz costing lives on both sides. Then another revolutionary, Francisco "Pancho" Villa, tried to provoke Wilson by killing U.S. citizens, expecting that Mexico's Carranza government would be blamed. But for Wilson's reaction to the loss of lives by his orders at Vera Cruz, this probably would have worked, but did not. After Villa next attacked Columbus, New Mexico, he could no longer be ignored. Wilson ordered General John J. "Black Jack" Pershing to invade Mexico with an American Expeditionary Force (AEF) to capture Villa. At first Carranza welcomed the help, but as Villa lured Pershing deeper into their country, Mexicans pressured their president to do something about the invasion. War likely would have occurred had Pershing and the AEF not been needed more in Europe.

Mexico also played a role in stimulating American anger against Germany through the publication of the Zimmerman Note. Wilson's anglophilia tilted him to the side of the British and the French and against the Germanic powers in the European conflict. Some Americans already wanted war with Germany because of that nation's unrestricted submarine warfare which had cost American lives and ships. The Zimmerman Note added another log to the fire, especially for Texans. German Foreign Minister Arthur Zimmerman proposed an alliance with Mexico which provided for the return of all U.S. territory formerly governed by that nation in return for their assistance if war developed between Germany and the U.S. Americans, especially Texans, were outraged. President Wilson asked Congress for a declaration of war on April 6, 1917.

Even before the war Edward M. House had traveled to Europe several times on missions for Wilson. So close was their relationship that Wilson admitted that he did not have to tell House what to say to European statesmen in his behalf, because "He will say I what I would say if I were there." Other Texans who played a significant role in the war effort included Congressman John Nance Garner, chairman of the House Ways and Means Committee, whose duties included finding ways to pay for the war; Congressman Tom Connally, a member of the Foreign Affairs Committee; and Congressman Sam Rayburn, who helped create the War Risk Insurance Board to insure the lives of servicemen for the protection of their families.

In Texas, training bases were expanded in El Paso, Brownsville, Houston, and San Antonio, and developed in many other locations. Military aviation had headquartered in Texas since 1911 when pilot Benny Foulois brought the Army's only airplane to San

Antonio to learn to fly. Foulois later flew observation for Pershing over Mexico and headed the Army's aviation arm in Europe during World War I.

On Registration Day, June 5, 1917, when all eligible males began registering for the draft, over 400,000 Texans signed up—eventually, over 900,000 registered.

Approximately 200,000 Texans served in the military during the war, and 5,171 died in service. Even more succumbed to influenza, especially during the national epidemic in 1918, and to other contagious diseases than to enemy action.

A Council of Defense coordinated state efforts to win the war. The National Guard and Texas Rangers were enlarged in response to the Zimmerman Note, and they patrolled the Mexican border. Patriotism was high, and sometimes carried beyond reason, as when Governor Hobby vetoed the appropriation for the German Department at the University of Texas. Texans along with other Americans "Hooverized," meaning they cooperated when Food Administrator Herbert Hoover requested they forego eating meat one day a week to spare a steak for a serviceman or an ally in Europe. And they purchased Liberty Bonds, part of Secretary of the Treasury William G. Madoo's plan to finance the war and spread the profits to purchasers of small denomination bonds.

At the end of the war, House returned to Europe with Wilson to advance the Fourteen Points, some of which were House's idea, to end the war in a way that would prevent future wars. Sadly, they failed, but it was not all their fault. Ill-treatment of Germany by the other allies generated a "get even" emotion. Partisanship in the U.S. Senate led by Henry Cabot Lodge, and the greed of our European allies to make Germany pay, literally in money, for their wartime expenses as well as confiscation of German territory, led the world to another war within twenty years.

War's end introduced the New Era, when Americans and Texans wanted to return to the "good old days" as rapidly as possible. Disillusionment followed the unsuccessful international crusade to make the world better and ushered in a period of inward focus

among most Americans. For example, labor unions did not strike during the war, but in 1919 Texas witnessed more labor stoppages than at any previous time. The New Era became "Normalcy" with the election of President Warren G. Harding, who meant to promise a return to prewar "normality" but in the process unwittingly contributed a new version of the word to the American language.

Pressure from the war upset many things, and changes continued during the 1920s despite the desire for "normalcy." Three significant amendments to the U.S. Constitution played a large role in changing the way people lived. The Seventeenth Amendment, sponsored by Texas Senator Joseph W. Bailey, partly because he knew the Texas legislature

Above: Theodore Roosevelt on the famous wolf hunt in the Texas Panhandle, April, 1905 with a group of noted West Texans that included Comanche chief Quanah Parker and Bill McDonald.

COURTESY, PANHANDLE-PLAINS HISTORICAL MUSEUM, CANYON, TEXAS.

Below: Photograph entitled "Friends" with the inscribed "Flying Dutchman and myself at his home; Grandpa." Shiner, Texas, March 22, 1907.

COURTESY, THE EDWIN WOLTERS MEMORIAL MUSEUM, SHINER, TEXAS, AND THE INSTITUTE OF TEXAN CULTURES, SAN ANTONIO, TEXAS.

would not return him to the Senate for another term, provided for the direct election of U.S. senators. The Eighteenth Amendment, introduced by Texas Senator Morris Sheppard, required national prohibition; concern for the morals of servicemen and the need for the grains that produced alcohol beverages made the dream of prohibition a legal reality. But Seymour Connor said that on the day prohibition went into effect 2,500 saloons in Texas closed and twice as many bootleggers and illegal stills went into operation. Texas was the first state in the South and the ninth in the nation to ratify the Nineteenth Amendment, which empowered women to vote. In fact, women voted in primary elections in Texas in 1918, even before they cast

their first ballots in national elections in 1920. Women still faced an uphill struggle for equality. They could not serve on juries until 1954. Married women could not exercise full property married until much later. Some discrimination, such as the state's community property law, was intended as protection but full gender equality was still to be achieved.

Progressivism continued in the 1920s, but often its negative side prevailed. For example, the Ku Klux Klan, outlawed and inoperative since the 1870s, was reborn in Georgia and spread to Texas and elsewhere. Hiram W. Evans of Dallas became the Imperial Wizard of the entire Klan. The Klan of the 1920s differed from its predecessor in that it had as many members in the North and West as in the South, and the second Klan focused more on controlling the lawless, Jews, and Catholics than on blacks—mostly because state segregation laws affecting blacks were providing effective control. Charles Alexander's study of the "second" KKK is an excellent source on Klan activities in the 1920s.

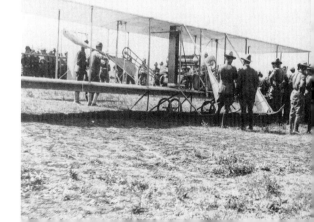

THE AGE OF OIL

Lynn Taliferro Barret, a resident of Melrose in Nacogdoches County before the Civil War, believed that oil lay beneath the surface of East Texas and determined to be the first to locate it. Actually, surface seepages were common in Texas and not welcome because they rendered the land unsuitable for agriculture and yielded little of value beyond some lubrication and medicinal use. Barret suspended his search in 1859, but resumed it as soon as the Civil War ended. In 1866 he successfully completed the first oil well in Texas, a 110-foot penetration that yielded about ten barrels per day, at a Nacogdoches County site known as Oil Springs where oil had surfaced along with spring water for a millennium. Not only was this the first oil well in Texas, it produced the first storage tanks and the first pipeline in the state. But production was low, and as yet there was no substantial market for the product.

Additional discoveries in Corsicana—when the city drilled for water and found oil—plus the arrival of Joseph S. Cullinan, gave the oil industry the stimulus needed to become a big business. Cullinan helped convince railroads to covert to oil as an energy source to produce steam, persuaded local governments to lay the substance on dirt roads to control dust, and built the first refinery in Texas.

The event that really ushered in the oil age in Texas occurred on January 10, 1901, near Beaumont, at a site known as Gladys Hill, although it is better known as Spindletop, a name used by oil field workers because of the shape of a tree that grew there. Patillo Higgins had predicted for a decade that oil could be found at the site. Finally he advertised for a driller, and the ad was answered by Anthony Lucas, an engineer. Higgins and Lucas traded away most of their interest in the well for supplies, but when the Spindletop gusher "blew in" it made several men millionaires. The field produced 3.5 million barrels during its first year, at least one-quarter of the total for the U.S., was rejuvenated in 1926 by deeper drilling that produced a second "boom," and continued to produced for the remainder of the century. So much oil, gas, and sulfur have

been produced from the salt dome known originally as Gladys Hill that it is now a sink. Gulf Oil, the Texas Oil Company (now Texaco, Incorporated) founded by Cullinan, J.W. Gates, and James S. Hogg), Magnolia Oil, and scores of lesser companies were founded as a result of Spindletop.

Major discoveries followed at Sour Lake, Batson, Humble, and Goose Creek in eastern Texas, and in Petrolia, Electra, Powell, and Burkburnett, in western Texas; each produced a million or more barrels per year. Oil production summoned the need for an expanded pipeline industry and made railroads and timber even more profitable, the latter because drilling rigs and plank roads to drilling sites demanded lumber. Howard Hughes made a fortune supplying drilling equipment, especially drilling bits. And for local governments oil produced a major new taxable resource that proved especially beneficial to school districts.

In 1900, Texans spent $9 million annually to educate just over 700,000 pupils; by 1920 the state spent $72 million on 1.2 million students, and increased the number of teachers from approximately 15,000 to 32,000. Per capita expenditure increased from $4.50 to

$14.50, although Texas still ranked thirty-ninth in the nation in educational support and seemed content with the ranking. Governor Ferguson's school consolidation program and free text books helped, but tax revenue from oil production, refining, and distribution made the greatest difference.

Institutions of higher education also increased in size and number between 1900 and 1920; although oil was less directly involved in their founding, its revenues often enriched them in later decades. Teacher preparation institutions were founded at Commerce (East Texas State), San Marcos (Southwest Texas, in 1899), Denton (North Texas and Texas Woman's), El Paso (Texas College of Mines), Kingsville (Texas A&I), Canyon (West Texas), and Alpine (Sul Ross), and authorized for Nacogdoches, although Stephen F. Austin State did not begin operating until 1923, the same year that Texas Tech began in Lubbock. Among private institutions, Rice was founded in 1912 and Southern Methodist University opened in 1915.

Oil discoveries continued, including the giant EasTex field in the area of Kilgore, Henderson, and Longview. Columbus M.

"Dad" Joiner completed his discovery well, the Daisey Bradford No. 3, near Kilgore in October 1930, still unaware that he had found the largest field in history. The major oil companies had been aware of oil in the area, but their geologists believed the amount was insufficient to justify a significant investment. Before the truth was known, leases were mostly held by "independents," or small producers. As the Depression deepened, they gloried in their sudden wealth and did not care that the volume of oil they produced had dropped its value from $1.00 to ten cents per barrel. The Railroad Commission, now the state regulator of oil production, and the rest of state government never succeeded in shutting off the flow of "hot oil," or production in excess of the commission's "daily allowable."

Within twenty-four hours of Joiner's discovery, 5,000 job seekers made their way to Kilgore, and most found jobs in the exploding industry. Many East Texans said they "never knew when the Depression began," meaning that the stock market crash in 1929 did not have much effect on an area that had always been economically depressed, with things only a little worse after agricultural supports were dropped after World War I. But the discovery of oil in East Texas made the Depression easier for all those who found jobs in the oil fields and refineries.

Texas politics remained colorful. Pat Neff served as governor from 1921 to 1925 and provided at least a rest between the Fergusons. In 1924, Jim Ferguson returned to power through the election of his wife, Miriam Amanda Ferguson, as governor. Soon reporters notice that her initials could be used as "MA," and of course Jim became "PA." Both Fergusons freely admitted that the former gov-

ernor would wield the power in her administration through the slogan "Two governors for the price of one."

One of the issues in the campaign was the KKK, which both Fergusons opposed vigorously. The Klan had succeeded in electing Earle Mayfield to the U.S. Senate, and supported Felix Robertson against Mrs. Ferguson. She won the Democratic nomination in a second primary, then faced Republican George C. Butte in the general election; Butte received more votes than any Republican candidate in decades, mostly from disgruntled Democrats who dreaded the return of "Fergusonism." And well they might have. Mrs. Ferguson's administration was mired in scandals: over 2,000 pardons for prisoners in two years, leading to charges that bribes were involved. Neff had pardoned only 200 in four years, and the mysterious connection between the awarding of state highway construction contracts and the size and number of ads that companies receiving them had placed in Ferguson's newspaper, the *Ferguson Forum*. Dan Moody defeated Mrs. Ferguson in the Democratic primary in 1926, and sponsored a reorganization of the way the highway department and public school text book contracts were let.

In 1928, Texas hosted its first national political convention when Democrats gathered in Houston to nominate the governor of New York, Al Smith, as their presidential candidate. Smith's northeastern origin, his religion (Catholic), and opposition to prohibition doomed his candidacy in Texas, which voted Republican for the first time since the Civil War. Herbert Hoover became president just in time to receive all the blame for the stock market crash and the Depression that gripped the nation until 1942. Mrs. Ferguson ran again in 1928 but was defeated by Ross Sterling, who was subsequently blamed for the Depression

Top: The Women Drum Corps of the Dallas Ku Klux Klan, c. 1920, at Union Terminal.
FROM THE COLLECTIONS OF THE TEXAS/DALLAS HISTORY AND ARCHIVES DIVISION, DALLAS PUBLIC LIBRARY.

Middle: Photograph of Local Council No. 4, "Order of Sons of America," taken on the steps of the First Methodist Church in Corpus Christi in 1927. This chapter, under the leadership of Ben Garza, was the driving force in unifying Latin American organizations under one title. That organization, the League of United Latin American Citizens (LULAC) held its first convention two years later in Corpus Christi.
COURTESY, CORPUS CHRISTI PUBLIC LIBRARY.

Bottom,left: "Shearing Wool by Hand."
COURTESY, ARCHIVES DIVISION - TEXAS STATE LIBRARY.

by Texas voters. Sterling's efforts to deal with the Depression focused on a state law to limit production of cotton, the state's leading agricultural crop, so that demand could catch up with supply and yield higher prices. This same philosophy advanced by the Agricultural Adjustment Administration during the New Deal, but was destined to fail when attempted by only one state since other cotton-producing states continued to plant without restriction.

The Depression and Sterling's unpopular attempts to curtail oil production in the EasTex field brought Mrs. Ferguson back to the governor's office after the 1932 election, when Franklin Delano Roosevelt replaced Hoover as president. By then, Texans and most other Americans had suffered severely from the Depression. Over 13,000,000 persons were unemployed and nearly 60,000,000 were directly affected. Banks experienced "runs;" businesses closed. "Bumming," or traveling to seek work, became a major factor long before the term "homeless" was coined. Migrants lived near the railroads they attempted to ride illegally from place to place in shantytowns inevitably called "Hooverville." In East Texas, armadillos, and in West Texas jackrabbits, became "Hoover Hogs." Newspapers under which migrants sometimes slept for warmth became "Hoover blankets." Certainly Hoover was not exclusively to blame for the Depression; both political parties had erred during the previous decades to produce this most trying economic time in U.S. history. But Hoover's method of dealing with the problem—principally to state that the national economy was basically sound and would eventually recover, while true, did little to offer hope in the

short run. Franklin D. Roosevelt, the familiar FDR, the first president since his since cousin Theodore Roosevelt (TR) to be known by his initials, provided hope with the New Deal. Roosevelt assured Americans that not they but the national economic system had failed, and he promised them a "new deal," the card-game metaphor for change and better luck, that would restore them and the nation to prosperity. Of course it did not; full employment did not return until 1942, and then it was produced by World War II But Roosevelt's smile, his willingness to try virtually anything to help, caught the attention of voters and sustained him in the presidency until his death on April 12, 1945. FDR led the fight against the Depression and against Germany, Japan, and Italy, and forever will remain the only person elected to more than two terms as president so long as the Twenty-Second Amendment, which a wary Congress proposed after his death to make sure that even his ghost could not arise and run again, remains a part of the Constitution.

Speaker of the House John Nance Garner of Texas had been a leading candidate for the presidential nomination in 1932, and he received the vice presidency as consolation. Garner stuck for two terms, chafing all the while, then fell out completely in 1940 over the third-term issue and returned to Texas. Garner was not alone in believing it was someone else's turn to be president, but FDR remained and Garner came home.

There really were two New Deals, the first of which was quickly enacted by a Democratic Congress grateful to be back in charge after Republican domination under Hoover. By 1935, however, the New Deal had largely been declared unconstitutional by the Supreme Court, which was still dominated by

Republican appointees. In form, the second New Deal, passed between 1936 and 1041, closely resembled the first. This time, however, the constitutionality of the program was affirmed by a Court which, through the intervening years and as a result of Roosevelt's appointments, had become more reflective of the Democratic administration. Each New Deal featured "Relief, Recovery, and Reform," although the first was heavier on "relief and recovery" and the second featured more "recovery and reform."

For agriculture, the New Deal established the Agricultural Adjustment Administration (AAA), and for industry, the National Recovery Administration (NRA), with a blue eagle as its symbol and "We Do Our Part" as its motto. The objectives of both were to increase demand by reducing supply through the pledged efforts of all producers to maintain uniform standards of quantity and quality. After these bills were enacted, however, the Supreme Court ruled that Congress had unconstitutionally passed along its exclusive lawmaking power to other groups. With appropriate revisions to subsequent legislation, Congress finally made the New Deal effective. Despite these efforts, the Depression continued. Per capita income for Americans in 1929 had been $462; by 1939, despite the New Deal, it had dropped to $401, and "official" unemployment figures in Texas had doubled. And they gratefully accepted employment with the Public Works Administration, the Civil Works Administration, or the Works Progress Administration to produce public buildings, facilities and works of art that, but for the impetus of the Depression-era programs, might have been long deferred or never achieved. Few later public assistance programs have so effectively equated effort with income while enabling workers to retain skills and dignity.

In state politics, Mrs. Ferguson's second administration (1933-1935) proved less controversial than her first and less associated with scandal except for her addition of over 2,000 "honorary" Texas Rangers purportedly to "get even" with the force for supporting Sterling for reelection. The Fergusons proposed a general consolidation of 129 state bureaus and agencies into twenty depart-

ments and a reorganization of the state's higher education programs, but little was accomplished. Ferguson's administration won legislative approval for a state relief program, legalized horse racing, and the production of 3.2% beer even before the Twenty-First Amendment repealing nationwide prohibition.

In 1935 James Allred replaced Mrs. Ferguson as governor after surviving a field of seven candidates in the previous year's Democratic primary. Allred proposed a tax on oil production and more state assistance for police to confront a national crime wave exacerbated by the Depression. He also combined the Rangers and the Highway Patrol in a Department of Public Safety, and increased old-aged pensions. Despite these efforts, the Depression lingered and worsened in Texas. Nevertheless Allred won reelection in 1936, along with FDR, because voters appreciated their efforts and had no better alternatives.

Above: Framed photograph by N.M. Wilcox of downtown San Antonio in the 1920s featuring the Long Barracks and the Alamo.
COURTESY, ARCHIVES DIVISION - TEXAS STATE LIBRARY.

Bottom: Hauling jail in oil boom town.
PHOTO BY SCHLUETER OF HOUSTON.
COURTESY, ARCHIVES DIVISION - TEXAS STATE LIBRARY.

Top: Aaron Arion's allegorical Spindletop Viewing Her Gusher. The painting celebrates the January 10, 1901 discovery of petroleum resources in the Beaumont area. As the Spindletop—or Lucas—Gusher blew in, oil sprayed over 100 feet above the derrick until it was finally capped nine days later. Subsequent major discoveries throughout the state further enhanced the quality of life in Texas, with oil revenues especially benefiting public education. Historian Joe B. Franz has written, for example, that prior to the Kilgore oil boom in the early 1930s, Deep East Texas was becoming "the Appalachia of the state."

COURTESY, TYRRELL HISTORICAL LIBRARY, BEAUMONT, TEXAS.

Middle, right: Contour plowing which created terracing in the Elm Creek watershed in Bell County near Temple following the Dust Bowl era.

SOIL CONSERVATION SERVICE OF USDA PHOTO BY JIM MITCHELL. COURTESY, CORPUS CHRISTI PUBLIC LIBRARY.

Bottom, right: Mildred "Babe" Didrikson Zaharius, world renowned athlete, posing October 1935 during the golf tour in which she played with Al Espinosa against Ken Rogers and Hank Williams at Willow Springs Golf Course in San Antonio. She has been honored with her own sports museum in her hometown of Beaumont.

COURTESY, THE INSTITUTE OF TEXAN CULTURES, SAN ANTONIO, TEXAS.

Bottom, left: During prohibition, law officers pose beside "EL FOOD MAYONNAISE" truck, with containers stamped "VICTORIA" on the ground."

COURTESY, CORPUS CHRISTI PUBLIC LIBRARY.

A different kind of political leader emerged in the gubernatorial election in 1938. W. Lee O'Daniel, known statewide as "Pappy" because of the "Pass the biscuits, Pappy" tag line in the theme song of a daily radio program he sponsored, disclosed that a listener had suggested he run for governor. O'Daniel asked his radio audience for advice and claimed that he received over 54,000 cards and letters urging him to make the race. O'Daniel's radio persona, made popular by biblical quotations and homilies and the music of the Light Crust Doughboys, a three-piece Western Swing band, ensured his election despite his having no experience in government, and he was continued in office for a second term in 1940. O'Daniel advocated a "transaction" tax, euphemism for a sales tax, that was not approved by the legislature;

instead, they passed the Morris Omnibus Tax Bill establishing taxes on gasoline, tobacco, and other items.

When Senator Morris Sheppard died in 1941 before O'Daniel's second term ended, some leg-

islators urged the governor to appoint himself temporarily to the Senate—to get him out of the state, because they disliked him, according to some. Instead O'Daniel appointed octogenarian Andrew Jackson Houston, a man so old that incumbency would not be an issue in the special election to complete Sheppard's term. Nearly thirty candidates entered the race, including Congressman Lyndon Baines Johnson, but O'Daniel won by the slender margin of just over 1,000 questionable votes, and LBJ vowed never to be cheated out of an election again. When O'Daniel moved to the Senate, Lt. Gov. Coke R. Stevenson became the governor of Texas on August 4, 1941—just in time to preside over the state during World War II.

TEXAS IN WORLD WAR II

World War II came to Asia and Europe during the 1930s, but it began for Texans and other Americans on sunday, September 7, 1941 with the shocking attack by the Japan's naval air forces on American military installations and civilians in Hawaii, and elsewhere in the Pacific soon afterwards. Texans were involved from the beginning. One of the heroes of Pearl Harbor was Doris Miller of Waco, a black steward aboard one of the attacked vessels. Miller manned an anti-aircraft gun with which he had no training or experience, and shot down one of the few Japanese aircraft felled that day. The next day

in Congress Texan Tom Connally introduced the war resolution against Japan.

The U.S. was unprepared for war, but not as unprepared as it might have been. Passage of the Burke-Wadsworth Act in 1940 had initiated the first peace-time draft in U.S. history, and industry was already beginning to gear for war, at least with those efforts that could escape the attention of isolationists in Congress and elsewhere. When war found them, Texans participated with the zeal they had demonstrated in each of the nation's previous international conflicts. Eventually 750,000 Texans participated in military service, a higher percentage of the population than in any other state; 15,764 Texans died while in the Army (10,839 as a direct result of combat) and an additional 7,259 died while serving in other military branches. The Congressional Medal of Honor was received by 36 Texans, including Audie Murphy, who at the time of his death in 1971 was the most decorated

Top: President Franklin D. Roosevelt spoke to a crowd of over 60,000 people gathered in the Cotton Bowl June 12, 1936 to hear his address the same day he dedicated the Robert E. Lee statue at Lee Park in Dallas.
FROM THE COLLECTIONS OF THE TEXAS/DALLAS HISTORY AND ARCHIVES DIVISION, DALLAS PUBLIC LIBRARY.

Bottom,left: Oil portrait of Audie Leon Murphy (1924-1971), painted in 1950 by artist Kipp Soldwedel. Murphy became the most highly decorated WWII American soldier, earning, among his thirty-three awards, the Congressional Medal of Honor in 1945. Murphy appeared on the cover of popular Life *magazine July 16, 1945. After returning to civilian life, he married and became a successful movie star and author and country and western songwriter.*
COURTESY, ARCHIVES DIVISION - TEXAS STATE LIBRARY.

Bottom, right: McDonald Observatory, located about forty miles northwest of Alpine in the Davis Mountains near Fort Davis.
COURTESY, TEXAS DEPARTMENT OF TRANSPORTATION. .

combat soldier in U.S. history, and Samuel Dealey, the nation's most decorated sailor. One hundred fifty general officers in the Army and twelve naval admirals had firm connections to Texas, including Denison-born Dwight David Eisenhower, Allied Supreme Commander in Europe, and Fredericksburg's Chester Nimitz, who served as Commander in Chief of the Pacific Fleet throughout the war. When the Women's Auxiliary Army Corps was created, Colonel Oveta Culp Hobby, wife of former Texas governor William P. Hobby, commanded them.

Texas became a training ground for many overseas-bound servicemen and women. San Antonio already served as headquarters for the Third Army, and the Fourth Army command was moved there during the war. San Antonio was the site of Randolph Field, where Army Air Corps pilots, bombardiers, and navigators received their initial training, and over forty advanced training fields were located elsewhere in the state, including Brooks, Kelly, and Lackland fields for the Army, and Grand Prairie and Corpus Christi for the Navy. Later in the war, the state hosted twenty-nine prisoner-of-war camps to house captured members of the armed forces of the Axis powers. These prisoners-of-war were employed in timber harvesting and in other industries.

For civilians, war brought many changes. The demand for workers in shipyards, aircraft manufacturing plants, and other defense installations brought in millions of dollars in federal payrolls and provided full employment for the first time in Texas history. Jobs previously denied to women, blacks, and Hispanics were now opened to them. Resulting social tensions surfaced, as manifested in Beaumont's 1943 race riot. Since the majority of the U.S. petro-chemical industry plants were located along the Gulf Coast near the source of its basic raw material, Texans also went to work in these plants to produce synthetic rubber and other products. Munitions plants appeared; the steel industry grew rapidly in the Daingerfield area of East Texas; and the nation's entire supply of helium was produced in fields in West Texas.

Texas agriculture underwent diversification during the war, but the state still led the nation in the production of cotton, cattle, horses, tomatoes, and other commodities, despite the loss of labor to the military service and a reduction in the number of farms in production. Texans accepted shortages and rationing of gasoline, tires, sugar, shoes, cigarettes, meat, oils, and other commodities with as much equanimity and as little "black market" activity as other Americans. They bought Series E War Bonds ($18.75 for a $25 bond maturing in ten years at 4% interest); tended victory gardens;

contributed scrap meat fats, metals, newspapers; even peeled the tinfoil from cigarette packages for reuse; and returned empty beverage bottles for refills because no more could be obtained by bottlers.

World War II drew Americans together as has no other event in the nation's history, with one possible exception. Texans' early "Pearl Harbor-like event" at the Alamo was featured in the words of a popular 1942 song: "Let's remember Pearl Harbor, as we go to meet the foe; Let's remember Pearl Harbor, as we did the Alamo." But there were political divisions.

Stevenson won full terms as governor in 1942 and 1944. Having presided during the state's return to prosperity, he remained popular throughout his tenure in office. O'Daniel, who won a full-term Senate seat in 1944, was also the leading campaigner for the "Texas Regulars," who deserted FDR when he sought a fourth term and lent their support to Republican Thomas E. Dewey. But the president won reelection anyway.

World War II ended in Europe on May 8, 1944, with the surrender of German forces, and on August 14 of the same year with surrender of Japanese forces, following the dropping of the first atomic bombs on the cities of Hiroshima on August 6 and Nagasaki on August 9. It had been a terrible war, costly in lives, resources, and even innocence, and, sadly, it did not end tensions among the nations of the world. But it did insure the continuation of freedom and democracy in the United States and Texas and in other parts of the world.

MODERN TEXAS

TEXAS IN POSTWAR AMERICA

*F*ranklin Delano Roosevelt, thirty-second president of the United States and provider of hope for Texans and other Americans during a decade of Depression and a half-decade of world war, died in Warm Springs, Georgia, on April 12, 1945, less than a month before the end of World War II in Europe and four months before victory over Japan. By then many Texans had ceased to support FDR over the issue of his running for a third and fourth term and because they disapproved of the enlargement of the federal role in the balance of federal-state relations. But all Americans were stunned by the news of his death. Quietly and quickly Harry S. Truman took charge of the government and the war and quickly made the decision to use America's new atomic bomb to hasten victory in the Pacific Theatre.

Victory over America's war-time foes brought home hundreds of thousands of Texans who had fought the war on three continents, numerous islands, on the seas, and in training and support capacities. The national GI Bill of Rights enabled many of them to begin or complete educational programs in academic or vocational schools, and a Texas GI Bill established a $100 million fund to assist veterans in the purchase of land. Returning veterans faced problems of adjustment, such as getting reacquainted with families and finding a place to live and a job. Legislation assisted veterans by guaranteeing them priority to the jobs they had left when entering the service, but after spending years separated from normal civilian life, some required time before they could settle down again. An Academy-Award winning film, "The Best Years Of Our Lives" (1946) provided a fictionalized account of problems faced by real people in the year of coming home.

In l946, when Governor Coke Stevenson, who had presided over the Texas government since 1941, did not seek reelection, a memorable contest ensued pitting former University of Texas President Homer Rainey against a field of thirteen opponents. Rainey had lost his job in 1944 in a dispute with university regents over appointments and the selection of University library books considered by some as corrupting, and he sought the governor's job to vindicate his defense of academic freedom. All the candidates except Beauford Jester of Navarro County joined into rancorous competition with Rainey for the office while Jester alone campaigned as the one who could enter the governor's office "without mud on his hands." Jester won, and Allan Shivers won the lieutenant governor's race.

Perhaps the most memorable political race in modern Texas history pitted Congressman Lyndon B. Johnson against former Governor Coke Stevenson in the 1948 Democratic primary to select the party's candidate for the U.S. Senate. When Governor W. Lee O'Daniel had defeated Johnson for the same post in the special election in 1941, O'Daniel's elevation to the Senate had moved then-Lieutenant Governor Stevenson into the governor's office. In 1948, Johnson and Stevenson both coveted the Senate seat, and Johnson also wanted vindication for what he regarded as O'Daniel's previous "stolen" election victory. Today, ironically, many believe that Johnson "stole" the 1948 election.

The campaign styles of the two candidates epitomized the "old" and the "new." Stevenson rode around the state in a Plymouth station wagon driven by his nephew, Bob Murphey, stopping frequently at crossroads to make appearances. Johnson whizzed across Texas in the "Johnson City Windmill," the first helicopter used for rapid transportation in a political campaign. Early returns showed that Stevenson had a slight lead, but the later tallies for the two candidates seesawed back and forth until, finally, the official count revealed that the Congressman had won by a margin of

Above: Two former SMU greats of the late 1940's, Doak Walker, left, and Kyle Rote, right, publicize an August 2, 1951 football game, with George Baldwin, president of the Salesmanship Club, looking on.

Buchanan Dam, built on the Colorado River, was dedicated in 1938. It has lessened flooding and provided power and recreational sites.

Below: When the Ridley turtles' chances for survival were endangered in the 1960's, Ila Loetscher, the "Turtle Lady," founded Sea Turtle, Inc. She is shown here in 1992 with one of these turtles on South Padre Island, where she stages shows to raise conservation funds and where sick turtles from throughout the Gulf Coast are sent to recuperate.

eighty-seven votes. That margin had been provided by late returns in Box 13 of Jim Wells County, which Johnson won by a 202-to-1 vote. Stevenson contested the election, but in the end the courts failed to sustain his charge that the election had been won fraudulently. Johnson went on to become Democratic majority leader in the Senate, vice president in the administration of John F. Kennedy, and then president following the assassination of Kennedy in 1963.

Governor Jester died on July 11, 1949. Shivers succeeded him as governor, and then won election to three two-year terms, making him the longest tenured governor to that time. While he was governor, Shivers used his strong leadership to strengthen the office, which is limited by the state constitution, by his strong leadership. The "tidelands" issue illustrates this leadership. In the courts, Attorney General Price Daniel led Texas' fight to control its tidelands, or the continental shelf, the site of significant deposits of oil and natural gas. Since 1946, the federal government had been engaged in efforts nationwide to assert federal ownership of all tidelands throughout the nation. Daniel and Shivers held that these claims were not valid in Texas, which had maintained and defended a three-league boundary in the Gulf of Mexico ever since the days of the Republic of Texas. At stake was millions of dollars in tax revenue and control of very valuable mineral resources. When the state's arguments failed in the courts, Speaker Sam Rayburn and Senator Lyndon B. Johnson pushed quit-claim legislation through the Congress awarding control of the disputed tidelands to the state, but President Harry S Truman vetoed the legislation. Truman's veto set up the tidelands controversy as the paramount issue in Texas in the presidential election in 1952.

The Democratic nominee, Governor Adlai Stevenson of Illinois, refused to pledge to

Shivers that he would not again veto quit-claim legislation, but the Republican candidate, General Dwight D. Eisenhower, committed to signing it. Shivers bolted from the Democratic Party and called on his supporters, known as "Shivercrats," to join him in voting for a Republican president while remaining loyal Democrats in down-ballot elections. In return, the Republicans did not run an opponent against Shivers or other Texas Democrats who supported Ike, and Texas voted Republican in a presidential election for the first time since 1928 and only the second time since Reconstruction.

Shivers is remembered for much positive legislation in the areas of public health, education, prison reform, and insurance regulation, largely supported by his lieutenant governor, Ben Ramsey. At the same time, his administration was marred by one of the infamous scandals that visit Texas politics occasionally, this time concerning the $100 million fund established to assist veterans to purchase land. Shivers, Attorney General John Ben Sheppard, and Land Commissioner Bascom Giles supervised the fund. Since the expenditures from the fund concerned land purchases and loans to veterans, Giles handled the day-to-day affairs of the program. The scandal involved buying land at an inflated price through a system of fraudulent appraisals and kickbacks to the officials who processed the purchases and loans. Veterans who obtained individual parcels of the land were unaware of the kickbacks. Giles received a six-year prison sentence for his part in the affair, and, although Shivers and Sheppard committed no wrong, their association with him tainted both careers.

Daniel, who had moved on to the U.S. Senate because "I thought Allan [Shivers] never would quit being governor," came home in 1956 to run for that office when Shivers did not seek reelection. Ralph Yarborough, who had run against Shivers previously, proved the most formidable of Daniel's five opponents. Following Daniel's victory,

Yarborough won the special election to fill out Daniel's remaining Senate term. Daniel won re-election as governor in 1958 and 1960, and concluded his career two decades later as a member of the state supreme court. Although he held nearly every elected office in Texas during his years of public service, he relished the role of governor above all others.

Lyndon B. Johnson again captured the spotlight in Texas politics during the presidential election in 1960. As the Democratic majority leader in the Senate, Johnson already wielded great power, but he wanted to be president. He kept to his job in the Senate during the primary election season while Senators John F. Kennedy and Hubert H. Humphrey battled for delegate support, hopeful that at the nominating convention in Los Angeles his maturity and good political connections around the country would make the slogan "All The Way With LBJ" a reality. But Kennedy had enough

delegates to win the nomination on the first ballot. For a few hours it appeared that Johnson would have to return to the Senate. Then Kennedy startled his own supporters, as well as Johnson's, by offering Johnson the vice presidency. Johnson accepted, and his place on the ticket helped carry Texas for the Democrats, who had to win in Texas in order to defeat Republican candidates Richard M. Nixon and Henry Cabot Lodge.

Because of special legislation passed by the Texas legislature, Johnson was able in 1960 to run simultaneously for vice president and for reelection to the Senate. He won both. The special election then made necessary to select his successor in the Senate drew over seventy candidates. Republicans and conservative Democrats rallied behind John Tower, who became the first Republican U.S. senator from Texas since Reconstruction.

The relationship between Kennedy's northeastern advisors and Johnson's southwestern supporters was not entirely harmonious, but the principals seemed to get along well enough, at least publicly. Johnson was never comfortable in the second position, and might have chosen not to run again as vice president in 1964 had tragedy not elevated him to the presidency on November 22, 1963.

Kennedy had come to Texas, some people thought, to kick off his reelection campaign. He was greeted warmly at appearances in Houston and Fort Worth before arriving in Dallas, a city that was reputed to oppose Kennedy as being too liberal. However, President and Mrs. Kennedy, accompanied by Governor and Mrs. John B. Connally, were well received by Dallas citizens, who came out to greet the presidential motorcade en route through downtown to the Trade Mart were Kennedy was to speak. Just as Mrs. Connally turned to the president to remark on the friendliness of the crowd, bullets struck both Kennedy and Connally, killing the president and gravely wounding the governor.

The motorcade sped to Parkland Hospital, where President Kennedy was pronounced dead. Johnson was

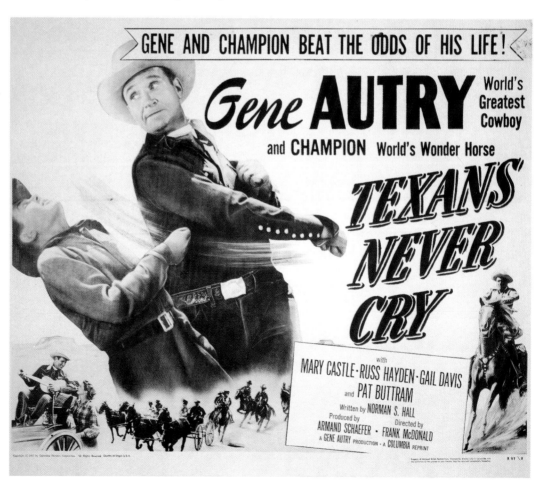

Top, right: Christmas lighting in Marshall, founded and incorporated during the Republic of Texas era. The city enjoyed early transportation advantages, including its location between the Sabine and Red rivers and its limited rail service prior to the Civil War. In 1861, citizens voted unanimously for secession, and during the Battle of Mansfield, Louisiana in 1864, many participated in order to avert a U.S. invasion of Texas. Reconstruction was bitter, with the city not only becoming the base for occupying federal forces but also hosting a Freedmen's Bureau office. In recent years, two national leaders have sought to deal with their historic hometown. Civil rights activist and son of Texas' first Black Ph. D., James Farmer, Jr., founded the Congress of Racial Equality (CORE), and Bill Moyers tackled the task of bringing coherence to the city's rich history.

PHOTO BY J. GRIFFIS SMITH. COURTESY, TEXAS DEPARTMENT OF TRANSPORTATION.

Below: The Majestic Theater, San Antonio.

COURTESY, TEXAS DEPARTMENT OF TRANSPORTATION

Bottom, right: Gene Autry, "World's Greatest Cowboy," and Champion, "World's Wonder Horse," featured on 1951 movie poster for western Texans Never Cry.

COURTESY, SOUTHWESTERN WRITERS COLLECTION, SAN MARCOS, TEXAS, AND THE CENTER FOR AMERICAN HISTORY, THE UNIVERSITY OF TEXAS AT AUSTIN.

taken immediately to Love Field and the safety of Air Force One, the presidential airplane, where Judge Sarah T. Hughes administered the presidential oath of office. As soon as Kennedy's body arrived, the aircraft flew both the slain president and the new president to Washington.

Police arrested Lee Harvey Oswald, an employee at the Texas School Book Depository, for firing the shots that killed the president. On the following Sunday morning, as he was being transferred to the Dallas County jail, Oswald himself was slain by Jack Ruby, a Dallas nightclub owner. The Warren Commission, appointed by President Johnson to investigate the tragedy, ruled that Oswald was the lone assassin of Kennedy, a conclusion still disputed by many who believe that Oswald was silenced to prevent the implication of others.

Connally recovered and won re-election in 1964 and 1966, and became one of Texas' most successful modern governors. Having seen during his tenure as secretary of the navy that the largest government contracts tended to go to states with superior education systems, Connally became a champion of public schools and higher education. He convinced the legislature to create the Coordinating Board for Higher Education in order to obtain the best results from the state's investment in education.

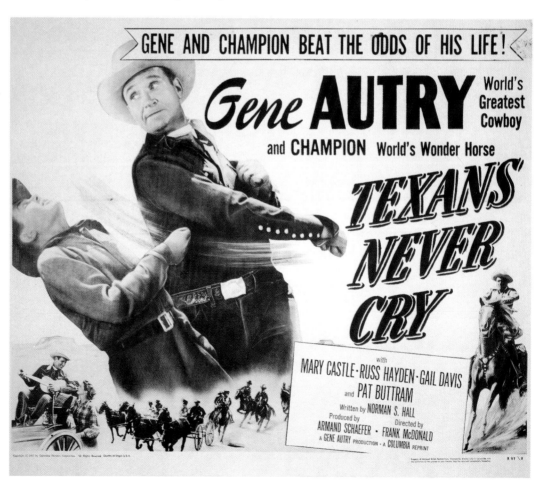

GENE AND CHAMPION BEAT THE ODDS OF HIS LIFE!

Gene AUTRY World's Greatest Cowboy

and CHAMPION World's Wonder Horse

TEXANS' NEVER CRY

with MARY CASTLE · RUSS HAYDEN · GAIL DAVIS and PAT BUTTRAM

Written by NORMAN S. HALL

Produced by ARMAND SCHAEFER · Directed by FRANK McDONALD

A GENE AUTRY PRODUCTION · A COLUMBIA REPRINT

During the following period of national grief over the murder of Kennedy, Johnson succeeded in pushing through Congress several previously defeated Kennedy initiatives. A tax cut was passed, as well as the 1964 Civil Rights Act dealing with public accommodations. In 1964 Johnson defeated Republican challenger Barry Goldwater to win a full term in his own right, and launched his Great Society program to end poverty in America. Historian Joe Frantz has argued that President Johnson changed the way Americans live more completely than any other modern president. Johnson's administration perhaps surpassed even that of Franklin D. Roosevelt in attempting to make a positive difference in the life of every American, regardless of race or any other factor. Unfortunately, Johnson was forced to shift his attention away from his domestic program because of America's escalating involvement in the war in Viet Nam. In 1968, noting the country's great division over the war, he chose not to seek a second term as president.

The same year, John Connally decided not to seek reelection as governor, opening the way for Lieutenant Governor Preston Smith, a Lubbock businessman who had waited in the wings for just such an opportunity. Smith subsequently won a second term in 1970, but before it ended, his administration became involved in scandal. Named for Houston entrepreneur Frank Sharp, the Sharpstown scandal involved illegal influence to pass banking legislation and eventually brought down not only the governor but Lieutenant Governor Ben Barns and House Speaker Gus Mutscher as well. Mutscher in particular became the target of a group of reform legislators who came to be called the "Dirty Thirty." Frances "Sissy" Farenthold, who emerged from this group to run for governor in 1972, was defeated in the Democratic primary by Dolph Briscoe, who

went on to win the general election. Briscoe's campaign slogan "No New Taxes" also became the theme of his administration and won for him the strong support of tax payers. In 1974, after the approval of a constitutional amendment, Briscoe was reelected to the first four-year governor's term in state history.

In l978, William Clements, president of an oil-well drilling company who had served in the Department of Defense in the Nixon Administration, defeated long-time Republican leader Ray Hutchison for that party's nomination for governor, and went on to defeat Democrat John Hill in the general election. This first Republican governor of Texas since Edmund J. Davis provided the state with a solid businessman's administration. His day-to-day conduct of the office was perhaps the best of any administration except Connally's, since the 1930s. But his plain-spoken manner, and what some considered an abrasive personality, left him vulnerable in 1982 to a Democratic Party united from the shock of its loss in the previous election.

Until Clements' victory, Texas' version of a two-party system featured clashes between "conservative" and "liberal" Democrats. The party primary was regarded as the "real" election. Clements' election changed that, and Democrats realized that they had to unite to reclaim the governorship, an office which controlled appointments to all state agency regulatory boards. Attorney General Mark White emerged from the Democratic primary as the nominee, and headed a slate of statewide office seekers as disparate as they were desperate: for state treasurer, Ann Richards; for agriculture commissioner, Jim Hightower; and for land commissioner, Gary Mauro.

Top, left: Ronald and Nancy Reagan, welcomed at Union Station on June 8, 1952 by James O. Cherry of the Interstate Theaters in Dallas, where the Texas Conference of the Council of Motion Picture Organizations was being held in 1952.

FROM THE COLLECTIONS OF THE TEXAS/DALLAS HISTORY AND ARCHIVES DIVISION, DALLAS PUBLIC LIBRARY.

Top, right: Henry Cisneros, first Mexican-American mayor of a major city, San Antonio.

PHOTO BY JACK LEWIS. COURTESY, TEXAS DEPARTMENT OF TRANSPORTATION.

Above: Van Cliburn, internationally renowned concert pianist, c. 1958.

FROM THE COLLECTIONS OF THE TEXAS/DALLAS HISTORY AND ARCHIVES DIVISION, DALLAS PUBLIC LIBRARY.

White served as governor for only one term. When Clements regained the office in 1986, some felt that his principal motive for running was to avenge his loss to White in 1982. Regardless of his goal, Clements used his victory to advance the fortunes of the Republican Party and helped make Texas a genuine two-party state.

Clements did not seek reelection in 1990, and Clayton Williams emerged to lead the Republican Party against Democrat Ann Richards, the state treasurer. A combination of Richards' colorful campaign style, which mixed humor with promises to reclaim the statehouse for the people, and William's occasionally tactless public performances—equating bad weather to rape, admitting he had paid no income taxes the previous year and refusing to shake Richards' hand when both appeared on the same program—enabled Richards to become the first woman governor of the state since 1935 and the first elected without being regarded her husband's surrogate.

Richards' "New Texas" program brought more Hispanics, African Americans, and women into state government than any previous administration. She initiated the most extensive prison construction program in state history, and as a recovering alcoholic, insisted that programs of rehabilitation be embodied in the correction process since eighty percent of the state's inmates had been imprisoned for crimes related to their chemical dependency. She also promoted business for the state elsewhere in the nation and the world more vigorously than any previous governor. In spite of these accomplishments, she failed her bid for reelection in 1994 and was defeated by George W. Bush, son of former president George Bush and managing partner of the Texas Rangers baseball team.

CONTEMPORARY TEXAS

Contemporary Texas is many things. With the third largest population in the nation and a party orientation that is no longer a "given," Texas plays an important role in national political processes. In 1996, Texans in congressional leadership posts under a Republican majority included Representatives

Richard Armey and Tom DeLay, Senators Phil Gramm and Kay Bailey Hutchison, all Republicans.

Hutchison won her post in 1993 in a special election to replace Democratic Senator Lloyd Bentsen, then chairman of the powerful Senate Finance Committee, who resigned to become secretary of the Treasury in the Clinton Administration. Gramm began his political career as a Democrat but switched to the Republican party during the administration of President Ronald Reagan. Since the Republican sweep in the congressional race of 1994, several other Democrats in Congress and in state offices have switched or have contemplated doing so. Even Democrat John Connally switched parties to seek the Republican nomination for president in 1980, although he never seemed comfortable in his new party and many traditional Republicans did not seem happy to have him.

Texas is now home to its second former occupant of the White House, President George Bush, who, with Mrs. Bush, returned establish residence in Houston following his defeat in the election of 1992. Although not a native Texan, Bush moved to the state after World War II to enter the oil business. In 1966 he entered into a long and varied career in politics, serving successively as a congressional representative, UN delegate, Chairman of the Republican National Committee, spe-

cial envoy to the People's Republic of China, director of the CIA, vice president in the Reagan administration and as president from 1988 until 1992. The Bush presidential library will be located at Texas A&M University.

Texas played a significant role in the modern civil rights movement. Many of the landmark desegregation cases, such as *Nixon v. Herndon* and *Smith v. Allright*, which dealt with segregated political primaries, and *Sweatt v. Painter*, which concerned education, were tried in Texas courts before advancing to the Supreme Court in Washington. NAACP attorney Thurgood

Marshall pioneered the sociological argument in *Sweatt v. Painter* that he later used successfully in *Brown v. Board of Education of Topeka* to end segregation in public schools throughout the nation. Hispanics constitute the largest ethnic minority in Texas, and a court case filed in behalf of their economically poorer school districts resulted in a revision of state funding for public education.

Texas continues to host the nerve center of America's space program at NASA's Johnson Space Center, located near Houston. Space probes are launched in Florida, but once airborne, all space activity is controlled from Houston. The city's citizens are proud that the first words spoken on the moon were, "Houston . . . the Eagle has landed."

Texans support, with varying degrees of enthusiasm depending on fortunes of the season, several professional sports franchises, including "America's Team," the Dallas Cowboys (who actually play in a stadium located in Irving), and

Above: Dr. Michael DeBakey, pioneer heart surgeon and winner of the national Medal of Freedom award.
COURTESY, METHODIST HOSPITAL, HOUSTON.

Top, left: Lyndon B. Johnson and crowd of well-wishers.
COURTESY, ARCHIVES DIVISION - TEXAS STATE LIBRARY.

Bottom: President and Mrs. John F. Kennedy being honored at a Chamber of Commerce event in Fort Worth on November 22, 1963, mere hours before his assassination in Dallas. Lady Bird and Vice President Lyndon B. Johnson, left, were among those accompanying the fallen leader back to the nation's capital.
COURTESY, ARCHIVES DIVISION - TEXAS STATE LIBRARY.

Above: Astronaut Neil Armstrong (1930-), speaking at Medal of Valor ceremonies before a Joint Session of the Texas Legislature honoring the Apollo II astronauts, October 17, 1970. Governor Preston Smith is seated left, with folded hands.

PHOTO BY BILL MALONE. COURTESY, ARCHIVES DIVISION - TEXAS STATE LIBRARY.

Top, right: Texas Senate President Pro Tempore Barbara Jordan poses for official photographer Bill Malone June 10, 1972 as she serves as Governor For A Day. A series of images was made throughout the day for the Current Events Photographic Documentation Program.

COURTESY, ARCHIVES DIVISION - TEXAS STATE LIBRARY.

Below: Sheridan Cowgirls, acrylic on photo linen by Bob "Daddy-O" Wade, 1996.

COURTESY, THE TORCH COLLECTION, HOUSTON, TEXAS.

the Houston Oilers, although franchise owner Bud Adams is moving his team to Nashville, Tennessee. Basketball enthusiasts support the Houston Rockets, San Antonio Spurs, or Dallas Mavericks; those who follow baseball have the Houston Astros and (Arlington) Texas Rangers; and Dallasites have the NHL Stars hockey team.

Texans boost a variety of amateur athletics at high school and collegiate levels. The famed Southwest Conference, which included most of the Division I schools in Texas involved in NCAA competition, played its last round during the 1995-1996 season, with The University of Texas winning the final football championship. Several universities located in the state compete in the Southland Conference, and in 1995 the Stephen F. Austin State University Lumberjacks advanced to the semi-finals in Division I-AA playoffs. In hundreds of communities the most anxiously awaited information on Friday evenings concerns the fate of local high school football teams. By spring, the emphasis shifts to basketball and then to baseball before the cycle repeats the following fall. The last two decades have witnessed a steadily increasing emphasis on and interest in women's athletics at collegiate and secondary levels, in part because of federal non-discrimination requirements, and in

part because of social trends that find women participating more fully in a wide variety of athletic activities, from individual physical conditioning to team sports. In the 1990s the Texas Tech University women's basketball team won an NCAA national championship and an enthusiastic following, a sign of the times and a token for the future of women's sports.

Texas continues to struggle with problems related to its education system. Since the issues of public and higher education dominate discussions over the state budget, education has been a continuing focus of both regular and special sessions of the legislature throughout the 1980s and 1990s. Concerns have proliferated that the state's schools are failing to instill among students meaningful work skill and citizenship values. Numerous lawsuits have been filed seeking to equalize financial support among the more than 1,000 public school districts. Support for state-financed vouchers to pay for private education has grown. Some improvements have been made, especially in specific school districts, but Texas still lags behind much of the rest of the nation and nearly all of the ten most populous states in scholastic performance and teacher pay rates. With some exceptions, in comparison with comparable institutions across the nation, Texas' facilities of higher education also fail to measure up.

Texans, like other Americans in the latter part of the twentieth century, face problems concerning the environment, poverty, homelessness, chemical dependency, and criminal activity, especially among juveniles. But, at the same time, Texans enjoy resources and advantages not shared by other Americans, including low unemployment, continuing abundance of most natural resources, and perhaps most significantly, a feeling that they share a special heritage. This sense of distinctiveness is exemplified in the story of a woman who always cleans her hotel room, especially when traveling out of state, because, she says, "They know we are from Texas."

Texas always means land. And this land has witnessed waves of invaders from Native Americans to Spaniards to Anglo Americans. All have left their mark, all have made history in Texas. The story of Texas has been retold countless times, but Texans never seem to tire of it. Above all, the story goes on. What awaits Texas in the twenty-first century?

Top,left: Former President George Bush, and son, Texas Governor George W. Bush. President Bush selected the campus of Texas A&M University at College Station as the site for his presidential library.
COURTESY, BUSH PRESIDENTIAL LIBRARY, COLLEGE STATION, TEXAS.

Below: The phrase "chromoly cowboy," coined by Lucille Enix from chrome and molybdenum (a strong, light-weight metal), connects the spirit of the cyclist to his precursor, the American cowboy. One of the National Bicycle Route Network trails passes through 1,050 miles of scenic and historic Texas as it connects Florida with California.
COURTESY, ADVENTURE CYCLING. PHOTO BY GREG SIPLE.

SHARING THE HERITAGE

historic profiles

of businesses and organizations

that have contributed

to the development and economic base

of Texas

Returning from a hunt.

CONTENTS

-C. C. ALLEN.
-521-

-STEAMING FIELD AS SEEN FROM F
-TEXAS GULF SULPHUR CO. - GU

MANUFACTURING & INDUSTRY

Texas' manufacturers produce goods

which contribute to economic growth

and stability of the state

Texas Gulf Sulphur Co., Gulf, Texas.
COURTESY, ARCHIVES DIVISION, TEXAS STATE LIBRARY

DR PEPPER / CADBURY NORTH AMERICA

Dr. Pepper came to life in a time and place of Texas legends. Created in 1885 by a Waco pharmacist whose job included working the drug store soda fountain, Dr. Pepper, like the mavericks of the Old West and the state the company grew up in, blazed many trails. It was the first soft drink to be sold in a can. It was literally made a class by itself, securing its own "pepper category" with the Food and Drug administration so as not to be classified in the "cola" category," and therefore legally could use the same bottlers as Coca Cola and Pepsi. Dr. Pepper was also instrumental in getting soft drink products declared "essential to the war effort" to ensure sugar use when the U.S. government rationed sugar in World War II.

In the late 1800's, Morrison's Old Corner Drug Store was a popular meeting place in Waco, a town then equally as famous for being the center of learning and culture as it was for its legalized prostitution and the gun fights that regularly broke out in the middle of its streets. Carbonated water was a new invention and was often mixed with fruit syrups and served as a refreshment at soda fountains. The most popular drink of the time was Sarsaparilla, made from the dried roots of the sarsaparilla plant. Soft drinks were formulated by pharmacists because they were the only ones with access to all the ingredients--basic raw materials such as natural fruit extracts and spices. Customers saddled up to the soda counter and told the soda jerk to "shoot a Waco." That was how a Dr. Pepper was ordered when it was first concocted by pharmacist Charles C. Alderton in Waco, Texas in 1885. Alderton earned his medical degree at the University of Texas in Galveston, but chose to pursue pharmacy instead of being a doctor. He took a job at the Old Corner Drug Store, on the corner of Fourth and Austin in one of Waco's busiest intersections, where he dispensed medicines at the pharmacy and soft drinks and confections at the soda fountain. Alderton experimented with with several mixtures of carbonated water, fruit juices, extracts and spices and came up with a mixture later named Dr. Pepper by the store's owner, pharmacist Wade Morrison. At the time, it was popular to make product names sound medicinal, so Morrison named the drink after a physician he had worked with in Virginia, Dr. Charles T. Pepper.

C.C. Alderton, 1913

R.S. Lazenby

The U.S. Patent Office cites December 1, 1885 as the official date when Dr. Pepper was first served at the Old Corner Drug Store. Morrison and Alderton experimented with the mixture and as the formula's popularity grew, they started selling large quantities of the syrup to area drug stores so the drink could be sold at other soda fountains. When the demand grew so great and there wasn't enough room at the drug store, Mr. Morrison rented a building on Bridge Street to produce Dr. Pepper flavoring. He hired Robert S. Lazenby to produce and promote Dr. Pepper. Six years after the drink was first introduced, Lazenby and Morrison formed the Artesian Manufacturing and Bottling Company in April 1891, with 50 shares of stock available at $50 each. The company moved to three other locations before 1906, when it moved to Fifth Avenue. The Artesian Manufacturing and Bottling Company headquartered there until 1923 when it became the Dr. Pepper Company and moved to Dallas. The Fifth Avenue location continued bottling operations until 1965, when a large facility was constructed in Waco, and it now houses the Dr. Pepper Museum, which was opened in 1991.

At the first stockholder meeting of The Artesian Manufacturing and Bottling Company in 1891, Morrison was appointed president and chairman of the board and Lazenby was made superintendent of works. As president, Morrison made a statement as part of the bylaws that the Dr. Pepper formula was owned by the stockholders and could not be revealed. Now, more than a hundred years later, only a handful of people within the Dr. Pepper organization know the complete formulas, and the people producing the products only know their part of the formula.

In the early days of The Artesian Manufacturing and Bottling Company, the company produced Dr. Pepper in the same facility as it produced Circle "A" Ginger Ale and Zu Zu Ginger Ale, Wine Coca and Celery Champagne, a line of fruit drinks and root beer. Early company advertisements and photos of delivery carriages feature the names of those multiple brands. Later, Blackberry Cordial and bitters, an alcoholic drink, were added to the company's product lines. All were

made form formulas developed by Lazenby, who also offered a purified mineral water product. At that time, the city of Waco received its water supply from 20 artesian wells about 1,800 feet deep--and the citizens got the very same water for free that Lazenby was bottling and selling as Aqua Lithia.

Lazenby was born in 1866 and grew up in Waco. He was instrumental in establishing Southern Methodist University in Dallas, and in 1991, he donated funds to build Dallas Hall, the school's first permanent structure, which is still in use. Lazenby's daughter, Virginia O'Hara, established an undergraduate chemistry trust fund which still honors the school's top chemistry student.

Robert Lazenby first produced Circle "A" Ginger Ale at the Artesian Manufacturing and Bottling Company from a formula he purchased from a man who had worked in a ginger ale plant in Dublin, Ireland. Circle "A" was named after the cattle brand used by Lazenby's mother's family. In 1898, Circle "A" won an exclusive contract with the U.S. government to the Army and Navy during the Spanish-American War. Circle "A" is till produced in St. Louis and small batches are made up in Waco for the Dr. Pepper Museum.

Dr. Pepper's inventor, Alderton, resigned from the Old Corner Drug Store in 1894 to become chief chemist for Behrens Drug Company of Waco. In 1896, Morrison resigned as president of the Artesian Manufacturing and Bottling Company and C.T. Young was elected president. On March 6, 1901, Young resigned and Lazenby became president.

By then, bottlers in Iowa, Illinois, Louisiana, Tennessee, Missouri, Nebraska, Oklahoma, and North and South Carolina were using Dr. Pepper syrup. Bottlers would buy the flavored in the form of syrup or concentrate and then add sweetener and carbonated water and would have exclusive rights to sell the soft drink in a designated territory. By 1911, more than 100 Texas bottling companies were producing Dr. Pepper.

On September 25, 1902, the Southwestern Soda Fountain company of Dallas changed its name The Dr. Pepper Company, which was the first a company used the name Dr. Pepper. The

John Bernard O'Hara

Completed in 1906, the Artesian Mfg. & Bottling Company at 5th and Mary Streets in Waco, was the fourth home of Dr Pepper. This Waco landmark also served as the Dr Pepper Bottling Company of Waco until 1965 when the current facility at 120 Villa Drive was completed.

newly named Dr. Pepper Company had exclusive rights to manufacture the syrup for fountain use, and the Artesian Manufacturing and Bottling Company, run by Lazenby, owned exclusive rights to produce Dr. Pepper for bottling purposes. Lazenby established a bottling plant in St. Louis, Missouri with bottling rights for Dr. Pepper and Circle "A" Ginger Ale. The

Advance Mineral Water Company then contracted with American Mineral Water Company of St. Louis to produce and sell Dr. Pepper in St. Louis, and in 1907 the two syrup manufacturing companies were consolidated so that the Artesian Manufacturing and Bottling Company was selling syrup for both fountain and bottle use. In 1905, the Artesia Bottling Company was founded in Fort Worth and Robert's brother, Henry Lazenby, became the Fort Worth manager.

In 1918, at the end of world War I, Lazenby's company was in financial trouble after heavy spending on Dallas and Waco operations that were later moved or consolidated. The Dallas operation moved to Waco in 1907 and the American Mineral Water Company stopped bottling Dr. Pepper on April 1, 1920, when Lazenby purchased all rights to the company in the copyright and trademark and license of the Circle "A" brand and the words and name Dr. Pepper. On June 12, 1923, Lazenby and his group declared bankruptcy and the company was reorganized. The new company was incorporated July 6, 1923 under the laws of the state of

Colorado and the name of the company was changed from the Circle "A" Corporation to the Dr. Pepper Company. The company moved from Waco to Dallas, where financing was more readily available. The company completed its magnificent new syrup plant and national headquarters building on Mockingbird Lane in Dallas in 1948. When the company first moved to Dallas, Robert Lazenby's son-in-law, John Bernard O'Hara was hired to assume production and distribution responsibilities for the new company. O'Hara was later credited with bringing the company back to life.

Soft drink advertising campaigns have changed drastically through the years, and many reflected the advertising of the times. In its first advertisements, Dr Pepper could cure any ailment--like other advertised products of the day. Prior to 1900, Dr Pepper advertised that it was free from both caffeine and cocaine, even though both substances were then legal. During that time, one of the company's advertising slogans read "Dr Pepper stands alone on the bridge defending your children against an army of caffeine doped beverages, as the great Horatius defended Rome" with an illustration of a Roman soldier warding off the enemy.

When Dr Pepper was first named, products sold better if they were perceived to be medicinal. Later, that association became a detriment, and Dr Pepper was faced with fighting the medicinal perception of its being a health tonic, a patent medicine, a laxative and/or a brain food. The company got rid of the period after the "Dr" for that reason. Through more than one hundred years, Dr Pepper's advertising ranged from "the best thing you ever swallowed" to "the king of beverages," a campaign started by Lazenby, who had always been interested in the English royal family.

Another ad campaign featured "Old Doc," a fictitious country doctor wearing a silk top hat and monocle, who appeared consistently in Dr Pepper advertising, as did the slogan: "Drink a bite to eat at 10, 2 and 4."

In 1981, Dr Pepper bought the soft drink division of Welch Food Company and established Premier Beverages to market Welch's. In 1982, Dr Pepper bought Canada Dry Corporation. In 1987, Premier Beverages began marketing IBC Root Beer, a brand it acquired in the Seven-Up merger in 1986.

The Dr Pepper Company was listed on the New York stock Exchange February 14, 1946, beginning with 800,000. By 1970, through stock splits and recapitalization, the number had increased to 9.6 million, and, by 1972, 25 million shares were offered. On February 29, 1984, Dr Pepper went private and was removed from the New York Stock Exchange. Two months after New York investment firm Forstmann Little acquired Dr Pepper, it sold Canada Dry to RJR Nabisco. The company's flagship bottling operations were sold in Waco, Dallas and Fort Worth, Texas in 1985 to Dallas investors Hicks & Haas, who had also that year purchased Seven-Up. In 1986, the Scaled-Down Dr. Pepper was purchased by equity owners consisting of several banks, Dr Pepper corporate management and Hicks & Haas.

In 1985, as part of a divestment plan, the Dallas headquarters property on Mockingbird Lane in Dallas was sold to a real estate firm, but the building was used as the Doctor Pepper/Seven-Up headquarters until it moved to a lease space on Walnut Hill Lane in Dallas in July 1988. the company announced in mid-1996 that Dr Pepper/Cadbury North America Inc. was consolidating Cadbury's headquarters in Dallas and would be building a campus complex in Plano, just north of Dallas. The new headquarters is scheduled for completion in mid-1998.

PILGRIM'S PRIDE

Glancing back over the last half century, one can see a Northeast Texas business that has become a legend of success. Pilgrim's Pride developed into a successful enterprise because of two daring men with courage and foresight.

Bo and Aubrey Pilgrim had a dream. Together, they envisioned a bright future for their families, customers and the community. But twenty years after the Pilgrim brothers started their modest business, Aubrey died leaving his brother to carry on the tradition.

From a meager start as Farmer's Feed and Seed Co. in the small Northeast Texas town of Pittsburg, Pilgrim's Pride became a Fortune 500 company that has exceeded the magical level of $1 billion in annual revenues after only fifty short years. Today, it is one of the largest agribusinesses operating in Texas. The company, still headquartered in Pittsburg, Texas, has over 11,000 employees, supports over 1,500 family farms and has facilities strategically positioned throughout the southwestern United States and Mexico.

Pilgrim's Pride today is a totally integrated broiler producer that produces over 1.5 million chickens and 175,000 dozen table eggs a day. The company has fully vertically integrated operations which include hatcheries, contract growing, feed milling, rendering, poultry and egg processing and further processed prepared food. Pilgrim's Pride sells branded items for retail, fast food and food service markets. In addition, the company's diversification includes feed and farm supplies. In 1996, Pilgrim's Pride will produce 1.8 billion pounds of dressed poultry and 50 million dozen table eggs, making it the fifth largest chicken company in America and the second largest in Mexico.

While building a thriving chicken business, the company assumed an increasingly important role in the development of the Northeast Texas economy. Pilgrim's Pride has progressed steadily over the past half century carrying on traditions established over the course of fifty years. It all started in 1946 with a common focus: "If the customer wants it, we can work together to make it happen." This same attitude remains today.

Reflecting on the successful history of the company, its vision — *To be a world class chicken company* — is credited for raising standards and keeping the company's clearly focused business strategy on track. It is the aggressive pursuit of this vision that will drive the Pilgrim's Pride success in the future while becoming the basis upon which the next fifty years will be built.

Farmer's Feed & Seed Co. store in Pittsburg, Texas was acquired in 1946 for $1,000 down and a $2,500 note.

TAYLOR PUBLISHING COMPANY

One might point to 1914 as the true beginning for Taylor Publishing Company of Dallas when H.C. Taylor, a student at Baylor University walked past the office of the school yearbook staff, looked inside and asked if anybody needed a hand. The rest, as they say, is history.

Back then, students had to start from scratch. There were no yearbook tools or how-to guides to rely upon. Each part of the yearbook had to be produced in different facilities, from the cover to the photographs, and it was difficult to get local printers enthusiastic about the project. It was so expensive and time-consuming, few schools produced a yearbook. But that would change.

In 1939, Bill, the youngest Taylor brother, found that a new printing technology, offset lithography, could produce higher quality at lower cost than the traditional engraving process. His brothers, E.M. and H.C., had owned an engraving company since 1923 specializing in graduation announcements and class rings. Bill, a sales representative for the company, presented his yearbook printing idea to them, and they were sold. Thus, Taylor introduced offset lithography to yearbook printing. Even more innovative was The Taylor Plan. It involved creating a kit of easy-to-use tools for yearbook staffs and then handling all steps of typesetting, printing, binding and cover production under one roof.

This was the beginning of Taylor's tradition of service. It was an immediate success and Taylor was on its way as a leader in publishing. The company led the yearbook market through the development of the Vision Series, the first yearbook-specific computer series of its kind. This easy-to-use program is now in thousands of yearbook staff rooms nationwide. UltraVision, Taylor's most intuitive release, allows schools to design, view and edit their pages with all elements in place.

In the early 1980s, many schools and commercial customers began to explore the benefits of desktop publishing tools. To meet these new production needs, Taylor developed the PageSetter product line, enabling staffs to submit PageMaker or QuarkXPress documents for high-resolution output, directly to film. With this production method, desktop publishing specialists place photographs electronically in both black-and-white and color, virtually eliminating the need for manual handling of pages prior to plate-making.

One of Taylor's recent innovations is the Automatic Picture Processing (APP) system. With this patented process, many pages are imaged directly to film, saving time and improving print quality. During the scanning process, photos are automatically sized and enhanced to improve contrast and detail.

Taylor is now exploring the creative possibilities of CD-ROM as a way to produce book supplements. Taylor is also committed to advancing methods so customers can submit and approve material on-line. As printing continues to evolve, direct-to-press technology -- printing straight from a customer's disk and bypassing pre-press steps entirely -- may soon become a common way to offer lower-cost color printing.

While the Taylor name is synonymous with yearbook quality, over the years the company has expanded its memory and publishing business to include Fine Books, Trade Books and Reunion Services. Taylor's Trade Books division is a leading publisher of adult non-fiction titles in the areas of sports, biographies, gardening, health and pop culture. In addition to publishing more than 30 original titles each year, Taylor also acts as a distributor for other publishers and sells books internationally through a network of distributors in various regions of the world.

Taylor's Fine Books Division also produces more commemorative books for organizations, businesses and institutions than any other publisher. Taylor has the resources to guarantee the success of commemorative publications: an in-house staff of specialists, a network of regional publishing consultants, state-of-the-art printing facilities and full-service marketing resources.

And, to complement its publishing expertise, Taylor introduced its Reunion Services Division in 1990. Organizing more than 400 school reunions each year, Taylor is the largest reunion services company in the United States.

Throughout its history, Taylor has been dedicated to helping people chronicle the memories of a lifetime and preserving them in yearbooks, fine books and special events. And, by offering innovative, quality products and services, Taylor continues to exceed its customers' expectations.

CASITA ENTERPRISES, INC.

Casita may mean "little house" in Spanish but in the language of recreational travel trailers, Casita stands for exceptional quality, graceful style and unbeatable customer satisfaction.

Casita Enterprises, Inc., which manufactures three sizes of these sleekly designed travel trailers, was purchased by its present owners John Lang and his father Dr. Robert Lang in 1984. In 1993, the Langs relocated their already successful business from its original home in Kerens, Texas to the company's current location in Rice, just north of Corsicana.

With a rounded, fiberglass design, Casita trailers have distinct advantages over traditionally built trailers. Unlike most other travel trailers, Casita trailers are constructed of two molded fiberglass sections, making them leak-free, lightweight alternatives to the traditional trailers which are usually made of wood, aluminum and plastic. Top and bottom sections are fiberglassed together, eliminating multiple seams which

often leak, as well as ensuring strength and durability.

With the fiberglass body attached to a heavy duty steel frame, Casita trailers are strong and durable. Trailer interiors are insulated, reducing noise levels and keeping occupants cool in summer and warm in winter. Casita's fiberglass interior furniture is easy to maintain and makes the trailer lighter.

Thanks to its lightweight, aerodynamic design, Casita trailers are easily pulled behind small vehicles with low wind resistance and excellent fuel efficiency. Aerodynamics also make Casita trailers safer to control on the road. When not being used, the trailers can be made to fit into many standard garages for storage

Standard features on all three standard models include a two-burner cooktop, range hood with light, ice box, silverware drawer, four-inch cushions, window drapes, storage for portable toilet, 20 lb. gas bottle, safety chains, 10 or 16-gallon fresh water tank, deluxe insulation, converter/battery charger and 12-volt lighting. Standard features on all three sizes deluxe models include three-way refrigerator, air conditioner, water heater, battery pack, 12-volt demand water pump, converter/battery charger, spare tire and cover, stabilizer jacks and most importantly, a bathroom with marine toilet, shower and lavatory.

The 17' model has several new features which may appeal to those traveling with children, grandchildren or additional guests. Larger interior headroom of 6 feet 3 inches and a rear bed area that is 54 inches wide add to the comfort and roomy feeling of this newest Casita trailer. Other special features of the largest in the Casita line of trailers include overhead storage wrapping around the rear of the unit over the bed, a higher capacity air conditioner and a larger refrigerator.

Deluxe models include additional amenities and more storage areas, as well as larger sleeping and sitting areas. The 17' Freedom Deluxe has swivel chairs beside a screened picture window for comfortable sitting and pleasant dining. In addition, a rear dinette area for four may be converted into a double bed. The 17' Liberty Deluxe can be made into a king-size bed. It has seating and dining for six when no beds are made out. In the 17' Spirit Deluxe, two separate sleeping areas both convert into dinette tables.

Casita travel trailers are built on-site in the Rice location. Although there is a showroom at that location, Lang says most purchases are orders, built to the customer's specifications. Forty employees of Casita Enterprises build some 400 to 500 trailers per year for people all over the United States, Canada, Mexico and Japan, where travel trailers with bunk beds are very popular.

Casita's referral program allows potential customers to view a Casita trailer near their home. Casita owners are asked to show their trailers to people who are interested in purchasing a trailer themselves and because customer satisfaction is so high, the referral program is a dynamic sales tool.

Most of Casita's customers are former owners of the larger, traditional travel trailers, according to Lang, and are delighted to trade in the big, heavier trailers for the lightweight efficiency and comfort of Casita trailers. Lang's company also has a contract with the United States government, selling about 50 trailers per year to the government for rental to military personnel.

The address is 3030 South McKinney, I-45, Exit 237 or 238, Rice, Texas 75155. The telephone number is (800) 442-9986.

HWC DISTRIBUTION CORP.

More than two decades ago, HWC Distribution Corp. set up shop near the Houston Ship Channel to take advantage of the area's concentration of petrochemical plants, prime users of the products the company planned to sell. Since then, it has grown into the largest electrical wire and cable master distributor in the country, with more than $200 million in annual sales and a customer base of more than 3,000 companies nationwide.

There are solid reasons behind this rapid growth, Eric Blankenship, vice president, sales and marketing, maintains. One is the mutually beneficial relationship HWC has developed with its customers nationwide.

"From the beginning, we've been a master distributor. That means our policy has been to sell exclusively to wholesalers, not directly to end users," he explains. "As a result, we don't compete with our own customers. In fact, our salespeople often visit with end users, acquainting them with the products we distribute and encouraging them to specify these products and to purchase them from wholesalers in their area. We've also gained business we might not have had otherwise because we can get involved in integrated supply programs, key supplier agreements and other strategic alliances with our customers."

In addition to its 166,000-square-foot headquarters building, which includes a 136,000-square-foot warehouse, HWC has opened eight other warehouses in strategic locations around the country. Using toll-free telephone numbers, customers can place orders around the clock and expect shipment within 24 hours. They will reach service representatives who are knowledgeable about the needs of their customers' industries and who can obtain expert consultation on HWC's product specifications and applications.

A huge inventory, valued at over $50 million and containing more than 45,000 reels, enables the company to fill almost 90 percent of its orders directly out of stock. Using a computerized inventory control system, its customer service representatives can locate a product, determine its price and schedule delivery — all in a matter of minutes.

"Our customers can come to a single source for their wire and cable needs," Blankenship points out. "They can count on quick turnaround—and that's important, since delays can be costly to the customers they serve."

Customers can also count on quality: in fact, HWC is the only master wire and cable distributor to receive ISO 9002 certification because of its commitment to vendor quality.

Blankenship cites still another critical success factor: his company's cable management program. This program helps eliminate job delays and surplus inventory investments of local distributors and contractors who are involved in turnkey projects.

In recent years, HWC has begun exploring additional opportunities for growth. Its acquisition in the late 1980s by Little Rock, Arkansas-based ALLTEL Corporation, a major telephone and information services corporation, not only provided financial stability for HWC but also expanded its expertise in a promising new field: voice and data telecommunications. In addition, the company set up a subsidiary, Worldwide Electric Sales, in 1994 to focus on international expansion.

A commitment to product quality and customer service have supported HWC Distribution Corp. growth in the last two decades. Those same characteristics, Blankenship believes, will contribute to its success in the future.

WILSONART INTERNATIONAL

Wilsonart International Inc. is the world's leading manufacturer of high-pressure decorative laminate and is poised to take a similar position in the laminate flooring market.

Laminate will always be the core business, but we are developing other businesses around that," said Bill Reeb, president of Wilsonart International. "Many people don't realize that we are the leading manufacturer of decorative laminate in the world," he said. "It's still very much a family organization. It's not family run, but everybody pulls together."

Founded in 1956, the company's world headquarters in Temple stands alongside the firm's first manufacturing plant. The brown brick structure is the focal point of eight production facilities and 3,000 employees, with distributors and service centers in more than 45 countries.

The company hardly resembles what it set out to be — a diversion between fishing trips for a retired Californian turned Texan named Ralph Wilson Sr. Wilson's career in California progressed from plaster and rubber to pressed plastics, co-founding the Wilson & Hoppe laminate company in 1946. Wilson sold his share of the business in 1955 after suffering a heart attack, but soon grew board with retirement and turned his attention toward Texas.

On a fact-finding tour of the Dallas area, Wilson learned that an institutional furniture manufacturer called American Desk was looking for a source of plastic surfacing convenient to its Temple plant. He visited Temple and liked the people he found there. Wilson gathered a team of skilled individuals he had encountered over the years and added some promising Temple natives to begin the new venture. Ralph Wilson Plastics Co. began production in April 1956, and a sales agreement with American Desk made the new company profitable by June.

Approaching the turn of the century, Wilsonart International stresses relationships as paramount. Many of those relationships date to the early days of the company. American Desk, just across the street from Wilsonart headquarters, remains an important customer. Other buy-

ers have grown up with Wilsonart, and like them, Ralph Wilson Sr.'s company now employs many of the children of its earliest employees.

Wilson directed his team to "serve the customer, serve the enterprise, and serve the people." In 1966, employees followed that directive in the form of a $500 collection to help the Wilsons establish a scholarship fund.

Working with George Hester, who would become vice president in charge of production, Wilson engineered a synchronized system from manufacturing through delivery. With the addition of company trucks, Ralph Wilson Plastics was able to offer delivery anywhere in the United States, usually within four days of order. The unprecedented turn-around allowed customers to save inventory space and vaulted Ralph Wilson Plastics ahead of competitors. "The fleet was started to ensure timely delivery," Reeb said. "That gives us a competitive advantage." At the time Wilsonart was founded, they were the smallest company in a pack of about 17, and now there are only about four domestic competitors left."

A division of Premark International Inc., Wilsonart International now uses 15 regional market centers to supply a network of 185 independent wholesale distributors and 30 flooring distributors across the globe. Wilsonart International employs the Total Quality Process, and has achieved ISO-9002 certification for its four manufacturing facilities. The Texas Natural Resource Conservation Commission recognized the company in 1996 with the Texas Clean Industry 2000 designation.

Looking to the future, Wilsonart plans to serve the international market through distribution centers and manufacturing abroad. Research and development efforts continue to bring improvements in decorative laminate and laminate products, and Wilsonart International is ready to deliver those innovations worldwide to the customers of the next century.

Copper Breaks State Park.

PHOTO BY LEROY WILLIAMSON

THE MARKETPLACE

Texas' retail establishments,

service industries and leisure/convention

facilities offer an impressive variety

of choices for Texans and visitors alike

Joe Bales' Warehouse.

RANDALLS FOOD MARKETS INC.

Fresh-baked breads and pastries; prepared meals from the deli ready to take home for lunch or dinner; colorful floral arrangements presented by master floral designers; full-service restaurant and catering; in-store banking services; pharmacy; video rental; Ticketmaster outlet; photo processing—even valet parking; these are only some of the many reasons why this home-grown Texas grocery is known as "Your Remarkable Store."

The trademark of every Randalls and Tom Thumb store is offering the best in food and groceries while providing courteous and friendly service in a pleasant shopping environment. That commitment has guided Houston-based Randalls Food Markets Inc., for more than 30 years as it has grown from a small two-store operation into one of the largest privately held enterprises in the Lone Star State.

"We do business by the Golden Rule," explains Randalls Chairman Robert Onstead. "We serve our customers the way we would want to be served."

Grocery stores were familiar territory to Onstead when he founded the company with Norman Frewin and R.C. Barclay in 1966. He had worked at his uncle's establishment on weekends in high school and summers while in college and had spent several years managing one of his father-in-law's Randall's Super Valu stores. His partners had also been in the business: Barclay,

a former route salesman for Mrs Baird's Bakeries, had run another Randalls store; Frewin, an experienced meat buyer, had managed the meat markets for Randalls and another store chain named Beldens.

They opened two outlets the first year, another one two years later and a fourth in 1970. Acquisition of four former Handy Andy stores followed in 1979. By the end of the decade, the three entrepreneurs owned 15 stores and had established themselves as key players in the market. The seeds of the future were planted when the founders' sons, Randall Onstead, Norm P. Frewin and Ron Barclay, joined the business.

The 1980s were a decade of growth for the company. The chain expanded to 42 stores with convenient locations, quality products, competitive prices and continued commitment to customer service and to the community. In 1986, the partners opened the company to associate ownership.

"The three of us were family, even though we were not related, and we considered all of our associates in the same way," Onstead says. "We wanted to give them a sense of ownership and a personal stake in the company. When you care about your associates, they will care about your business and your customers. That philosophy is still prevalent to this very day."

Below, left: The three founding partners (left to right): R. C. Barclay (deceased), Robert R. Onstead, and Norman N. Frewin (deceased).

Below, right: President and CEO Randall Onstead (left) and his father, Chairman Bob Onstead.

By 1991, Randalls had passed the billion-dollar mark in sales, making it the fastest-growing company in Houston as well as the leader among grocery store chains in Texas. In recent years, new store construction and acquisitions have broadened its base of operations and strengthened the company's position even further.

In August 1992, Randalls purchased Cullum Companies, Inc., a Dallas-based supermarket retailer and owner of Tom Thumb Food and Pharmacy in Dallas, Fort Worth and Austin. The move doubled Randalls' size, and the company became a dominant player in the Dallas/Fort Worth metroplex. A year later, the company reopened nine former AppleTree and Tom Thumb outlets under the Randalls banner in Austin, Killeen and San Marcos, giving the company a significant presence in the Texas Hill Country.

The year 1996 marks two significant historical occasions for Randalls Food Markets Inc. — its 30th anniversary, and the naming of Randall Onstead as president and CEO of the company. Robert Onstead continues as chairman, and will oversee operations of the Tom Thumb division in Dallas.

"I am most proud of the reputation we've developed throughout the state for customer service and corporate citizenship," Onstead says. "We have the best bakeries, the best floral departments, the fastest checkout service and the best associates who are dedicated to serving our customers."

Onstead credits the success of Randalls Food Markets Inc. to the pride and unity of TEAM Texas—25,000 remarkable Randalls and Tom Thumb associates across the state who make it all happen. He also attributes the TEAM Texas spirit to the company's excellent reputation for community responsibility and leadership through its many ongoing philanthropic efforts.

In the last 30 years, grocery stores have evolved to meat new market demands. Yet the level of commitment to quality, service and value that epitomizes the Randalls/Tom Thumb TEAM Texas culture has remained steadfast.

"To be successful, you have to ENJOY satisfying the customer," Onstead concludes. "We strive to give our customers what they want and a little extra—superior service."

And that's what will keep Randalls Food Markets, Inc., "Your Remarkable Store."

Houston-based Randalls Food Markets Inc.,
widely known as "Your Remarkable Store,"
maintains family traditions by providing
high quality products, excellent service and
responsible corporate citizenship in the
Houston and Austin areas.

Tom Thumb, with deep roots in the Dallas and Fort Worth
communities, joined the Randalls Food Markets family in
1992, bringing nearly fifty years of service and dedication to
Texas families.

Simon David, the pride of Tom Thumb and
Randalls, is a one-of-a-kind full-scale
gourmet grocery store specializing in hard-
to-find culinary items, professional catering,
and expert customer service.

Horse and buggies still outnumbered cars in the 1920s, a time when country roads were invariably narrow, and often unpaved and rutted as well. Flat tires and mechanical problems were commonplace, but filling stations and auto mechanics were rare. The grand opening of a filling station in the little town of Vickery, north of Dallas, was cause for celebration among the local farmers and travelers driving the road to Greenville.

Owner W.H. Loveless hired a band and attracted what was said to be the biggest crowd assembled in Vickery. The price of gasoline on opening day was 17 cents per gallon, a hefty price when workmen earned just $2.50 a day. With miles of farm land—and little else—the little filling station, visible from any direction, was a welcome sight to travelers for decades. It's said outlaws Bonnie and Clyde were frequent customers. For many years it operated as a Mobil station with the trademark red neon flying horse revolving high atop a pole fronting Greenville Avenue.

The Dallas suburbs began marching northward as the years passed. Increased traffic brought the filling station booming business, but open countryside remained plentiful until the 1960s. By the early 1970s, the little station's uniqueness had long passed. Greenville Avenue was now a congested thoroughfare flanked by homes and apartments as the tiny town of Vickery became absorbed into Dallas. Larger and far more modern filling stations were built in the area, but the old station remained as a vestige of days gone by.

When Loveless' widow broke her leg in the early 1970s, internist Sam Dorfman, M.D., bought the station, located at 6862 Greenville Avenue at Park Lane. He thought it would make a distinctive casual theme restaurant for the eatery row then blossoming in the area.

In a humorous twist arising from his medical background, Dorfman first considered naming his new restaurant "Dr. Quack's." But, perceiving the great potential in capitalizing on the old station's heritage, he ultimately selected "The Filling Station Restaurant & Bar"—keeping "Dr. Quack's" as the name of the owning corporation.

Dorfman restored the station's exterior, including the original, now antique, gasoline pumps. To heighten the effect, he parked a black 1920s convertible pickup under the porte-cochere.

Inside the popular restaurant the old-time filling station theme is continued. The original red neon horse revolves on a post, two booths hunker cozily beneath Model T convertible car tops and old license plates share the walls with oil company emblems.

Hanging from the open rafters are an engine fan and an old steering column assembly. Focal point of the large bar is the top portion of an antique see-

through gas pump, bubbling with ersatz "beer." (The real stuff is piped from a proper container into the pump's dispenser.) Even the tables further the theme with embedded license plates, gears and car tools.

The Filling Station's Menu — printed on old oil cans used until the oil companies changed to plastic bottles — follows the theme faithfully as well. Categories bear designations like "Starters," "Turbo Chargers," "STP (Salads to Perfection)," "Front Grill," "Additives," and "Fluids & Lubricants." Hamburgers are ordered under such monikers such as "Ethyl," "Highbeam," "Lowbeam," and "T-Bird." Hot dogs are "Diesel Dogs"; if rolled in flour tortillas and fried, they are "Tailpipes." Customers can also order "O-Rings" —onion rings—Radiator Chili, and a variety of more conventionally designated items. The Filling Station's "Special Fuels" are unique drinks (Tune Up, Overhaul and Grease Job) each in a stop light color.

The Filling Station's period decor attracts customers in every age bracket. Referring to the television program, Dorfman called the restaurant "A 'Cheers' kind of place, where everyone knows everyone. Some customers come in nearly every day. They tell us what's happening in their lives, and we listen. You don't find many places anymore where it's obvious that people really care."

"We're a good family restaurant," he continued. "We have customers from 8 to 80. Parents can feed their children here for less than at many fast-food restaurants." There is live entertainment Tuesday through Saturday evenings and big-screen broadcast sports on Saturdays and Sundays. Dorfman said the Filling Station's friendly atmosphere shows his philosophy of restauranting: "You can get a hamburger and a drink anywhere. So what can we do differently? Well, there's our decor, which certainly is unique, and more importantly, we really care about our customers."

The doctor plunged into the restaurant business, and after 15 years of maintaining a dual life as doctor and restaurateur, he ultimately chose the restaurant. He owns a second Dallas-area Filling Station in an old Addison "parts building" just north of Beltline on Addison Road. Dorfman's third restaurant is in Austin, located in a converted dry cleaner's store.

Once the vanguard of advancing progress, but ultimately bypassed by time, the auto service station has been reborn in a new guise — The Filling Station Restaurant & Bar.

THE FILLING STATION RESTAURANT AND BAR

CONTINENTAL AIRLINES

In 1995, employees of Houston-based Continental Airlines purchased the chief executive officer a Harley-Davidson for Christmas. That's how they expressed their gratitude for the leadership Gordon Bethune had exhibited since taking the company's helm late in 1994.

The gift reflected the fact that Continental, whose history had been characterized by two bankruptcies and years of financial losses, had reported a record $224 million profit for Bethune's first year, sending its stock prices soaring from $6.50 to $47.50 per share. Furthermore, it had managed to move from dead-last in its industry to at or near the top in several critical success factors. In 1996, Continental was rated first by frequent fliers in the J. D. Power & Associates survey for best airline on long flights.

Continental's rise from the ashes can be credited, in part, to the Go Forward Plan, a program instituted by Bethune and chief operating officer Greg Brenneman in early 1995. Its first component, Fly to Win, focused on enhancing assets and activities that boost profits and eliminating those that don't. To contain costs, for example, Continental began withdrawing from unprofitable routes and hubs and unpopular services, replacing big jets with smaller ones to eliminate empty seats and reducing staff. To enhance travel agent allegiance, it restored competitive commissions.

The second component, Fund the Future, was designed to improve Continental's financial picture. Steps were taken to reduce debt and interest payments, build cash reserves and invest in technology and other aspects of its business.

Until early 1995, the Department of Transportation (DOT) reports, Continental placed last among major U.S. airlines in two key success factors—on-time performance and baggage handling—and it led the list in customer complaints. Thee plan's third component, Make Reliability a Reality, awarded bonuses to every employee for improvements in these statistics. It also called for such enhancements as a unified look for the jet fleet and telephones at every seat. As a result, Continental has become an industry leader in all three of the DOT Consumer Report categories.

The fourth element, Working Together, focused on improving work force satisfaction by rewarding cooperation, enhancing communication, minimizing management interference and encouraging employees to treat each other with dignity and respect. Successful implementation of this program component has led to reduced absenteeism and attrition rates, improved morale and labor relations and an increase in the number of job applications.

Continental's rise from the ashes marks a new beginning for the airline, whose history dates to 1934, when the single-engine, four-passenger plane that comprised Varney's Speed Lines' Southwest Division took off from El Paso en route to Pueblo, Colorado. Two years later, Walter T. Varney sold out to his partner, Louis Mueller, who, in turn, sold 40 percent of his stake to Robert F. Six. The two entrepreneurs changed the company's name to Continental Airlines and mortgaged their homes to upgrade its fleet.

By 1945, Continental boasted 400 employees and six DC-3s serving 26 cities. Still, it remained only a secondary, regional airline. Then in 1951, the company entered into an interchange agreement with two other airlines—a turning point in its quest for growth. The move gave passengers direct, one-plane service on the major Houston-to-Los Angeles route. By year-end, Continental's annual profits had reached $400,000—a company record.

As its 20th anniversary approached, Continental had almost 1,000 employees and a net worth of more than $4.5 million. Then in 1955, it received authorization from the Civil Aeronautics Board to serve three transcontinental routes from Denver to Los Angeles, San Francisco and Chicago—and ordered $60 million worth of planes to fly them. As the 1950s came to a close, Continental's attractive fleet,

aggressive marketing and outstanding in-flight service had made it a top competitor in these new cross-country markets.

The next two decades were glory years as the company expanded service to such distant destinations as Hawaii and Southeast Asia. But with deregulation in 1978, the commercial airlines industry changed profoundly. Operating costs skyrocketed, and Continental's long period of profitability came to an end.

As losses continued to mount, in 1982 the company merged with Texas Air Corporation, the holding company of Texas International. Still, it was forced to file bankruptcy in 1983.

Continental began its return to profitability, and by 1986 it reported record earnings of $60.9 million. The late 1980s were characterized by phenomenal growth as the company acquired Eastern Airlines, PeoplExpress, New York Air and most of the assets of Frontier Airlines. It also formed an alliance with Scandinavian Airlines System—the industry's first global partnership—and continued to add routes.

However, the logistical challenges associated with such rapid expansion sent the company into a tailspin. Performance and customer perception suffered. In 1989, Continental reported an unprecedented $315.5 million loss for the previous year. Then as rapidly rising fuel prices in the wake of the Middle East War exacerbat-

ed its losses, in 1990 the company declared bankruptcy for the second time in seven years.

Continental didn't struggle alone. Eastern, Pan American and Midway shut their doors, while American West and TWA also found themselves in bankruptcy court. Through efforts to improve efficiency and reduce costs, Continental survived and even saw improvements in performance and customer satisfaction. However, a continuing industry recession and the devastating effects of fare wars kept it mired in red ink.

A $450 million investment by Air Partners/Air Canada brought the company out of bankruptcy in 1993. Then a year later, Bethune took over at the top and introduced, among other innovative measures, his Go Forward Plan.

Today, Continental is more secure, operationally and financially, than it has been for many years. It's well on its way to becoming the best airline anywhere, as measured by its employees, its customers and its shareholders around the world.

CONQUEST
AIRLINES

Conquest Airlines, is a regional commuter air carrier linking small and mid-sized East Texas cities such as Tyler with San Antonio and Rio Grande Valley cities including Laredo and McAllen. In addition, the airline serves Abilene, Austin, Beaumont/Port Arthur, Corpus Christi, and San Angelo. Because air service links people across a vast territory and creates new economic possibilities for smaller cities, the company slogan reads: "Tying Texas Together...Conquest Airlines." Its current President and CEO, James McClean, and chief operating officer, Jim Echols, are both active pilots. McClean, an official and maintenance director with major carriers for twenty years, also founded his own aircraft maintenance company Worldwide Aircraft Services, Inc. of Springfield, Missouri.

The airline began when brothers Victor and Rafael Rivas responded to 1978 deregulation legislation that allowed air carriers to determine their own routes and caused many major airlines to discontinue service to small and mid-sized cities. Seeing an opportunity to control a niche market with a strong potential for growth, the entrepreneurs decided to offer service to cities then underserved, overpriced or abandoned by the major airlines. They noted that the effect on local business communities that relied on air service for travel, freight and cargo movement had been particularly devastating. With

Conquest's first scheduled commuter flights from Jefferson County Airport in Beaumont, Texas, on April 13, 1988, the Rivas brothers joined a distinguished group of Texas aviators including the founders of many of today's major carriers.

By flying where no other carrier flew, Conquest was able to issue its first public offering after one year, by which time forty daily flights had been added and company headquarters moved to Robert F. Mueller Airport at Austin, Texas. Demand for air service has risen along with interest in commuter service from smaller markets to larger metropolitan Texas cities, particularly for business travelers. By 1991 Conquest served Dallas' Love Field, Tyler,

Houston, Sugarland, Abilene, San Angelo, Beaumont/Port Arthur, San Antonio, Corpus Christi, McAllen, Laredo and Monterrey, Mexico. Two years later, flights reached destinations in states outside Texas including Little Rock, Arkansas; Birmingham and Mobile, Alabama, Greenville/Spartanburg, South Carolina, Knoxville, Tennessee, and Atlanta, Georgia. Roughly ninety per cent of the airline's passengers today are business travelers.

As Conquest grew, the Rivas brothers divided responsibility for overseeing the airline's management. Victor Rivas worked in New York, while Rafael, its visionary leader, led the firm in Texas. Consequently, when Rafael died in 1994, expansion ended temporarily, including plans for a jet service that would operate under the name "Conquest Sun." Although aircraft, licenses and certification already had been obtained, Victor Rivas decided to sell this operation to an Orlando-based firm that operated it subsequently under the name Air Tran. Concentrating his own efforts on Texas, Rivas consolidated company resources, people and equipment within the state. What remained was acquired WECO, Inc. and subsequently to Air LA, a West-Coast regional air carrier that made it a wholly-owned subsidiary with headquarters in Austin. By 1996 Conquest contemplated expanding its service to Dallas, Houston, New Orleans, Jackson, Mississippi, Little Rock, Arkansas, Bryan-College Station, and Galveston.

Conquest's eight nineteen-passenger Metro III turbo-prop airplanes, are manufactured exclusively in Texas by San Antonio's Fairchild Aircraft Company. Using jet engines to turn their propellers, these planes are highly economical and efficient, cruising at speeds up to 300 mph that allow them to rapidly reach short-haul destinations and to perform point-to-point service and is capable of flying at altitudes permitting the use of advantageous tail winds. Other Fairchild airplanes are currently used by the US Navy, US Air Force, corporate aviation departments and commuter airlines worldwide.

Conquest's Airlines has never experienced an accident or injuries in its 10 year history. Its pilots come from major civilian carriers or military backgrounds, and many have received commendations from the Federal Aviation Administration for their exceptional training in

excess of standard requirements. Recently, Conquest lessened the threat of in-air collisions to its aircraft by installing a traffic alert-and-avoidance system meeting the same standards as those of the largest American airlines. Conquest prides itself on safety, quality on-time travel, low cost, and convenient point-to-point service. Non-stop or one-stop service arrives at all its destinations in fifty-five minutes or less. Reaching customers through travel agencies, the corporate community and an in-house reservation center, the airline caters to individuals and charter groups flying for business or leisure, and handles freight, cargo and small packages at competitive rates.

PRESTIGE FORD

For Randall Reed, success didn't seem to come naturally. Although in the automobile industry his achievements are nothing short of extraordinary. His youthfulness, complimented by his neat well-groomed physical appearance, elegantly tailored suits, and confident stride, only hint at the disciplined person that he truly is.

Forever a visionary, at 37, Reed is president of "World Class Automotive Operations," the Dallas based headquarters of his award winning automotive and consulting group. He and his partners also own six of the top automobile dealerships in the country. Both Prestige and Park Cities Ford have been awarded the Ford Motor Company's top dealership honor - the coveted "Chairman's Award." This distinction is only presented to Ford dealerships that place in the top 1% nationally in customer service and satisfaction. Having now won a total of five "Chairman's Awards," between the two stores, Randall Reed has already made a powerful impact on the face of complacency in the automobile industry.

Ask Randall Reed what makes him so successful and he'll tell you. "Our people." "Our successes come from the dedication of our employees. We hire and train people who are truly committed to customer service, and create our own family environment." Himself being no stranger to hard work, Reed has genuine compassion and an open door policy toward his employees.

After the death of his mother, Reed took a temporary job as a salesperson at a Denver Colorado Ford dealership. His goal was to save enough money to go back to school at Western State, in Gunnison. However, he learned that selling cars came naturally to him. It was there that he began developing his unique customer satisfaction processes. In two years he was promoted to Finance Manager. As he continued to overcome many odds, due to his young age, it was always predicted by his subordinates that he would fail within ninety days. However, time and time again, he would prove them wrong.

In 1988 Reed bought his first dealership in a Dallas suburb, making him the youngest dealer in the country. The dealership was ranked 42 out of 42 in customer service in the region. Prestige is now the number one retail Ford dealership in Texas, and ranked 11 nationally. It also won "Chairman's Awards" in 1991, 1992 and 1995. With the success of Prestige, Reed took on a greater challenge in 1992. Park Cities Ford held the record for the most money lost in its four owner, 17 year history. Using the same "success formula" from Prestige, the store began to turn a profit from day one, and has progressively set records every since. In addition, Park Cities Ford also won consecutive "Chairman's Awards" for 1994 and 1995. A more than $1.5 million expansion of Park Cities has recently been accomplished, and the current renovation of Prestige will make it a state of the art facility. Prestige will also house a new parts and service center that will offer an array of client services. It will also be the largest in the southwest.

Reed's successes in sales and customer satisfaction have led to national and international speaking engagements. He enjoys sharing his organizational processes with other Ford and Lincoln Mercury dealers. Although the visionary, Randall Reed never likes to accept full credit for his accomplishments. He, along with the help of his staff and employees, continually develops innovative "success formulas" for a constantly change resistant industry. When asked about his phenomenal achievements, Reed appears uncomfortable when the subject is focused too long on himself. "Pleasing customers generates revenue, and its word of mouth advertising that drives friends, business associates and family members into your dealership...We're creating new and exciting ways to get things done. We're all family and everyone plays a critical part."

Reed and his wife, Sherry, have three children and, when he's not planning future business ventures, he enjoys quality time with his family, such as camp-outs as a Troop Guide.

EL FENIX

As every Texan knows, there's nothing like a good Mexican dinner when it's time to celebrate or relax. But it hasn't always been that way. In fact, Mexican food was unknown to most Anglo Texans when Miguel "Mike" Martinez opened his first El Fenix restaurant in 1918.

El Fenix, more than any other restaurant, popularized the unique Tex-Mex style of Mexican cooking that originated among Texas' Spanish-speaking population. With 14 Dallas-area restaurants and two in neighboring Ft. Worth today, El Fenix is the nation's oldest family-owned Mexican food chain.

Born in the tiny Mexican village of El Potrero in 1890, Martinez began working at age 7, driving burros to and from the local mines. By age 15, he was working deep in the mines. But young Martinez had other ambitions and came to the United States in 1911 at age 21. He worked first as a dishwasher in Dallas' Oriental Hotel, learning cooking from watching and helping its chef. After seven years, Martinez opened his own small cafe, which initially served traditional American foods.

Customers, though, asked him to include spicy Mexican dishes, which soon became more popular than his American menu. On Sept. 15, 1918, Martinez reopened as El Fenix, named for the legend of the Phoenix rising from its own ashes.

"My father created Tex-Mex in the sense that he popularized the dishes with the sauces he developed," said son Reuben Martinez, president and chief executive officer today. El Fenix quickly became renowned for its enchiladas, chili, tamales and frijoles a la Mexicana.

Mike Martinez also created the combination plate that is a staple at Mexican restaurants today. Restaurants of the era typically served foods in separate dishes, as cafeterias do now. But the young El Fenix was understaffed, leading Mike to combine foods onto one plate so he wouldn't have to stay all night washing dishes.

It wasn't long before El Fenix outgrew the small cafe, and Martinez bought a larger building near downtown. During the 1940s and 1950s, El Fenix became Dallas' late-night destination. "Dallas still didn't have many restau-

rants then, and certainly not many that stayed open after 10 p.m., so we got the nightclub crowd and all the movie stars in town," Reuben Martinez said.

The eight Martinez children were brought up in the restaurant business. They did everything. After school every day, they washed dishes, waited on tables, made tortillas and helped out anywhere needed.

"Papa Mike" turned El Fenix over to his children in 1946, after his sons returned from World War II military service. Eager to make their own mark, the younger Martinezes in 1947 opened El Fenix's second restaurant, in suburban Oak Cliff. "We all needed jobs," laughed Reuben. Other locations followed over the years as the family knew they could manage them properly.

The six surviving siblings still own and manage the growing restaurant chain. Irene Martinez Garcia, Alfred Martinez, Reuben D. Martinez, Gilbert Martinez is executive vice president, Tina Martinez and Hortencia Martinez Stickle. With five of Mike Martinez' 21 grandchildren involved in various management positions, family ownership is ensured well into the coming century.

Mike Martinez died in 1956 at age 65, but his conviction of quality and strong family management still guides El Fenix. "The family is continuing the tradition that Papa Mike set for us," said Reuben Martinez. "We remain successful, when so many have come and gone, because of the consistent quality of our food and our service. El Fenix is going to stay El Fenix, serving good Mexican food at reasonable prices."

Hansueli and Annemarie Schlunegger are living the American dream. In 1959 they immigrated from Switzerland with one son, and Hans took a job with the Olympic Westin Hotel in Seattle, Washington. Today the couple has two more children -- a daughter and another son -- and owns four hotels, their adjacent restaurants and a catering service.

In 1962 the Schluneggers moved from Seattle to Houston. Hans worked at the Rice Hotel as the assistant to the executive chef. In 1963, he was responsible for preparing John F. Kennedy's dinner, which turned out to be JFK's last meal, since he was assassinated in Dallas the next day.

From the Rice Hotel, he went to work as the executive chef for Warwick Hotel in Houston, which was considered to be "the plush hotel" in the United States at the time. He served such people as the Duke and Duchess of Windsor, John Wayne and countless other celebrities.

In 1969, the family moved to Kerrville where they were leasing the food and beverage operation at the Inn of the Hills resort for three years. When the Inn was bought out, the Schluneggers canceled their contract and opened the extremely popular Alpine Lodge Restaurant, which they have operated for 20 years.

The Alpine Lodge is known throughout the Hill Country and serves continental and American cuisine. The customers are very loyal. "I think we have some customers who never miss a meal with us, and Annemarie is the key to this sustained success," said Hans.

Finally in 1993, the Schluneggers came back home to the Inn of the Hills. When they took over the hotel, it was seriously deteriorated, so they undertook a huge refurbishment project. Now the resort, decorated in a unique Hill Country style, remains a landmark in Kerrville. They are currently completing the process of renovating the hotel, including the addition of 20 more rooms.

The Inn, built in the 1960s, is a full-service resort hotel. It has 175 rooms and meeting space for up to 800 people. Catering of Central Texas, Inc., also owned by the Schluneggers, provides a full-service catering option. "We like to think of it as catering to our guests," said Hans.

The Olympic-sized pool is a great place to spend the afternoon. And the beautifully landscaped gardens, well-kept grounds and nearby Guadalupe River provide a serene setting to take a relaxing evening stroll. In addition, the Schluneggers control 64 condominiums adjacent to the hotel available for daily or monthly rentals.

The family owns three other hotels. The Best Western Swiss Chalet Resort in Ruidoso, New Mexico has been refurbished, and the Best Western Swiss Clock Inns in Fort Stockton and Pecos, Texas offer the full range of hotel services.

All members of the family are involved in the business, including their son-in-law, who is general manager of the Inn of the Hills.

Why have the Schluneggers been so successful? It's all in their philosophy. "We feel we are superior operators," said Hans. "Our first priority is to take care of the people -- both guests and employees."

INN OF THE HILLS/ CATERING OF CENTRAL TEXAS

Top, left: Annemarie inspects the buffet table.

Bottom, left: A family portrait

Above: Hans tending one of the many beautiful Swiss cuckoo clocks.

Below: Diners enjoying a meal in the Alpine Lodge Restaurant in Kerrville.

MENGER HOTEL

Rich in hospitality, the Menger Hotel stands at the crossroads of Southwestern history in the heart of San Antonio. Located on Alamo Plaza behind the shrine to Texas heroes who died for independence, the hotel overlooks the Riverwalk and shopping, entertainment and business districts of a thriving modern community while offering an atmosphere that combines the Old West with the graciousness of southern living. Eisenhower spent his honeymoon here. President Bill Clinton ordered the hotel's famous mango ice cream sent all the way to Washington for his inauguration.

Hotels have long served as meeting places for the notorious and anonymous, adventurers and eccentrics, and the Menger is no exception. For over 137 years this grand hotel has offered rest and refreshment to trail-dusty cowboys, local society, civic leaders, itinerant celebrities, and politicians, including twelve U.S. presidents. Listed in the National Register of Historic Places, the Menger claims to be the oldest enterprise of its kind offering uninterrupted service west of the Mississippi.

It all began when German immigrant William A. Menger married the owner of a local boarding house and began making beer at the equivalent of a modern microbrewery. The malt and hops came from New York, and the beer cooled on ice all the way from Boston. The neighborhood was rougher in those days. The adjacent site occupied today by Dillards department store was a holding pen for cattle being driven north on the Chisolm Trail, and often the place cowboys settled their disputes with gunfire. Down the way were stables and water tanks for soldiers passing through to secure the frontier.

Passengers on arriving stagecoaches raced to get a room and play billiards in Menger's bar. Other pioneers came to imbibe the brew by mule-drawn wagon or on foot and spent the night on tables in the bar before the host built lodgings. Eventually, the Menger constructed rooms and began to offer more lavish fare: potted antelope and dried buffalo tongue, wild turkey, quail, home-made German sausage and other delicacies. A German chef carries on the tradition today at the hotel's Colonial Restaurant, still offering examples of nineteenth century cuisine.

More than a hotel, the Menger is a landmark worth seeing. When it opened in 1859, the newspapers called its "shining furniture, fine carpets and beautiful curtains...a spectacle of exceeding

brilliancy." At a cost to build of just over $15,000, the Menger brought civilization to the frontier. Menger's Parisian furnishings, now fine antiques, recreate the fashion of the past throughout the establishment. The painting of cattle herding that hung in Rock Hudson's ranch house in the film Giant adorns the hotel lobby. The elegant solid cherry bar with paneled ceiling and French mirrors is a replica of London's House of Lords Club and the place where Teddy Roosevelt recruited some of Texas' finest fighters to become Rough Riders in the Spanish-American War. The hotel's most recent renovation applied nine million dollars to restore some of the elegance of the Old West. A reminder of its glory, the Menger prides itself on attention to every guest's individual needs and remains one the unique experiences in the city of San Antonio.

Celebrity, fame and local social prominence have been associated with the Menger from the start. In a graceful garden in its inner courtyard, English playwright Oscar Wilde sipped mint juleps from silver tumblers by the pond. Alligators swam in the pool there after an adventurer settled his bill with partial payment in reptiles. Sam Houston, Ulysses S. Grant, Cornelius Vanderbilt, Robert E. Lee, Judge Roy Bean and a host of lawmen, outlaws, soldiers, cattlemen and traveling salesman number among the thousands of guests entertained since opening day. Geronimo was housed here briefly before his transfer to nearby Fort Sam Houston. French actress Sarah Bernhardt, Mae West, Bob Hope, Beverly Sills, and Jose Ferrer came later.

After Menger sold the hotel it was owned for a time by another prominent San Antonio businessman, J.H. Kampman. Since 1943, when entrepreneur William J. Moody, Jr. bought it, the hotel has been operated by the Texas-based Gal-Tex Hotel Corporation, Inc. as part of the Moody family empire.

AEROMEXICO

Aeronaves de Mexico began operations in 1934. In 1988 this Mexican airline was privatized and emerged as "Aerovias de Mexico," opening as Aeromexico after being purchased by a visionary and ambitious investor group.

Establishing outstanding on-time performance as its primary goal, Aeromexico achieved a 97% on-time performance within its first three years. It has maintained this level in 1996, making it one of the world's most punctual airlines.

In addition Aeromexico became known for its new fleet manned by professionally trained crews; Mexico's first frequent flyer program; and continuous employee training at University of Aeromexico. It has gone on to become the largest carrier in the Mexican passenger market, and one of Latin America's preeminent airlines, currently serving over 70 destinations in the U.S., Europe, Central and South America, with its main hub in Mexico City.

Aeromexico has maintained continuous ties with Texas through the years, not only providing services to and from its Houston and Dallas/Ft. Worth gateways, but also because in 1991 Aeromexico acquired a majority position in Aerolitoral, a regional carrier with hubs in Monterrey and Guadalajara. Aerolitoral currently links various Mexican cities with San Antonio, Harlingen and El Paso.

Positioning itself as a prominent Latin American airline, Aeromexico acquired a majority position in Peru's largest airline, Aeroperu, in January 1993. One month later, Aeromexico raised its stake in Mexicana airlines, thus securing a large portion of the Mexican domestic market between both airlines.

Aeromexico is following a strategic flight plan carefully designed to strengthen its position as Mexico's leading airline while expanding its role as Latin America's dominant carrier.

Aeromexico's maintenance systems are so highly regarded within the airline industry that they have been approved by the FAA to service other international carriers consisting of some of the best-known names in air travel today, including Iberia, Continental, Delta, American and Northwest to name a few.

Today the 5317 dedicated employees of the Aeromexico family -- pilots, flight crews, maintenance specialists, marketing personnel and ticket agents -- are committed to delivering the high performance standards you have come to expect.

Aeromexico is proud to be a major link between Texas and Mexico and is dedicated to ensuring that the bonds of commerce and tourism between the two countries remain close -- as close as we are together.

FAIRMOUNT HOTEL

Folks in Texas love a challenge and moving the Fairmount Hotel six blocks through Downtown San Antonio certainly spurred on the "can do" Texas spirit.

Undaunted by curbs, corners, driveways, medians, a bridge with unknown capacity, and the nay-sayers, the historic Fairmount Hotel was moved six blocks from its original site at Bowie and Commerce Streets to Nueva and South Alamo, and into the Guinness Book of World Records as the heaviest building ever moved on wheels.

The world watched as the 3.2 million-pound former railway travelers hotel made its way on its six-day journey. Cameras from the BBC, ITV, CNN and TV network affiliates recorded the feat, and it was rumored that Las Vegas bookmakers were giving 5-1 odds that the hotel wouldn't make it off its foundation and into the street, and then 7-3 odds that the building wouldn't make it across the Market Street bridge.

The bridge was estimated to be capable of holding one million pounds, but its exact strength and capacity were unknown. Guido Bros. Construction Company shored up the bridge with steel scaffolding anchored in steel shoring plates placed on the bed of the drained San Antonio River. Beer bottles were placed at strategic locations in the scaffolding to measure the bridge's "give" as the building rolled over it. If the bottles broke, the building would be considered too heavy to go over the reinforced bridge. The beer bottles didn't break and spectators cheered the successful bridge crossing.

After its memorable move in April 1985, the Fairmount Hotel was meticulously restored to its Italianate Victorian splendor and designated a State Archaeological Landmark by the Texas Antiquities Committee in 1986. It is San Antonio's only member of the prestigious Small Luxury Hotels of the World Consortium.

Once featured on the TV show "Lifestyles of the Rich and Famous" the Fairmount has hosted many "rich and famous" celebrity guests. The Fairmount has hosted such notables as King Juan Carlos and Queen Sofia of Spain, Joan Collins, David Rockefeller, Dionne Warwick, Molly Ringwald, Dick Clark, Walter Cronkite, Donald Sutherland, Vanna White, and many others.

In addition to meeting and party facilities for small groups, the Fairmount has twenty guest rooms and seventeen deluxe suites, each designed to pamper guests with a luxurious decor that includes Italian marble baths, solid brass fixtures, overstuffed chairs, basketed plants, and such amenities as plush terry robes and oversized towels, lighted makeup mirrors, twice-daily maid service, and other comforts that guests expect in a world class luxury hotel. The concierge is available to look after guests' special

needs and can arrange for massage or beauty salon service in their rooms in addition to other requests.

In both public and private areas, the Fairmount offers the ambiance of a fine home with its understated soft colors, rich natural woodwork, fine stone and marble, high ceilings, chandeliers, and fine art, all complimented by fresh flower arrangements. The lobby displays numerous artifacts found when the foundation for the building was excavated, including china, a bayonet, rifle balls, and other evidence of San Antonio's history.

Along with its luxurious accommodations, the Fairmount offers fine dining and a cozy place to visit with friends in its award winning Polo's Restaurant and Bar. Polo's has been honored as one of the United States' top 250 restaurants by *Conde Naste,* "one of the most innovative in the country" by *Esquire Magazine,* one of 10 Best Restaurants in San Antonio by the Concierge Association of San Antonio, and has received numerous AAA Four Diamond Awards.

Chef Sander Edmondson presents a menu that incorporates different cultures — Asian, French, Southwestern, and features a variety of game and fish signature dishes. His grilled fish specialties, such as salmon or tuna, are served with innovative sauces such as his signature citrusy fruit and peppercorn sauce. Polo's menus change seasonally to take advantage of produce abundance. Grilled vegetable plates are popular "lighter fare" in the summer and game is featured in the fall. Hunters often bring the chef game and fishermen their catch to cook and serve guests at private dinners held in the hotel's party rooms. The Fairmount Hotel is at 401 South Alamo Street, San Antonio TX 78205; Phone: 210-224-8800; Reservations: 1-800-642-3363; Fax: 210-224-2767. The North American Office of Small Luxury Hotels of the World is at 3525 Sage Road, Suite 508, Houston Texas 77056; Phone: 1-713-522-9512; Fax: 1-713-524-7412.

Guests at the 1923 grand opening of the Stoneleigh Court Apartment Hotel in Dallas were dazzled by what they saw. Walking between the twin recumbent lion statues flanking the entrance, elegantly dressed couples gazed up 11 stories at the tallest hotel west of the Mississippi. Inside, the plush ballroom vibrated periodically to the lively beat of the newest dance rage, the Charleston.

Gentlemen tried out the Stoneleigh's billiard room, admired the gymnasium's recreational facilities and noted the in-house barber shop. Many took their wives or sweethearts to the building's rooftop garden, where the couples relished a panoramic view, for the Stoneleigh was the tallest building of any kind outside downtown.

Built of fine marbles, woods and stone, the Stoneleigh quickly became known as one of the city's finest hotels, a premier site for lavish wedding receptions and society balls. Its elegant yet cozy atmosphere made it the Dallas "home" for many Hollywood celebrities over the decades.

Theirs was an era of gracious service many hotels have forgotten in today's harried rush, but the Stoneleigh Hotel's distinctive classical European-style hospitality still thrives. "The Stoneleigh is the definition of a small, personal service, luxury hotel," said owner Al Granoff. "It is our heritage and we continue to build on that special tradition."

That tradition's most recent addition is the Stoneleigh's newly renovated Celebrity Level, an all-concierge floor with special amenities such as thick bathrobes, honor bars, stocked bookcases, coffeemakers, hairdryers and mementos. Furnishings feature 18th Century English mahogany furniture, fine wood trims, granite bathroom countertops and custom wood vanities.

"This floor, in particular, has the special touches celebrities expect," said Lisa Lantz, the Stoneleigh's general manager. "But anyone can reserve a room on this floor and be pampered like a celebrity." Guest rooms on the Celebrity Level — and indeed, all Stoneleigh guest rooms — carry a distinctive aura because they are not simply one or two room designs endlessly repeated, as is typical in hotels today. Each room has its own unique ambiance, varying in size, configuration, color scheme and decor, just as it would in a comfortable home. There are, in fact, about 20 different room combinations.

One guest room even matches the rooftop penthouse, with stained glass windows, dark paneling and hand-carved stone fireplace mantel imported from England. Stoneleigh legend says that decades ago the room was a colorful owner's

refuge for late night card games, and may even contain a never-found secret passage to the penthouse. About half of the Stoneleigh's 153 oversized rooms are suites, including junior suites (one large room that includes a living area) and king parlors (bedroom and separate living room). Some even include a full kitchen, making them the perfect temporary home for relocating executives and others living in Dallas for several weeks or months.

"There is absolutely no cookie-cutter appearance here," Lantz said. "One reason the Stoneleigh is so special is because the rooms aren't all alike. That makes the hotel very residential in feel. Many people today want to get away from the huge chain hotels. We want our guests to feel like they are staying in a friend's home."

The Stoneleigh's service and surroundings reflect the same inviting home-like atmosphere. "We offer very personalized service," Granoff said. "Whether a person is an overnight guest or a customer of one of our three restaurants, our concierge will know their name on the way in. Our staff is oriented to that personal touch. There's a warmth here that makes a wonderful difference."

The Stoneleigh may be small and intimate in flavor, but it includes all the amenities expected in a fine hotel. Its English pub, the Lion's Den, serves burgers and sandwiches in a cozy, casual atmosphere. Ewald's restaurant, on the other hand, has been a Dallas fine-dining institution for more than a quarter century. Known for its gourmet continental cuisine, Ewald's also caters to today's health conscious guests with lighter fare. A few steps down the hall — but half a world away in cuisine — is the venerable hotel's newest restaurant, Sushi at The Stoneleigh, serving sushi and Dallas' most extensive variety of sake.

The Stoneleigh is still the setting for society wedding receptions and large banquets, but today is also reserved for business meetings. Settings range from the hotel's large and graceful Renaissance Ballroom to the Penthouse, with its warmly evocative English decor and grand view of the Dallas skyline. That skyline is mere blocks away. Guests looking for evening entertainment step out into the heart of Dallas' vibrant Uptown neighborhood. Located just north of downtown Dallas and adjacent to the city's finest neighborhood, the historic area is filled with antique shops, art galleries, fine shopping and enough restaurants to satisfy every taste.

The Stoneleigh Hotel has it all — the best of today's variety and conveniences, combined with the best of yesterday's elegance and service.

STONELEIGH HOTEL

SOUTHWEST AIRLINES

Twenty-five years ago a little upstart Texas airline finally made its inaugural flight and began a revolution in the airline industry.

Against overwhelming odds, Southwest Airlines became the maverick of the airline establishment with a handful of planes and a lot of guts. By offering low fares and frequent flights, its mission was to make air travel affordable and convenient for everyone. Southwest is a genuine American success story with deep roots in Texas.

San Antonio entrepreneur Rollin King devised the novel idea of starting a new airline to serve Houston, Dallas, and San Antonio, because it was inconvenient to drive and expensive to fly between these cities. King presented the plan to San Antonio attorney Herb Kelleher at the St. Anthony Club. Kelleher replied, "Rollin, you're crazy. Let's do it!"

The Texas Aeronautics Commission's 1968 approval for Southwest to fly between the three Texas cities unwittingly started a legal battle between Southwest and incumbent airlines. This war lasted more than three years, severely tested Kelleher's litigation skills, and almost put Southwest out of business before it launched its first plane on June 18, 1971. Southwest's early struggle to survive sparked a special spirit that keeps the company at record levels of performance year after year. See for yourself.

PROFITABILITY

Southwest is the only U.S. airline to earn a profit every year since 1973, despite billion dollar losses in the industry.

LOWEST FARES

The U.S. Department of Transportation described Southwest's low fares as "the principal driving force behind dramatic fundamental changes" in the airline industry.

MOST PRODUCTIVE WORKFORCE

Southwest has more daily departures per gate, gets more productive hours out of a plane, and services twice the number of passengers per employee of any other airline.

NO FURLOUGHS

Southwest has never laid off employees, not even during the jet fuel crisis of 1979, the recession of 1982-1983, or the recession of 1990-1994. Kelleher, Southwest Chairman, President, and CEO, says, "If your focus is on the long term, the well-being of your business and its people, you don't do it."

HIGHEST CUSTOMER SERVICE RATING

Southwest is the only U.S. carrier to win the industry's "Triple Crown," based on baggage handling, on-time performance, and customer service -- and they won it four consecutive years.

BEST SAFETY RECORD

Conde Nast Traveler magazine called Southwest "the safest airline in the world."

In 1971, Southwest's low fares and friendly service to three Texas cities were as outrageous as its uniforms -- orange hot pants and white lace-up go-go boots. Today, employees sport khakis and polo shirts and Southwest flies to 49 cities in 24 states, but the airline still prides itself on providing "positively outrageous service."

The people of Southwest are crusaders with an egalitarian spirit who truly believe they are in the business of freedom -- to give ordinary people the chance to see and do things they never dreamed possible.

For a more detailed account, read NUTS! Southwest Airlines' Crazy Recipe for Business and Personal Success by Kevin and Jackie Freiberg published by Bard Books, Inc., Austin, Texas.

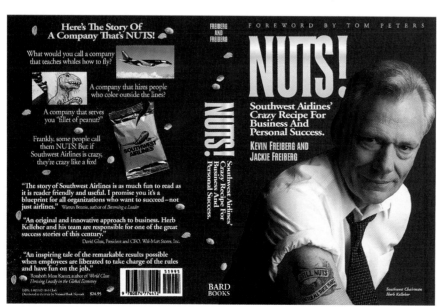

The Ramada Inn Bayfront, at 601 N. Water Streets located one block from the Bay and Marina in the heart of Corpus Christi's downtown business district. Each of the hotel's 200 spacious guest rooms provides a private balcony, and many offer bay views. Currently managed by HIMC Ltd., Partnership, or High Plains Management Company of St. Charles, Missouri, with corporate headquarters in Colorado Springs, Colorado, the hotel stands on the site formerly occupied by the historic Nueces Hotel, once considered the finest in the state. HIMC also manages the Radisson Inn Airport at Colorado Springs, Twin Palms Hotel in Tempe, Arizona, and the Comfort Inn at St. Charles, Missouri.

For fifty years, the Nueces served as a center for civic and social activities as well as a haven for vacationers. Registered guests included such famous names as politician William Jennings Bryan, General John J. Pershing, and Lyndon Baines Johnson. At the time it was built by local investors, few towns in America with a population of only 10,000 had a 200-room hotel, but the extension of railroad lines across the state promised a burgeoning clientele.

In 1919, a colorful new owner, South Texas rancher and financier William Whitby Jones and his three daughters, bought out the other stockholders and built a 103-room addition. The hotel fared well in the 1920s due to improved railroad transportation and the opening of the port of Corpus Christi in 1926, but subsequently declined. In 1961 it was sold by the Jones estate at public auction to Greater Corpus Enterprises, Inc. For a half million dollars, and then leased for use as a retirement home to an operator form Miami Beach, Florida. Principal stockholder, Joe J. Barshop of San Antonio who had built the Ramada Inn across Water Street in 1964, operated the hotel for a time, but in 1970, after Hurricane Celia brought destruction to the community, the old hotel was demolished and its contents sold. On the site of the old Nueces arose the current ten-story hotel which was known for a time as the La Quinta Royale, Corpus Christi Royale and Royale Nueces.

Corpus-HIMC Ltd. Partnership acquired it in 1990, and undertook extensive remodeling.

The lavish newly redecorated hotel was renamed the Ramada Inn-Bayfront and became part of the Ramada franchise in 1994.

Situated to allow vacationers ready access to deep sea fishing, sailing and windsurfing as well as full privileges at the nearby Country Club for golf and tennis, the current Ramada Inn-Bayfront Hotel is only fifteen minutes from the Corpus Christi International Airport. Offering many amenities in addition to its Palms Restaurant and atrium piano bar and lounge, it provides guests with over 15,000 square feet of flexible meeting space, the city's largest hotel ballroom, exercise facilities, a business center and more. A tenth floor reception area offers a spectacular view of Corpus Christi Art Museum and Botanical Gardens, Greyhound Race Track, specialty and antique shops, and miles of white sandy beaches along the Gulf Coast. From trade shows to football clinics, military reunions to weddings, the 1992 American Bowling Congress to gatherings of nurses and plumbers, the Ramada annually hosts numerous conferences and visiting business groups. With over eighty employees, the hotel prides itself on a professional conference and catering staff that can assist with any requirement from personalized menus to board room space.

RAMADA INN BAYFRONT

BUILDING A GREATER TEXAS

Texas' real estate, construction

and energy industries shape

tomorrow's skyline, providing

working and living space

for Texans and fuel for the nation

Early train in South Texas, locomotive probably belonging to the Rio Grande Railway Co.
COURTESY, ARCHIVES DIVISION, TEXAS STATE LIBRARY

STEWART TITLE

Carlotta Barker painting of Stewart Title Building in Galveston.

Carlotta Barker painting of Stewart Title's corporate offices in Houston.

When William Henry Stewart, a young Maryland-born attorney, stepped ashore on Galveston Island in 1844, he had no reason to expect that his role in the development of Texas would be such a profound one. Nor could he know his descendants would continue that involvement, and in so doing, would enhance the development of Texas — and the nation — for generations to come.

William H. Stewart settled in Gonzales, established his law practice, and after serving as the town's mayor, was elected to the Texas Legislature. During the War Between the States, Stewart served as a major in the Army of Northern Virginia. Upon his return to Texas, he made Galveston his home, setting up a private law practice while continuing his involvement in state legislative matters.

As a delegate to the convention in 1876 which formulated the Texas Constitution still in use, he wrote the resolution transferring 3,000,000 acres of public land to finance construction of the present State Capitol building. For this contribution, William H. Stewart was named "Father of the State Capitol of Texas," and his portrait occupies a prominent place in the Senate Chambers. In 1876, he was named judge for the Tenth Judicial District in Galveston, a position he held until his death in 1903.

Judge Stewart's children and grandchildren would also play major roles in the growth and development of Texas. In 1892, Maco Stewart, then 20, an attorney, established his Law and Land Title office in Galveston to examine titles statewide. In 1893, he purchased a Galveston abstract company, a step which marks the beginning of the Stewart companies. Ever visionary, Maco Stewart recognized the importance of providing greater security and guarantees to property owners, and with his brother Minor, he founded the Maco and Minor Stewart Title Guarantee Company in 1905. Maco was instrumental in encouraging legislation to allow title insurance to be written within the state, and in 1908,

Stewart Title Guaranty Company was chartered with capital stock of $150,000, and issued the state's first title insurance policy. Original directors included Maco and Minor Stewart and their brother-in-law, W.C. Morris.

In 1905, Maco Stewart purchased the Kauffman and Runge Building which was designed by noted architect Eugene Heiner, and completed in 1882. The impressive Neo-Renaissance style four-story Philadelphia pressed brick structure is in the heart of Galveston's commercial district. The building became Galveston's premier business address when the Stewarts introduced the latest inventions of the period, including on-premise wireless telegraph, an innovative atrium design within the structure's interior, a bird-cage elevator, and the first postal letter drop in an office building in Galveston. Stewart Title Guaranty Company and the first national bank of Texas were headquartered in the Stewart Building. To this day, Stewart Title continues to maintain its offices in the historic building.

Stewart Title Guaranty and its subsidiary, Stewart Abstract company — later renamed Stewart Title Company — began to expand in 1910. The first office outside of Galveston was located in Dallas. Offices were subsequently opened in San Antonio and Houston, and operations expanded to El Paso and Fort Worth in the 1920's. W.C. Morris, who began with the company in 1897, assumed an ever-increasing role in its expansion, directing day-to-day operations and setting up new companies statewide. Through careful growth, the company increased its insurance reserves and established a network of owned offices and independent title agents throughout the state. By the end of World War II, Stewart Title

Malcom Morris and Stewart Morris, Jr., sons of Carloss and of Stewart Morris, joined the management team. In 1972, Stewart Information became a publicly-traded stock with its first offering providing capital for further expansion. In 1975, through its Landata subsidiaries, the company launched an intensive effort of developing computer technology to pave the path toward the ultimate goal of providing paperless real estate transactions, aiding customers to save time and reduce costs.

Few publicly-held international companies can boast of three generations of family leadership to provide the consistency of decision-making that assures optimum growth. This continuity has allowed Stewart to establish a vision of developing companies with business technologies which enhance the security of land

Guaranty Company was the largest title insurance company in the state, a distinction it continues to hold.

With the death of Maco Stewart in 1938, and subsequent deaths of W.C. Morris and Maco Stewart, Jr., in 1950, the continuity of family involvement was perpetuated by the election of Carloss and Stewart Morris, sons of W.C. Morris, as president of Stewart Title Guaranty Company and Stewart Title Company, respectively. Under second-generation leadership, Stewart Title first ventured outside Texas into neighboring New Mexico in 1956. By 1960, the company had issuing offices throughout the Sun Belt states and began a vigorous expansion nationwide.

Stewart Information Services Corporation, the holding company, was formed in 1970 to allow the company to form new real estate information companies, building on the base of its principal subsidiary, Stewart Title Guaranty Company. At this time, the third generation began to assume their roles in operations when

ownership. With offices and agents throughout the United States and new ventures added internationally each year, the company carries an "A Double Prime" rating from Demotech, the highest rating available for the field of 100 title insurance companies.

Stewart's commitment to leadership in automation of real estate information has top priority. Productivity and electronic commerce in the real estate process is the task of the Landata group of companies. Landata has become the industry leader and continues developing technology to reduce costs and speed transfer of title to real estate safely.

Other subsidiaries provide ancillary products essential to the real estate transfer process. Landata Geo Services provides digital geographic information systems and digital imagery for government agencies as well as for engineering firms and real estate developers. The information superhighway provides the opportunity to offer new services through another Stewart Information subsidiary,

Gordon Gray Award from the
National Trust for Historic Preservation

The first title insurance policy

Mortgage Management Services Corporation, which interfaces with mortgage lenders to provide electronic data interchange (EDI) for real estate settlements, to provide flood determination information, document preparation and other real estate information, and to develop processes which will lead toward a paperless and less cumbersome, yet protected, conveyance process, and reliable document storage system.

The security of land ownership that has been so essential to the prosperity of the United States, coupled with technological advances, allows Stewart to play a major role internationally in helping other countries enhance and manage geographic information systems as well as to introduce good land records, a secure land title conveyance process as the stabilizing influence of private ownership of land and the entire national economy, as well as security for mortgage lenders. Stewart Information International, Inc., has brought the organization recognition as an expert in global real estate.

The past is prelude to the future, indeed. As evidence of their commitment to the sound investment and the enduring value of real estate, the Morris family and the Stewart companies have been active in the historic preservation movement for decades. In 1979, the National Trust for Historic Preservation awarded the prestigious Gordon Gray Award to Stewart and Joella Morris and Stewart Title Guaranty Company for the painstaking restoration of the landmark Stewart Title building in Galveston. The company proudly dedicated the William H. Stewart Room to house treasured historic documents relating to the history of the company and of Galveston. Among those items available for viewing are the original 1838 Menard Grant providing for establishment of the city of Galveston, signed by Sam Houston; the first title policy issued in 1905 by Maco and Minor Stewart Title Guarantee Company; the Galveston City Company safe which houses original minute books and records of the City's early history; hundreds of early abstracts relating to Galveston County property, and many valuable old maps.

In keeping with its emphasis on history and historic preservation, the company sponsors symposia and holds special events in historic structures throughout the United States, and periodically presents the Stewart Title Historic Preservation Award to deserving projects. During the company's Centennial celebration in 1993, the rich history and traditions so vitally nurtured were the focus of the company's achievements and expansion during its first 100-years.

Bonding past to present while building for the future has been a Stewart tradition for more than a century. Three generations have provided management continuity in ensuring the company remains true to its mission: to enhance the real estate closing process.

Technology has changed the title industry drastically.

Houston Engineers, Inc. was founded in 1924 by Charles Ross Edwards, an inventor, entrepreneur, and "transplanted" Texan. Born in 1876 near Phillipsburg, Kansas, Edwards fought in the Spanish-American War before pursuing his engineering and technical education at Kansas State A&M College. After moving to Houston in 1907, Edwards worked as a general supervisor for Southern Pacific Railroad while developing an interest in the growing Houston oil industry. Recognizing the need for a tool capable of recovering pipe lodged or "stuck" in an oil and gas well, he invented and developed the Reversing Tool. Edwards patented the tool in 1920 and founded Houston Engineers, Inc. (also known as HE) to manufacture and market it. Over the next twenty years, Edwards presided over HE as its product line and domestic sales grew.

Charles Edwards' daughter, Rea, and her husband, Art Britton, managed HE after Edwards' death in 1946. The Brittons continued the Edwards legacy of adding new tools to HE's product line, presiding over the company until its sale to Wilson Industries, Inc. in 1968.

Wilson Industries appointed William "Bill" Miller president. Under Miller's leadership, HE began to expand into the international drilling market. Charles Bartley stepped in as president in 1973 and helped HE establish a successful joint venture with Weir Pumps Ltd. of Scotland to market HE products and services in the North Sea and Europe. International expansion was further fueled by the development of the Hydra-Jar®, a uniquely-designed impact tool used to free or recover drilling equipment lodged in a well.

After Bartley's retirement in 1982, Dwight E. Beach, Jr. became HE's president. Beach, a West Point graduate and M.I.T. engineer, directed the company during the severe downturn of the oil industry in the 1980's. Under his leadership, HE successfully weathered the storm and continued its growth as the market improved. In 1995, HE added Wilson Downhole Services, a directional drilling company, as a division. HE is now a major supplier of innovative drilling and fishing equipment to oil companies, service companies, and drilling contractors worldwide. HE manufactures, sells, and rents its product line of drilling and fishing jars, Accelerator® and shock tools, downhole motors, and MWD (measurement while drilling) equipment.

Houston Engineers, Inc. continues to expand as it enters the 21st century with a solid product line and strong management. Its worldwide headquarters and manufacturing plant are located in Houston only a few blocks away from Charles Edwards' original office. HE's domestic interests are served by district offices in Texas, Oklahoma, Louisiana, Michigan, and Wyoming. International operations are augmented by HE's subsidiary offices in Singapore and Perth, Australia. The company has come a long way since 1924 and the future of Houston Engineers, Inc. is indeed bright.

(Written by Kirsten Jonrowe Coats and researched by Cristine S. Davila. Mrs. Coats is an HE employee and student of history and psychology at the University of Houston-Downtown. Ms. Davila is also an HE employee and researcher of the company's history.)

HOUSTON ENGINEERS, INC.

The Houston Engineers test rig at sunset against Houston's downtown skyline, 1996
PHOTOGRAPH BY CRISTINE S. DAVILA

Houston Engineers truck on a rig site, early 1930's.
PHOTOGRAPH COURTESY OF DIANE DORMANT

TEXACO

A truck delivers in the Port Arthur area in 1927.

A 1907 "family" portrait of employees at the Port Neches office.

TEXACO: THE STAR SHINES BRIGHT

When the world's first great oil gusher blew black gold into the sky at Spindletop, a field near Beaumont, in 1901, it ushered in an oil boom that made Texas the energy capital of the world. Hundreds of companies were created as entrepreneurs crowded into the southeastern part of the state. Almost a century later, the Texas Company, predecessor of Texaco Inc., is the only one that has survived.

Competitive spirit and innovation and a willingness to take reasonable risks and expand technological boundaries has brought Texaco a long way since its early days. Now, almost a century later, it is a fully integrated international energy company involved in all phases of the petroleum industry, from exploring and producing crude oil and natural gas to transporting, refining and marketing fuels and lubricants in some 150 countries.

A STAR IS BORN

Oil flowed freely from Spindletop when the Texas Company was formed on January 2, 1902. But as underground saltwater seeped into the field, production plummeted, putting many competitors out of business. Fortunately, Texaco's discovery of oil at nearby Sour Lake put the company back on firm footing.

Business boomed as oil replaced coal as a power source for industrial plants and locomotives and as the "horseless carriage" boosted gasoline demand. By the end of its first decade, Texaco had opened five refineries and extended its product sales into all but five

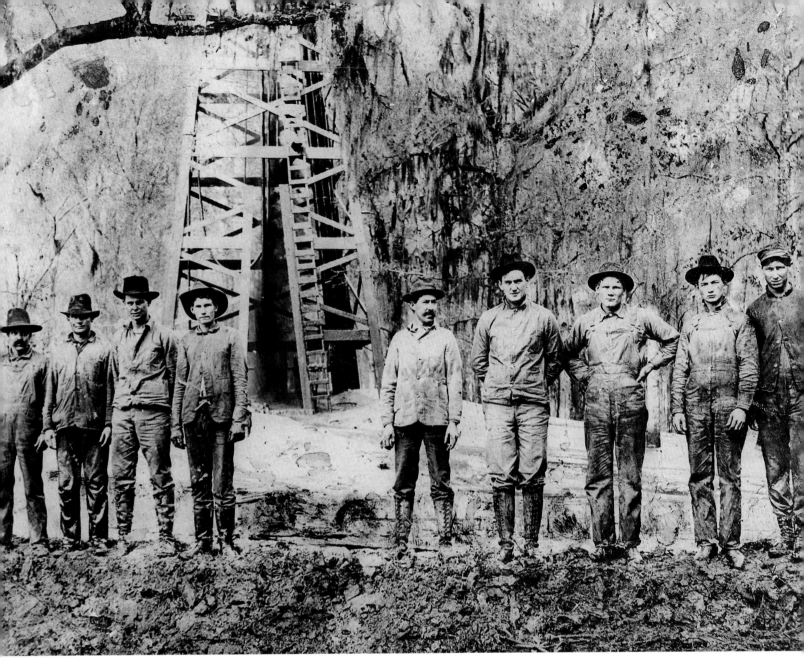

states -- the largest operating area of any independent oil company. It had also begun entering markets overseas.

Expansion continued into the 1920s and early `30s as Texaco enlarged its market territory and pipeline system and became one of the largest U.S. refiners. It proved technological superiority by developing the first offshore drilling barge, combining the portability of a barge with the stability of a permanent derrick.

Texaco also created the Holmes-Manley refining process, the first commercially feasible continuous thermal cracking process to increase the volume of gasoline which could be gleaned from a barrel of oil. Today, Texaco maintains its position as an industry technology leader with such innovations as 3-D vertical-cable seismic imaging and new horizontal drilling techniques and the development of state-of-the-art gasoline such as

CleanSystem[3] and lubricants such as Havoline Formula[3] motor oils.

In 1936, the company established exploration and production interests in the Middle East through a joint venture with Standard Oil of California (now Chevron) in Saudi Arabia, which later became the Arabian American Oil Company (Aramco). Other joint ventures in 1936 which have proved pivotal in the company's success were Caltex Petroleum Corporation, founded through the consolidation of Texaco's marketing facilities east of Suez with the producing and refining interests of Chevron on Bahrain Island in the Middle East, and P.T. Caltex Pacific Indonesia, a company holding concessions in Sumatra. In the process, Texaco became one of the first American oil companies to engage in large-scale, fully integrated operations in the Eastern Hemisphere.

Shown in this picture are members of the drilling crew which drilled and brought in the Fee No. 3 well at Sour Lake, Texas oilfield, the grandaddy of all Texaco producers, in January 1903. They are standing in front of the derrick. A monument stands on the site today.

Above, left: The Texaco brand is a symbol of quality and convenience to motorists around the world.

Above, right: Probing the deep waters of the Gulf of Mexico for oil and gas reserves is a key element of Texaco's growth plan.

Below: Texaco maintains its position as a technology leader with innovations like 3-D vertical-cable seismic imaging and new horizontal drilling techniques.

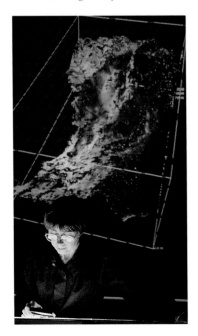

During the post-war era of prosperity, Texaco spent hundreds of millions of dollars for plants and equipment to meet the growing demand for gasoline, lubricants and other petroleum products. It enlarged and upgraded its retail service station chain. And, it invested heavily in pipelines, including the Trans-Arabian Pipeline (TAPLINE), which reduced the distance for shipping Middle Eastern crude to Western Hemisphere refineries by thousands of miles.

In 1984, Texaco acquired Getty Oil Company, more than doubling its liquids reserves, increasing its domestic gas reserves by 45% and adding more than 21 million acres to its worldwide undeveloped exploration holdings. Then in the late 1980s, it teamed up with Saudi Aramco to form Star Enterprise, a Houston-based company which refines, distributes and markets petroleum products under the Texaco brand in 26 East and Gulf Coast states. This provided Saudi Arabia with an outlet for its oil in the U.S., while providing three key refineries with a secure, long-term supply of crude oil.

POSITIONED FOR THE FUTURE

Texaco has come a long way since those early days when only a handful of employees appeared on the company payroll. With assets of more than $25 billion and some 28,000 employees, this Fortune 50 company is among the leaders in industry on a worldwide scale.

Though based in White Plains, N.Y., near America's financial markets, Texaco has a major presence in Houston, not far from its East Texas roots and in proximity to the oil-rich areas of Texas, Louisiana, Oklahoma and the Gulf of Mexico. About 3,000 employees work out of a variety of facilities here.

The success which the company has experienced in the past has provided a firm foundation for the present. For example, Texaco continues to be an industry technology leader through such initiatives as DeepStar, an industry consortium that is developing technology needed to produce oil and gas reserves in the deep waters of the Gulf of Mexico and elsewhere.

One of the company's key accomplishments has been its continued focus on developing and marketing top-of-the-line products. Texaco offers a full range of fuels and lubricants, including CleanSystem^3 gasolines, the family of Havoline Formula^3 motor oils, Havoline Extended Life Antifreeze/Coolants and a full spectrum of commercial and industrial lubricants.

To position itself for the future, in mid-1994 Texaco announced a major growth plan designed to thrust the company into top-quartile performance among petroleum industry competitors. The aggressive plan has focused on asset redeployment, the reduction of overhead and improved operating efficiencies through cost controls and strengthened core businesses. Success of the plan is evidenced by strong returns to shareholders, lower operating costs and a healthy capital budget.

Texaco is poised to enter the next millennium as a financially strong energy company with a bright future, driven by technological excellence, vigorous leadership, highest ethical standards and a commitment to providing superior value to its customers, investors and partners.

As a young oil and gas law attorney unable to get an industry job in the 1950s, when women lawyers were rare, Norma Beasley took a "general flunky" job with a Dallas title insurance company. Attending Southern Methodist University's graduate school of law had been her reason for moving to Dallas, and a primary attraction of the title company job was that it gave her the time to pursue her goal.

Still, taking the menial job was a huge step down at the time. It proved fortuitous, however, for Beasley today owns Safeco Land Title of Dallas and the largest group of independent title operations in the nation.

"The company president promised to teach me the business if I would do whatever needed doing," she recalls. "I found, to my surprise, that I loved the title business." Six years later, at age 28, she headed the company's legal department — though paid just half what her male predecessor had earned.

Later, as executive vice president of a major Dallas title company, Beasley conceived her dream of owning a string of title companies. She saw particular opportunity in the counties surrounding Dallas, where it was often difficult to obtain all but the most basic title services from the existing independent companies.

Her dream excited two friends in the business, accountant Imogene Walker and title abstractor Oscar Jones. "They pushed me to go faster than I probably would have on my own," Beasley said. "They deserve great credit."

The result was Trinity Abstract & Title Co., which opened in Ellis County's county seat, Waxahachie, in late 1965 after the trio laboriously microfilmed and indexed county records at night and on weekends. Walker, who soon became a certified public accountant, remained a partner with Beasley and today is chief financial officer for Safeco Land Title of Dallas and the other eight title companies.

Beasley added five more operations in the ensuing decade, in Rockwall, Kaufman, Hunt, Collin and Denton Counties. By then, her six operations surrounded Dallas County and she decided to tackle a bigger challenge: opening an office in the competitive Dallas market.

The opportunity came in 1979 when she was approached by California-based Safeco Title Insurance Co. to provide attorney closing services for their relatively new Dallas operation. Though the corporation's intent was contracting for specific services, she persuaded its executives to sell their Dallas oper-

Norma Beasley, owner of Safeco Land Title.
PHOTO BY GITTINGS

SAFECO LAND TITLE

ations outright to her and partners Walker and Paul Pulliam.

She calls the Safeco acquisition "lucky Number Seven" that enabled fulfillment of her dream. Beasley today is chief executive officer over nine title companies, most of which operate today under the Safeco Land Title name. Safeco's nearly 300 employees work in 42 branch offices in Dallas County and eight north Texas counties. In addition to being the largest group of independent title operations in the nation, Safeco Land Title is one of the largest woman-owned businesses — of any kind — in the Metroplex.

Safeco is so successful because of its high level of professionalism, experience and willingness to resolve the most complicated title problems of customers. "My partners and associates are the reason for the company's success. I am tremendously fortunate to have wonderful people with me," said Beasley.

After more than 40 years in the title business, Beasley says part of its enduring fascination is that it allows the practice of a broad spectrum of business, corporate and family law to resolve often complicated title issues.

"It's a people business. Real estate represents the majority of the nation's wealth and is the largest single investment for most families," she said. "It's a wonderful way to help people."

The address is 1510 Pacific Avenue, Dallas, Texas 75201. The telephone number is (214) 720-1100.

WALTER P. MOORE AND ASSOCIATES

Few companies have their fingerprints on the underpinnings of Texas as fully as Walter P. Moore and Associates. The Houston-based engineering firm has designed superstructures, foundations and infrastructures from El Paso to Beaumont, from Brownsville to Texarkana. For over 65 years the Moore organization has supported the growth of Texas with premier engineering design for tall buildings, schools, highways, arenas, stadiums,

convention centers, sewer systems and performance centers.

Walter P. Moore, Sr. launched his structural engineering firm in 1931, selling his Stutz Bearcat automobile for capital. His earliest job was designing foundations for homes in the posh River Oaks neighborhood for $10 apiece. But by 1950, he would sign onto a local project that would mark the turning point of Moore's firm: Rice Stadium.

The massive concrete stadium, nestled comfortably between some of Houston's most beautiful tree-lined boulevards, is still regarded as one of the most elegant and functional sports facilities in the country. Although many other more complex engineering projects would follow in Houston and across the country, Walter P. Moore, Jr. still regards Rice Stadium as one of the ground-breaking achievements of Walter P. Moore and Associates because of its scale and enduring importance to the city and to the then-Rice Institute, now known as Rice University.

Walter P. Moore, Sr. was joined in his firm by his namesake son in 1953, and the two worked alongside each other until the elder Moore's death in 1983. During the two decades that followed the construction of Rice Stadium, Walter P. Moore and Associates would serve as structural engineer to most of the major architectural firms in Houston.

Walter P. Moore, Sr. was mentor, collaborator and friend to many local architects who gave Houston its distinctive architectural character.

Moore's finished products stand as a testimony to the evolution of Houston from a small Gulf Coast town to a major urban hub, not the least of which is the Astrodome. The Harris County Domed Stadium would be meticulously designed and revamped by teams of engineers which included Moore in 1961, years before number-crunching computers were in widespread use by engineering firms.

When the domed stadium, dubbed the Eighth Wonder of the World, was finally completed in 1963, observers stood nervously as steel erection towers supporting the roof during construction were removed. The 642-foot clear span domed roof performed beautifully, sagging 1/16-inch less than predicted by the design team. As a structural engineer responsible for the Dome, Walter P. Moore and Associates had performed what other structural engineering firms only dreamed could be accomplished.

The success of the Astrodome helped launch the firm in the heady national world of sports facility design. After completing major arenas and stadiums in El Paso, Beaumont, Waco, Dallas, Galveston, Austin, College Station and Houston, Walter P. Moore and Associates took their sports game on the road. Today the firm is one of the country's leading sports facility designers, with completed or current work in over two dozen cities throughout the U.S.

Walter P. Moore and Associates' designs are the underpinning of most of the Texas Medical Center, now the world's largest health care center. Over the last 46 years, the firm has designed structural systems and infrastructure for more than 60 major buildings for 21 different Texas Medical Center institutions. Milestones include all the buildings in the M.D. Anderson Cancer Center, Texas Children's Hospital, Baylor College of Medicine, Ben Taub Hospital and the original Methodist Hospital and its neurosensory clinic. The firm was also an integral part of the team that designed Houston's Veterans Administration Replacement Medical Center, the world's largest VA hospital.

Space exploration continues to play a prominent role in Houston's economy, and Walter P. Moore and Associates has supported the city's emergence as one of the nation's major centers for the aerospace industry. Design work has included numerous facilities at NASA's Johnson Space Center, notably the Mission Control Building, the

Astronaut Training Building and, most recently, Space Center Houston. Similarly, the firm has designed many of Houston's major governmental and justice buildings, such as the award-winning Harris County Jail, the Harris County Administration Building and Family Law Center and the soon-to-be-built downtown County Justice Center.

As Houston's growth and success fueled more cultural and entertainment facilities, Walter P. Moore and Associates was again called to contribute. The firm's design work on Astroworld, Busch Gardens, Sea World, the Houston Zoo and Fiesta Texas in San Antonio established the firm as a leader in the new world of entertainment design. Today, Walter P. Moore and Associates continues to support Galveston's Moody Gardens, the Houston Museum of Natural Science and the Museum of Fine Arts/Houston with major ongoing expansion programs. Walter P. Moore's elegant design of Moody's Tropical Rain Forest and the new Butterfly House at the Houston Museum of Natural Science have helped cement these buildings as new Houston-area landmarks.

As Texas' economy grew, the Moore practice spread. The firm helped the Dallas/Ft. Worth metroplex boom with such memorable contributions as MBank's 60-story downtown skyscraper, Frito Lay's suburban campus, the Ballpark at Arlington and much of the development in Las Colinas, one of America's most favored corporate addresses. Today the firm continues to contribute to to the area's skyline with the new Fort Worth Performing Arts A\Center and projects at Texas Christian University.

San Antonio, the state's most popular tourist attraction, drew on the firm's expertise for the design of Fiesta Texas and Rivercenter Mall along the River Walk. Currently the firm is helping the city stay competitive in convention and tourism with an $85 million expansion and modernization of Henry B. Gonzalez Convention Center.

In Austin, Texas' seat of political power, Walter P. Moore and Associates has made a lasting impression. Since designing Frank Erwin Center in the mid-1970s, the firm has contributed to the design of over a quarter billion dollars of state buildings, including the Supreme Court building and the recent underground expansion of the historic State of Texas Capitol Building.

Moore's world for the major university systems has taken the firm to campuses throughout the state. The firm has completed major projects for Texas A&M University in College Station, Laredo, Corpus Christi and Prairie View and for the University of Texas system in Austin, Galveston, Houston, Tyler and Edinburg. Current and recent projects include a new state of the art Student Recreation Center, the soon-to-open George Bush Presidential Library and Archives, and a new 12,500-seat sports arena, all on the College Station campus of TAMU. The firm is also helping the University of Texas prepare for entry into the Big 12 Conference with an improvement and expansion program at Memorial Stadium in Austin.

Recognizing the need to diversify, the firm branched out to civil engineering services in the mid-'60s, designing roadways, utility and water systems and drainage structures throughout Houston and Texas. The firm was often called upon by the City of Houston, Metropolitan Transit Authority of Harris County, Dallas County and other agencies to assist in dealing with its mobility challenges through traffic analyses and designs. Moore's designs have sped the city's traffic and made parking easier in many of the city's major employment centers, including the Texas Medical Center, Greenspoint, Greenway Plaza, Uptown Houston and downtown Houston. Taking that experience a step further, the firm was commissioned to complete a high-profile traffic improvement and graphic identity program for the world-famous Galleria area, complete with signposts, utility relocation and traffic improvements. The results -- a striking combination of stainless steel arches, light poles and signage -- has created yet another memorable landmark in Houston.

In many ways, the rise of Walter P. Moore and Associates as one of Houston's best-established structural, civil and traffic engineering firms reflects the growth of the City of Houston itself. As Texas has grown, expanded and reached out to a global market, so has Walter P. Moore and Associates. With regional offices in Dallas, Tampa and Atlanta, the 65-year-old Houston-based firm has completed work in 35 states and 13 countries to date.

For the last 25 years, the quality of Walter P. Moore's design work has been consistently recognized with state and national awards, including Texas' highest award for engineering excellence in four consecutive years, from 1990 to 1993.

Ray Messer was named president of Walter P. Moore and Associates in 1993 and has guided the firm's transition from a family-owned and operated business to a modern organization with broad horizons and diverse ownership. The firm is poised to support Texas, literally, as it continues to grow, change and prosper in the 21st Century.

MOBIL

In 1866, just seven years after oil was discovered, a perceptive young grocer realized that an excellent lubricant existed in the slick residue remaining after vacuum distilling crude oil for kerosene. He and a partner formed the Vacuum Oil Company in their home town of Rochester, N.Y., initially concentrating on manufacturing lubricants for tanning harness leather.

From that tiny beginning, the company that became today's Mobil Corporation burgeoned into one of the world's largest corporations, with operations in more than 100 countries.

Texas has been a crucial part of Mobil since the earliest days of the state's oil industry. Its Texas heritage traces to the 1898 founding of Magnolia Petroleum Co., in which a Mobil predecessor purchased part-interest in 1918 and fully acquired in 1926.

Mobil's Texas investments befit its deep roots in the state, with key divisions here that support the corporation's global operations. Indeed, Mobil's giant refinery in Beaumont is the company's largest.

Mobil Exploration & Producing U.S. Inc. (MEPUS) oversees the exploration and production aspects of Mobil's U.S. operations. Formed in 1987 to consolidate three U.S. exploration and production units, MEPUS manages a large and diverse asset base — much of which is located in Texas.

Headquartered in Dallas, MEPUS directs Midland and Houston operations. Midland coordinates Permian Basin operations, which include many waterflood and CO2 injection projects, as well as significant levels of gas production. Houston manages properties in Louisiana, east and south Texas and Oklahoma, plus properties operated by other companies.

MEPUS is known as an innovator. One highly successful strategy, for example, uses an Enhanced Oil Recovery/CO2 process to target light oil reserves in west Texas and Oklahoma.

While developing and expanding its reserve base, MEPUS focuses on managing efficient and successful operations. In Texas alone, MEPUS produces oil at an average rate of 46 million barrels per day and natural gas at an average of 376 million cubic feet per day.

Designed to apply new technology swiftly to MEPUS' needs, the Mobil Exploration & Producing Technical Center (MEPTEC) provides worldwide research, development and technical support of Mobil's exploration and producing activities.

Based in Dallas, MEPTEC manages a state-of-the-art laboratory complex that uses leading-edge computer capabilities. Its technologists span the vast range of exploration and producing disciplines, encompassing geology, geophysics and engineering. Four divisions comprise MEPTEC: Geosciences, Subsurface Production Engineering, Surface Production Engineering, and Technology Application and Data Management Systems.

Mobil's Beaumont Refinery, built in 1902, played a crucial role in ensuring Beaumont's leading position in the Texas — and eventually the world's — petrochemical industry.

The largest and most complex plant in Mobil's worldwide refining system, the Beaumont Refinery occupies approximately 1,200 acres along the Neches River in Jefferson County. That vast span, measuring two miles long by one mile wide, encompasses more than 30 processing units. The plant can refine 325,000 barrels per day of crude oil and a total input of 450,000 barrels a day.

The Beaumont Refinery's products fuel the modern world. It makes all grades of gasoline, home heating oil, highway diesel fuel, petroleum feedstocks, household and industrial waxes, kerosene, sulfur, liquid petroleum gas, petroleum coke, base stocks for lubricants, jet fuel, and marine fuel oil. Refinery products are shipped by pipeline, barge, tanker, rail and truck, to be distributed throughout the world.

Mobil Chemical Company has become one of the world's top petrochemical manufacturers, with significant investments in three Beaumont and Houston facilities that take

advantage of strategic opportunities in growing petrochemicals markets. These plants produce the raw materials for an array of consumer products, including plastics, antifreeze, clothing fibers, synthetic lubricants, paints and pharmaceuticals.

A key product produced at one of the Beaumont facilities, ethylene, is the world's largest primary petrochemical in volume, number of derivatives and sales value. Mobil has expanded and modernized its production facilities repeatedly since 1961, when the first Beaumont ethylene unit was streamed.

A new grassroots aromatics plant in Beaumont will help Mobil Chemical become the world's largest merchant marketer of paraxylene (a raw material used to make polyester). Also located in Beaumont is Mobil's Chemical Specialty plant that manufactures ZSM-5 catalyst, used in many petrochemical manufacturing processes around the globe.

Mobil's Houston olefins plant has undergone steady improvements during the past decade to sharply increase ethylene and propylene production.

Mobil Pipe Line Company's long and colorful history in Texas traces to Magnolia Pipe Line Co., an arm of Magnolia Petroleum Company. The company began with a small network of pipelines serving Magnolia's original Corsicana refinery, built in 1898. Its pipelines grew to traverse Texas and extend into the Gulf of Mexico.

For many years, Magnolia Pipe Line's headquarters were in the landmark Magnolia Building in downtown Dallas, home of the "flying red horse." It was renamed Mobil Pipe Line Company in 1966 and moved to its current Renaissance Tower location in 1977.

Mobil Pipe Line owns about 7,000 miles of common carrier pipeline in Texas and other states, transporting 600 thousands of barrels per day (TBD) of crude oil, 350 TBD of refined products and 115 TBD of natural gas. They are controlled and monitored by the Pipe Line Oil Control Center in Dallas. It also shares joint ownership in numerous other pipelines, including two of the world's largest, Colonial Pipeline and the Trans Alaska Pipeline.

Providing sales and distribution for Mobil's regional interests is the Texas and Louisiana Sales & Distribution unit, which sells more than 500 million gallons of Mobil brand gasoline and 30 million gallons of diesel fuel in the two states each year.

These are sold through Mobil's company-operated stations, lessees and independent dealers, as well as other distributors. Mobil's "Friendly Serve" was implemented in October 1995, providing personalized customer service to consumers and creating more than 400 new jobs.

The Mobil Business Resources Corporation encompasses support organizations providing services to Mobil's business units. Those with a Texas presence are: Global Procurement, Real Estate and Global Facilities, Financial Operations Center, Human Resources, Office of Legal Counsel, Environmental, Health and Safety Global Professional Services, Global Aircraft Services, Global Security, Global Medical and Public Affairs.

Like so many companies today, Mobil is undergoing restructuring. Texas, however, will remain fundamental well into the coming century. "If you look at the distribution of Mobil people in the U.S., Texas has one of the largest concentrations of Mobil employees," said Tim Felt, vice president of Mobil Pipe Line. "Texas plays a prominent role in the corporation and likely will do so far into the future."

WALTER OIL & GAS CORPORATION

Walter Oil & Gas Corporation ranks among the top independent oil companies operating in the energy-rich waters of the Gulf of Mexico. Thanks to its financial strength, technical expertise and pioneer spirit, this Houston enterprise is one of the most prolific natural gas producers in the Gulf, and it consistently places among the top 20 companies in wells drilled there annually.

WOGC's history dates back to 1981, when Houston Oil and Minerals Corp., which was founded by J. C. Walter, Jr., merged with Tenneco. Walter's industry track record enabled him to raise money from pension funds and other investors that he needed to launch a new enterprise: Walter Oil & Gas Corporation.

Petroleum prices plummeted just after Walter set up shop. Though that spelled disaster for companies that had borrowed or invested heavily during the boom days, well-capitalized ventures like WOGC were able to acquire leases that major oil companies were farming out to cut their domestic operating costs.

Initially, WOGC focused its efforts inland along the Texas-Louisiana coast. Then in 1984, it became one of the first independents to begin operating in the Gulf.

"That enabled us to build strong working relationships with the majors before our competitors could," says J. C. "Rusty" Walter III, who joined his father's company in 1982 and serves as its president and chief executive officer.

Expanding its operations, WOGC formed gas and oil trading companies in 1988 and 1990. Then as rising energy prices increased competition in the Gulf, in 1990 WOGC became one of the first independents to explore internationally.

"We employed the same strategy that had worked for us in the Gulf," Walter recalls. "We sought opportunities that were too small for the majors to pursue profitably."

Today, WOGC and its affiliates have some 60 employees. The company owns, wholly or in part, and operates over 100 producing wells that yield about 450 million cubic feet of gas equivalent a day.

Walter attributes this success in part to the company's entrepreneurial spirit. "We're risk takers. We're willing to try new things," he notes.

"Since we're not a public company, we can make decisions based on economics rather than on public market evaluations," he adds. "We can react quickly when opportunities arise."

WOGC prides itself on its ability to find oil and gas consistently at a lower-than-average cost per barrel or cubic foot. As Walter explains, "We've been profitable at times when others were struggling."

Over the years, the company has assembled a team of highly qualified geologists, geophysicists and engineers. That expertise plus the use of such advanced technology as 3D seismic have contributed to WOGC's success as well. In addition, the company contributed to the development and use of subsea production systems, which represented a major advancement in offshore technology.

In the last 15 years, Walter says, WOGC has built a firm foundation for further expansion and growth and is well-positioned to take advantage of opportunities as they arise. It already has moved into the Gulf's deeper waters, increasing its risks and costs, he adds. But as he concludes, "We're not afraid of taking risk—as long as we can reap the rewards."

*McKittrick Canyon, Guadalupe Mountains
National Park*

PHOTO BY LEROY WILLIAMSON

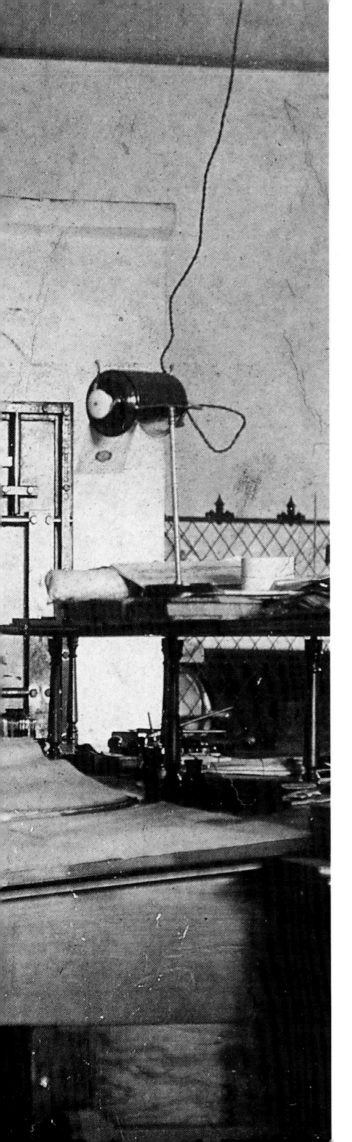

BANKING & FINANCE

investment banking

and securities brokerage

provide the financial foundation

for a host of Texas enterprises

Wettermark Bank, Nacogdoches, Texas.

FIRST VALLEY BANK

On June 1, 1995, FirstBank Group, Inc., and Raymondville State Bancshares, Inc., formally merged as First Valley Bank Group, Inc. The merger brought together FirstBank and First Valley Bank, combining the resources of two of the Rio Grande Valley's oldest banks and creating one of the Valley's largest locally-owned banking systems. Designated as First Valley Bank -- "The Valley's Bank," the network of community banks emerged with total assets exceeding $351 million as of June 30, 1995, and fifteen banking locations in three counties. By July 1, 1996, First Valley Bank had grown to exceed $420 million in assets and to include 19 banking locations. With added locations in Harlingen (Dixieland Rd.) and in Pharr (the former Security State Bank) and new locations in Weslaco and Mission, First Valley Bank has a growing recognition as being "The Valley's Bank".

First Valley Bank is a lineal descendant of Raymondville State Bank, chartered in 1907, and Los Fresnos State Bank, chartered in 1928.

The bank originated in the land rush following the arrival of the St. Louis, Brownsville and Mexico Railroad (now part of Union Pacific) in the Valley in 1904. Among the landseekers was Charles Henry Pease (attorney, banker and first Winter Texan), formerly associated with the Flushing, Michigan Bank, an institution largely owned by Ira Sayre and a man named Packard. The Packard organization, seeking to expand its interests, agreed to back Pease in the establishment of a bank in the recently formed Raymondville settlement.

Soon after arriving, Pease met Colonel E.B. Raymond, who was developing the town (Raymondville-named after Col. Raymond), and William F. Sprague, a prominent rancher who also participated in railroad development. After they agreed to subscribe for new bank stock, Pease met with major shareholders of First National Bank in Brownsville who subscribed to the remaining shares.

On January 31, 1907, Raymondville State Bank, capitalized at $10,000 was organized. Ten of the first hundred shares were owned by Ira T. Sayre of the Packard Group in Michigan, with the balance owned by ranchers and businessmen between Corpus Christi and Brownsville. Directors were Col. Raymond, Sprague, Judge James B. Wells, Jr., William Kelly, Pease, Marcus Phillips, Robert J. Kleberg (of King Ranch), Charles H. Flato, Jr., S.L. Dworman and B.J. Frazier.

The bank's articles of incorporation were filed with the Texas Secretary of State on March 1, 1907. Five days later the bank opened in temporary headquarters in the Raymondville Lumber Yard Company, using the lumber company's safe as a vault. A pine shelf with a wooden grill served as the first teller window. Colonel E.B. Raymond was president with William F. Sprague, vice president, and Charles Henry Pease, cashier. By the end of the first day, the bank had fourteen accounts totaling $5,624.90, and by the end of the first week, it reported $10,000.

While Raymondville State Bank provided financial services to northern Cameron County (which was later changed to Willacy County), a new bank in Los Fresnos was helping the agricultural community of central Cameron County. Southern Pacific followed the St. Louis, Brownsville and Mexico Railroad, arriving in Los Fresnos in 1927, augmenting an already booming land and agricultural business in the area. Juan G. Fernandez, whose family had owned the land since colonial times, was president of First National Bank of Brownsville. He decided to center the newly-established Los Fresnos near the tracks to best serve the farming community in shipping cotton, citrus and vegetables.

Since the farming community needed financial services, Alfred N. Tandy, one of the area's leading growers, led a movement to establish a bank in Los Fresnos. Tandy had come to the Valley in 1907 from Meridian, Texas, with his wife, Louella, and sons, Cleve and Clyde, to take advantage of the land boom.

The Tandy effort to open a bank was supported by H.C. Aldridge, whose Aldridge-Washmon Company was a leading implement dealer in Cameron County, and E.C. Couch, a prominent land developer in eastern

Los Fresnos State Bank, chartered in 1928.

Raymondville State Bank, chartered in 1907.

Hidalgo County. The new institution, chartered as Los Fresnos State Bank, opened in October 1928 with Alfred N. Tandy, president; E.C. Couch, vice president; and Nolan Taylor, cashier. Other original organizers and stockholders were John [Juan] Fernandez, Clyde Tandy, Cleve G. Tandy, Aldridge, and W.L. Forbes.

The timing of the bank's organization was not ideal. The stock market crash of 1929 and ensuing Depression threatened Los Fresnos State Bank's existence. However, the bank continued operations despite the failure of many other Valley financial institutions and the unpredictable effects of the weather. In 1931, a potato blight ruined the crop. The following year, a freeze crippled the citrus industry. A third disaster struck in 1933 when a ruinous hurricane landed in the Valley.

By 1935, the discouraging financial climate threatened Los Fresnos State Bank with closure. Cleve Tandy personally assumed operations. With an additional investment of Capital and personal guarantees, the Tandy family prevented possible failure. The family's reputation maintained confidence among the depositors.

Ura Breedlove joined the bank in 1935. The husband of Cleve Tandy's first cousin, Helen Tandy, he served as the bank's only teller, bookkeeper, cashier and secretary of the board at $100 a month. With the ailing A.N. Tandy and Cleve Tandy, Ura Breedlove kept the bank operating for many years and built a reputation of integrity and service.

Ura Breedlove was one of three brothers who eventually became synonymous with banking in the eastern end of the Valley. A second brother, H.C. (Cleo), worked his way up through the ranks at Raymondville State Bank, ultimately becoming president. The third brother, E.C., worked for many years with Raymondville State Bank before becoming president of the former First National Bank of Harlingen. Thus, through the Breedlove family, a rapport was established between Los Fresnos State Bank and Raymondville State Bank long before any consideration was given to a merger.

The Second World War revitalized the economy of both the nation and the area's banks. As the "History of FirstBank" notes, "The war effort needed the backing of the agricultural community and the farmers were again in business".

The Breedlove's rose in the banking community in the 1940s. When Cleve Tandy succeeded his father as president in 1944, Ura Breedlove became vice president and cashier.

On January 4, 1947, Cleo was named a director of Raymondville State Bank and, eight months later,

became vice president and cashier. E.C. became assistant cashier. In Los Fresnos in 1949, Cleve Tandy's promotion to chairman of the board raised Ura to chief executive officer. With Tandy's retirement in 1951, Ura Breedlove succeeded him to become president and CEO.

Meanwhile, Raymondville State Bank prospered. In 1960, the bank moved to its present location at 400 W. Hidalgo. With Cleo Breedlove's elevation to the presidency in 1964, G.L. McDonald became vice president. McDonald later resigned and was succeeded by John A. Calkins on December 14, 1965. On Cleo Breedlove's death in 1969, Calkins became the 5th president. John A. Calkins served as president until 1988 when he was elected Chairman of the Board/CEO and C. Michael Scott became president (the fourth generation Scott to take part in bank management of Raymondville State Bank).

Calkins feels he is fortunate that, when he assumed the leadership of the bank, he worked with mature, solid, experienced directors and good managers. The directors allowed the managers to run the bank while overseeing the operation.

The 1970s and '80s were exhilarating years for Valley banking. The oil boom in Mexico and the stable peso brought extensive Mexican investment, particularly in real estate. Additionally, state and federal banking policies allowed the establishment of more banks with less capitalization than was traditionally required. By the late 1970s, however, the bottom started to fall out of the oil industry and Mexico-oriented businesses ran into trouble. In the 1980s, as the move toward deregulation accelerated, there was a strong push toward consolidated banking. In both Los Fresnos and Raymondville, the banking community began adjusting for a new era which would leave financial institutions either stronger or in ruins.

First Valley Bank, Raymondville facility as it appears today.

At Los Fresnos State Bank, Ura Breedlove's son, Cleve, used experience gained from managing banks in the Western United States to thrive during the changes in Texas banking. After finishing college, Cleve joined People's National Bank, a 55-branch institution headquartered in Washington State.

"The West Coast opened my eyes to progressive banking," he recalled. "I could see the time when we [in Texas] would have branch banking, and where there would be some advance through holding companies."

First Valley Bank, Los Fresnos facility as it appears today.

With that experience, Cleve T. Breedlove joined Los Fresnos State Bank as vice president in October 1970, three months before his father's death.

"When I came on board, all the directors, who had been through the depression, were peers of my father," he remembered. He said their background and experience allowed them to be innovative without being careless as the bank explored ways to provide services outside of traditional banking.

Guided by R.B. (Ray) Stewart, who succeeded Ura Breedlove as president, one of Cleve T. Breedlove's first moves in 1971 was to computerize the bookkeeping system, replacing the old "Boston Ledger" system; and to introduce drive-thru banking in 1973. Upon Stewart's retirement in 1975, the board elevated the newest Breedlove banker to the presidency. Six years after becoming president, Cleve T. Breedlove formed Fresnos Bancshares, Inc., a one-bank holding company which gave Los Fresnos State Bank more flexibility, allowing it to acquire more capital. In 1984 it was able to purchase Sunrise Bank, a five-year-old Brownsville institution with deposits of $32 million and a staff of 40. Breedlove also organized FirstBank of Port Isabel, which opened in January 1985.

Meanwhile, in Willacy County, Raymondville State Bank's officers and directors were preparing for a new era while striving to serve the traditional farming community. In 1982, approval was granted for Raymondville State Bancshares, Inc., to become a holding company. The bank was also involved in a $1.2 million remodeling and modernization of its building, completed in 1986.

During the 1980s, the Mexican economic collapse continued to spill over into the Valley. Examiners forced

banks to write off billions of dollars in uncollectible loans. The result was that less capitalized banks began to fail.

Texas banking was beginning to modernize, and restrictions were being lifted. Among the changes occurring in the fall of 1986 was a lifting of the constitutional restriction prohibiting banks to cross county lines. This amendment coincided with the failure of Citizens State Bank of Donna. Raymondville State Bank's bid for the failed institution was accepted by the Federal Deposit Insurance Corporation. With this acquisition, Raymondville State Bank became the first bank in Texas to cross a county line.

While other banks in the Valley continued to fail, Raymondville State Bank and Los Fresnos State Bank survived and grew.

"We had seasoned directors [in Los Fresnos] who set reasonable standards, and didn't get loose and overly competitive," Breedlove explained. "We tried to offer consistent, conservative service and remain focused on the needs of the community."

In 1987, Fresnos Bancshares became FirstBank Group, Inc., and the three subsidiary banks — Los Fresnos State Bank, Sunrise Bank and FirstBank of Port Isabel — were renamed FirstBank. In that year, Data processing was modernized with an in-house computer system, and Valley National Bank of Harlingen was added to the group. In 1988, all four banks merged into a single institution with four locations, which ultimately developed into additional locations in Rio Hondo, South Padre Island, Rancho Viejo and Harlingen.

Raymondville State Bank also survived the '80s. Calkins states it was because it "continued to serve the community with local loans. The loan demand was not great, but they were good, solid loans, which allowed us to expand, add shareholder value and protect our investors". As approved by the Board of Directors on March 19, 1991, Raymondville State Bank became First Valley Bank to emphasize that it was not only the first bank in the Valley since 1907 but also served the Valley with branches in Pharr and McAllen in addition to those in Raymondville and Donna.

The emerging bank has more resources, is better positioned to offer convenience, products, and service to customers, and is committed to being "The Valley's Bank". The community-oriented banking tradition of both Raymondville State Bank and Los Fresnos State Bank has been carried over to the present First Valley Bank.

"We consider ourselves a network of community banks," Breedlove explained. "We are strong on people from those communities to serve those communities."

On March 18, 1852, westward-looking New Yorkers Henry Wells and William George Fargo formed Wells, Fargo & Co. to offer Gold Rush Californians banking and the rapid delivery of treasure and letters. Express agencies in general stores, drug stores, and elsewhere, along with Wells Fargo's interstate banks in Oregon, Nevada, Utah, Idaho, and New York, supplied "Anytime, Anywhere Banking"™. The Company was indeed "the omnipresent, universal business agent" of the West, as a traveler reported in the mid-1860s, when Wells Fargo's stagecoach lines connected Nebraska to California and the states in between.

Stagecoaching brought Wells Fargo to the Lone Star State. It was one of four express firms forming the Overland Mail Company, which between 1858 and 1861, carried mail between Missouri and California, by way of "the wilds of Texas," according to one passenger. Twenty years later, Wells Fargo crossed Texas by railroad to become the first express to offer "Ocean to Ocean" service. Agents sent money primarily, but armadillos and agriculture, cotton and Corsicana fruitcake also went by express. When Wells, Fargo & Co's Express joined American Railway Express in 1918, it operated one thousand Texas offices.

Meantime in San Francisco, Wells, Fargo & Co's Bank merged with Nevada National Bank (1905), Union Trust Company (1923), American Trust Company (1960), and The Crocker Bank (1986). "Our ambition is not to be the largest bank," Wells Fargo's president declared in 1918, "but to be the soundest and the best." Good banking preserved Wells Fargo during numerous financial panics. On April 1, 1996, Wells Fargo bought First Interstate Bank, entering nine other Western states: Wells Fargo is back in Texas!

In mid-1996, Wells Fargo holds $109 billion in assets, while 52,000 employees serve 11 million Western households through 2,000 branches and 4,500 Automated Teller Machines. "Technology facilitates good service," CEO Paul Hazen emphasizes. Wells Fargo is pioneering "electronic cash" and the payment of funds on the Internet, while seven telephone banking centers (one near Dallas) serve customers 24 hours daily. Demonstrating its historical flexibility, Wells Fargo has moved beyond traditional branches to place half of 1,200 California offices in eight of the state's top ten supermarkets. "We're like a jaguar" in action, Hazen quipped, and the vast increase in shareholder value proves his point.

As "The Oldest Bank in the West"™ Wells Fargo blends old with new. In California, five historical museums welcome worldwide visitors, while around the West, millions of people see the Wells Fargo Stagecoach on parade. The Concord Coach, says Hazen, is "a link to Western history that symbolizes a tradition of innovation, technology leadership, customer service, and dependability."

A Wells Fargo coach leads a parade past the company's office in Houston in 1912.
PHOTO FROM THE WELLS FARGO ARCHIVES.

Henry Wells (left) and William George Fargo (right)
PHOTOS FROM THE WELLS FARGO ARCHIVES.

FIRST VICTORIA NATIONAL BANK

A reliable system for banking was essential to the success of the rugged farm and ranch communities of early Texas, and for the City of Victoria, First Victoria National Bank provided that service.

Located approximately 100 miles southeast of San Antonio, Victoria is a South Texas town rich in heritage. What is now one of the state's thriving mid-sized cities was once Nuestra Senora de Guadalupe de Jesus Victoria, established by empresario Martín DeLeon in 1824. After the Texas Revolution ended in 1836, the community, at one time known as the City of Roses, was simply known as Victoria.

Victoria's roots come from its immigrant families. In fact, First Victoria National Bank is still directed by members of some of the pioneer ranching families that laid the foundation for the rock-solid institution well over a century ago.

To that list of Victoria's pioneers can be added the name of John Milton Brownson, who founded Brownson's Bank, now called First Victoria National Bank. Brownson established the first bank in the town of Victoria in 1867. At the time, the population was recorded at 2,000 residents, and the city also served as a stopover between the Lavaca Bay port and final destinations such as San Antonio, Austin and northern Mexico.

Within a decade, Brownson was joined by Eugene Sibley, creating a bank known as Brownson and Sibley. Already, the city was a stop on the San Antonio and Mexican Gulf Railroad.

In the 129 years that have followed its inception, First Victoria National Bank, once known as "The Cattleman's Bank," has evolved with the times, initiating many of the banking services current-day residents of Victoria take for granted. First Victoria National Bank was the first in Victoria to offer drive-in banking in 1959, and the first to provide a mini-bank in 1975. As the city grew, the bank broadened its services to eventually add two additional branches in Victoria County. In the summer of 1996, the bank's first branch outside the county, in Port Lavaca, was opened for business.

Although the two prime founders of First Victoria National Bank were born in other states, by the time they joined forces John Milton Brownson and Eugene Sibley were both Texan by nature. Brownson moved to DeWitt County with his parents from Illinois in 1852. By the time he formed Victoria's first bank, he had already served in the Civil War as a private in the Confederate Army, bearing the wounds of the Battle of Shiloh. Brownson's calvary regiment was commonly known as Terry's Texas Rangers, and the future Victoria leader did not consider his service to

the Confederacy done until the war ended in 1865.

After the Civil War, Brownson returned to DeWitt County. Shortly thereafter he relocated to the booming South Texas town of Victoria and opened the town's first bank. The original banking establishment was called Brownson's Bank and the year was 1867.

In 1883, the red-brick Brownson Building was built in the 100 block of North Main Street to hold the bank. Today, the original building site is a row of businesses, some with old facades and some remodeled. When Brownson was named president of Second National Bank in San Antonio, Sibley took the reins as bank vice president, overseeing the day-to-day operations of the bank while Brownson served as president of the Victoria bank from San Antonio until 1905, the year prior to his death. Sibley, an Alabama native, had moved to Victoria soon after the Civil War to help his brothers, Origin and Frank, operate a steam mill. As Brownson moved north, Sibley continued to be a faithful steward of the bank. Records indicate Sibley left Victoria in 1906 and died in San Antonio in 1911.

First National Bank of Victoria served as the cattleman's lifeline by providing much-needed capital. When the Organization Certificate creating the First National Bank of Victoria was issued in December, 1889, the bank had 22 shareholders. The number of shareholders showed the strength of the bank, which was considered an asset to both Victoria and the region. The capital stock of the new financial institution was $150,000, a sizable amount at the time.

According to the bank's original records, the first cashier of the First National Bank of Victoria was Theodore Buhler, a German immigrant who had worked for both railroads and a steamship company. By 1889, the bank was issuing its own currency. Still in the era of the gold standard, the notes would be issued by First National Bank of Victoria against the institution's assets. The bank's assets steadily grew.

The history of First Victoria National Bank runs rich with the area's cattle heritage. Past presidents and directors of the bank include John James

Welder and James Francis Welder, both of the famous Welder clan. The Welder family originally immigrated to Texas from Germany to establish a ranching empire of several thousand acres. The efforts of former bank director Clarence St. Elmo Holland created the Gulf Intracoastal Waterway, essential to barge travel from the Mississippi River to the Texas Gulf Coast.

Other distinguished Victoria residents who oversaw the bank's operations included Alfred Brown Peticolos, a local attorney and director for the bank, who wrote the Index Digest of Civil and Criminal Law of Texas, which for many years was the standard text used by the Texas Bar Association. Allen Minor McFaddin, another former director, was a cattleman and rancher who was also one of the founders of the Texas and Southwestern Cattle Raisers Association.

Former chairman of the board Martin O'Connor was a member of one of the area's earliest families, who came to Victoria from Ireland in 1833. Another chairman of the board, Claude McCan, was a rancher and cattle breeder who served as chairman of the Production and Marketing Administration during the 1950s. He also developed a Hereford-Brahman cross-breed known as the Victoria Breed.

In the past nine decades, First Victoria National Bank has grown through determination, as well as the faith of the bank's leaders in the people and economy of South Texas.

It would not be until 1963 that the bank would alter its name from Victoria National Bank to First Victoria National Bank. Today the bank's location constitutes an entire city block, running from Main to Bridge Street downtown only one block away from its original location. A staff of 250 employees— a far cry from the early days of Theodore Buhler— now run the bank's various branches.

As First Victoria National Bank pioneered new ways of banking in South Texas, the financial institution was known for its conservative lending practices. During the Panic of 1907, First Victoria National Bank was one of the few banking establishments in the nation solvent enough to put no limits on withdrawal of deposits. Through the difficult struggle of the Great Depression, the bank continued its normal operations until President Franklin D. Roosevelt ordered the closure of all U.S. Banks. When First Victoria National Bank was permitted to reopen, it did so without being burdened with the restriction laid down for many of the nation's banks. The citizens of Victoria knew their money was safe at First Victoria National Bank.

The growth of First Victoria National Bank can be marked by its expansions. Since the purchase of the John J. Welder Building in 1928, the bank has renovated and expanded every 20 years or so, including a major exterior renovation in 1937, a $1 million addition in 1959 and the addition of a mini-bank and drive-in in 1975. In 1980, First Victoria National Bank completed a three-and-a-half year expansion project that doubled the bank's size, from 40,000 square feet to 80,000 square feet. A convenient four-story parking garage was constructed adjacent to the bank. In addition to the downtown bank, First Victoria National Bank has added two additional branch offices in Victoria: Colony Creek and North Branch.

As proof of its growth, First Victoria National Bank recently opened a location in Port Lavaca, the fourth full-service location for First Victoria National Bank and the bank's first full-service office outside Victoria County. As of June 1996, the bank had assets totaling $437 million, making it one of the largest independent banks in South Texas.

Moving into the next century has meant new ventures for First Victoria National Bank, such as expanding the Trust and Investment Services division of the bank with a special emphasis on employee benefit plans, asset management and investment management. Along with an expanding discount brokerage service, First Victoria National Bank has developed new deposit products such as First Free Checking, Cash Management and the Investor Sweep Account. A recognition of technology has led the bank to enhance its 24-hour bank-by-phone service and unveil a new "home page" on the Internet.

In the last 100 years, Victoria has grown from a small ranching community to a mid-sized Texas city of more than 58,000. Encouraged by the bank to be active in its community, employees contribute their time to some 84 local clubs and agencies, including the state's "Adopt a Highway" program. Hoping to strengthen their community, employees recently completed the construction of a home through Habitat for Humanity. The bank regularly participates in the Victoria Livestock Show, which raises scholarships for deserving students. As First Victoria National Bank moves into a new millennium, it will carry forward the tradition of building lasting relationships through quality financial services.

John Milton Brownson was born in Illinois on December 20, 1836. He came to Texas with his parents, Theron and Agnes J. Brownson, in 1852. They settled in DeWitt County, where John's father operated a general store.

At the outset of the Civil War Brownson enlisted in Terry's Texas Rangers. He remained with the Eighth Texas Cavalry Regiment for the duration of the war. Brownson settled in Victoria in 1866. In 1867 he opened Brownson's Bank, the town's first banking establishment.

He is remembered as an entrepreneur, philanthropist, community leader and pioneer banker. Brownson Street bears his name, as did the first school building built by the Victoria Independent School District in 1910. Also named for him is the Brownson Home for Youth.

First Victoria National Bank

COASTAL SECURITIES

Executive staff, left to right, Frank J. Klaus; David J. Master; Christopher L. LaPorte and R. Dwayne Whitehead.

In 1990 David J. Master was a man with a vision. Having served as President and CEO of a major broker/dealer, he desired to organize and build from the ground floor a unique financial services firm located in Houston that could eventually become known as the premier regional investment banking firm in the nation. With that desire, he founded Coastal Securities, L.P. (originally Coastal Securities Corporation) in 1991. The principals of the firm have a long history of business success in the regional securities markets and have been employed in the business for an average of over twenty years.

Coastal Securities L.P. (Coastal) has developed leadership roles in several specialized markets and initially focused in the areas of financial advisory services for municipalities, municipal underwriting, sales and trading of fixed income taxable and tax-exempt securities, NASDAQ over-the-counter (OTC) market making, funds advisory services, distressed securities analysis, and cash flow management through its proprietary portfolio analysis tool called CoastalView.

The fixed income marketplace is the critical component of the capital formation process for financing our nation's infrastructure. Coastal proudly participates in nationally syndicated underwritings on a regular basis

and was involved with over $6 billion in underwritings for Texas municipalities alone from 1993 through 1995. Coastal was also honored by being selected as the financial adviser for Harris County (Houston), Texas in 1995.

In May 1996, Coastal made a huge jump forward in time by joining forces and operations with another well known Houston broker/dealer, Government Securities Corporation (GSC). This combination enabled Coastal to double its capital base and number of employees and become the largest regional broker/dealer domiciled in Houston, Texas. With this added staffing, capital, and expertise, Coastal is even better prepared to offer its clients the best in investment services available now and well into the twenty-first century.

GSC was founded in 1979 by Christopher LaPorte. Having relocated to Houston after graduating from the University of Tennessee Law School and passing the Tennessee Bar exam, he was eager to chart a career path. The company's initial objective was to establish a secondary market for U. S. Small Business Administration (SBA) guaranteed loans. The SBA was established by the federal government to support the country's small businesses, the backbone of our nation's economy. The SBA 7(a) loan guaranty program provides long term financing for these small businesses not normally available through conventional commercial lending channels. Displaying the innovative thinking which would become a company trademark, GSC was among the first brokerage firms in the country to specialize in the purchase and sale of adjustable rate SBA loans. A good indicator of its success in this market was the company's position in 1995 as the third largest pool assembler for SBA guaranteed loans in the country. Overall, through fiscal 1995, GSC had ranked first among all SBA pool assemblers in volume issued since the inception of the pooling program in 1985.

Today, Coastal continues to maintain a large presence in the SBA market. Coastal is also a leading market maker for loans guaranteed by the Farmers Home Administration (FmHA) [now RECD], the Agency for International Development (AID), and the National Oceanic and Atmospheric Administration (NOAA). GSC had traded over $500 million in AID loans since 1990 and provided financing for the first-ever AID loan to South Africa in 1995 as well as the first

OPIC loan to a joint venture between U.S. and Russian corporations.

Coastal clears its securities transactions and holds its customer accounts for safekeeping at Pershing, a division of Donaldson, Lufkin and Jenrette Securities Corporation. Its customers enjoy $50 million in account insurance protection. Coastal's customers include banks, credit unions, savings and loans, investment advisors, insurance companies, public funds, and other institutional investors across the country. A strong commitment to identifying and satisfying those clients' needs is a primary focus of the company, and every member of the Coastal team strives to meet that challenge.

The senior management staff is comprised of individuals with diverse backgrounds and many years of experience in trading, marketing, banking, and financial analysis. The company's brokers spend extensive time traveling across the country developing long-term relationships as they work one-on-one with clients and prospects. Experienced support personnel are available to assist in settlement of transactions as well as to address customer inquiries. Both before and after the sale, clients have access to many support services, such as asset liability modeling, portfolio management, accounting systems, and other analytical tools. Coastal's proprietary data processing and analytical systems represent a significant investment and commitment to state-of-the-art communications and customer support.

As a result of superior analytical abilities, many years of experience, substantial inventory levels, and superior trading and retail capabilities, Coastal maintains a competitive edge which enables its representatives to offer sage market advice and efficient execution for its customers.

Continuing education for employees is critical in Coastal's business culture. Training programs and classes are regularly conducted for all employees. Adhering to the policy that quality communication is essential to successful relationships, Coastal employees are encouraged to maintain frequent interaction with clients. In fact, the company's bankers

and brokers are known for combining a high level of individualized attention with established expertise to deliver consistent performance in all markets.

Coastal is a member of the National Association of Securities Dealers (NASD). Securities Investor Protection Corporation (SIPC), and the Municipal Securities Rulemaking Board (MSRB). In recognition of their leadership in the securities industry, Coastal's Christopher LaPorte was elected in 1996 to the board of Directors of the National Association of Government Guaranteed Lenders (NAGGL), the nation's largest trade association for small-business lenders; and David Master, Chairman and Chief Executive Officer, is currently a member of the NASD's Fixed Income Committee. Mr. Master was also a member of the MSRB and co-chaired the Regional Municipal Security Dealers' Association which authored the "Bank Qualified" bond provisions of the 1986 Tax Reform Act.

As Houston and Coastal Securities approach the twenty-first century together, Coastal's commitment remains constant: to provide quality investment and financial services characterized by a degree of skill, efficiency, and integrity unmatched by other firms in the industry.

The address is 1160 Dairy Ashford, Fifth Floor, Houston, Texas 77079. The telephone number is (713) 558-8855 or (800) 231-5783.

Coastal Securities trading and sales floor.

SOUTHWEST SECURITIES

Southwest Securities Bond Trading Floor

Southwest Securities Founders, Don Buchholz, Chairman of the Board (left), and Allen Cobb, Vice Chairman.

A dynamic management team, sophisticated business and information technology and an enduring reputation for superior client services pave the road to success for Southwest Securities as it approaches its twenty-fifth year of business.

Southwest Securities provides fully disclosed securities clearing, securities brokerage, investment banking and asset management services. Founded in April 1972 by Don A. Buchholz and Allen B. Cobb as a private broker/dealer, the business has grown from twelve original employees to more than 600 employees and today has $2 billion in assets, $182 million in revenues and $84 million in shareholders' equity.

Southwest Securities Group, Inc., holding company for all of the operating subsidiaries, issued stock to the public in October 1991. Today, approximately 4,200 beneficial owners hold the company's common stock which is trading on The Nasdaq Stock Market's National Market System under the symbol "SWST." Approximately 47 percent of the shares are owned by directors, officers and employees of the company and its subsidiaries. Southwest Securities Group has been recognized by Forbes as one of the 200 best companies in American with revenues under $350 million, and by Texas Business Magazine as one of the "100 Fastest Growing Texas Companies."

In the spring of 1995, Southwest acquired Barre & Company, Incorporated and Barre founder David Glatstein became president of Southwest. A year later, CEO was added to his list of responsibilities when Raymond E. Wooldridge was named vice chairman and chairman of the executive committee. Company founders Buchholz and Cobb continue to serve as chairman of the board and vice chairman, respectively.

As a result of the acquisition of Barre, Southwest's work force gained 41 new associates, including several key executives who now play important management roles. Many areas of the company have experienced growth and expansion, including research, investment banking, institutional equity sales and syndicate, clearing services and the Fixed Income Division.

Early in its history, Southwest was one of the first securities firms to enter the fully disclosed clearing business. Regulatory changes made soon after Southwest's founding created this market niche which became Southwest's core business. In 1972, the New York Stock Exchange amended its regulations to permit NYSE member firms to rebate commissions of up to 40 percent to non-member firms on their customer transactions. Then in May 1975, the SEC eliminated all fixed commission rates on securities transactions and eliminated the 40 percent limitation on rebates to non-member firms. As a result of these changes, Southwest became the "back office" to a growing number of other brokerage houses, executing and clearing their trades, issuing confirmations and checks to their customers and providing a myriad of related services. Today, the company's extensive sales and distribution network includes approximately 580 registered representatives at Southwest Securities and its sister firm, Brokers Transaction Services, and more than 4,500 affiliated sales people at 228 correspondent firms in 33 states, Europe and the Pacific Rim.

Acquisitions of Pine Securities in 1974, Lentz Newton & Co. in 1975, Institutional Equity in 1984, Quinn and Company in 1987, Trust Company of Texas in 1992 and Westwood Management Corporation in 1993 have built a steady foundation for a company which is today considered the largest regional brokerage and investment services organization headquartered in Texas.

Primary subsidiaries of Southwest Securities Group, Inc. are:

Southwest Securities, Inc., a broker/dealer and major clearing firm with over 228 correspondents nationally and internationally, is the company's principal subsidiary. In addition, it operates a securities brokerage business with 14 offices and account executives in Texas, Oklahoma and New Mexico. The firm provides a full range of investment banking services to corporations, municipalities and other political subdivisions. Southwest Securities, Inc. is a member of the New York Stock Exchange, the American Stock Exchange, major regional exchanges and the National Association of Securities Dealers.

Brokers Transaction Services, Inc. is a broker/dealer that services the securities business of more than 460 independent contractors. Considered a leader in this area, BTS provides administrative and home office support to independent registered representatives.

Westwood Management Corporation is a registered investment advisor, managing pension and profit sharing funds as well as other assets for institutions and individuals. Westwood consistently ranks among the top 20 of "America's Best Money Managers" as rated by Nelson's. The firm also serves as investment manager for The Westwood Funds, a family of high-quality, registered mutual funds which includes balanced, equity and intermediate bond portfolios. Westwood President & CEO Susan Byrne's expertise is sought by many national and regional publications, including Barron's and Money, and she has appeared on Wall Street With Louis Rukeyser.

The Trust Company of Texas provides a full-line of trust and executor services to successful families and companies. The Trust Company offers a portfolio of trust and investment services designed specifically for the clients of securities account executives SW Capital Corporation administers the Local Government Investment Cooperative (LOGIC), a $900-million-plus investment pool for cities, counties, school districts and other public entities in Texas.

The strength of Southwest Securities Group, Inc. lies within its financial soundness. With virtually no long-term debt, the company's assets consist of cash, marketable securities and receivables from clients, broker/dealer firms, their clients and clearing organizations. Revenues in the past ten years have gone from under $30 million to over $182 million and have increased by 51 percent from fiscal 1995 to fiscal 1996.

Top quality customer service remains the focus of Southwest, as improvements are made in the areas of information systems and technology. Identifying ways automation can improve efficiency, investigating alternatives to creating paper reports and mailing documents and enhancing existing computer capabilities are top priorities for company leaders.

Since the 1980's, the company's correspondents have benefited from on-line, real-time computing, and Southwest continues to upgrade and improve its information systems to meet the changing needs of its customers. In the implementation stages is a new computer software system known as CSS - Comprehensive Software Systems. Over the next few years, CSS will replace all of the currently used software and provide an impressive array of expanded capabilities. This new generation of open architecture software is expected to improve contact management and customer service with on-screen portfolios and to open the door for internet communication with correspondents and their customers. Southwest is a founding member of the CSS consortium.

Southwest Securities Group President and CEO David Glatstein says the key to the investment business is intellectual property. "The only thing that people buy from us other than our processing is our brain. Research is our brain at Southwest Securities," says Glatstein. Under his leadership, the Research Department has expanded from one person to nine analysts plus support staff. As "young" as the research team is, it has already earned a reputation in the investment industry and media for its accurate recommendations. Each analyst deals with companies in his or her area of specialization. Coverage includes retail, oil and gas, distressed and special situations, real estate investment trusts, hotels, telecommunications, finance, high tech and restaurants. Through relationships developed with high level management at companies throughout the United States, Southwest analysts are able to track investment trends and opportunities in the Southwest to benefit the firm's customers.

Its dynamic growth has placed Southwest in an enviable position within the financial industry. The company's mission of building wealth and preserving capital for clients has proven to be the most valuable source of new business. On the eve of its 25 anniversary, Southwest Securities faces its future with a solid financial base and the components of a winning team. After all, nobody knows the Southwest better!

Southwest Securities is located at 1201 Elm Street, Suite 3500 in Dallas, Texas, (214) 651-1800.

David Glatstein, President and Chief Executive Officer

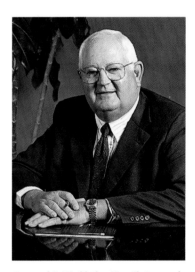

Raymond E. Wooldridge, Vice Chairman of the Board and Chairman of the Executive Committee.

Galveston Bathing Girls Revue.
Panoramic photograph by E.O. Goldbeck.
The sign in the panoramic picture carries
the information: "Third Annual Bathing Girl
Revue, Galveston, Tex. May 14th 1922."
Goldbeck's largest panoramic group
photograph included 21,765 members of the
United States Army Air Force at Lackaland
Air Base in San Antonio.

QUALITY OF LIFE

recreation and leisure-oriented companies and historical and civic

organizations contribute to Texans' quality of life

DENTON COUNTY SESQUICENTENNIAL CELEBRATION

Above: Decorative metalwork, restored courthouse.

Above right: May House, built in 1878, when Denton's prosperity was just beginning.

Below: Denton County Courthouse, 1895-97.

One hundred and fifty years ago, in 1846, when the new state of Texas passed the legislation that created Denton County, few people lived there. Most of those who did were very recent immigrants, the product of a colonization scheme begun when Texas was an independent republic. The plan was to attract settlers to those areas that lay between Indian domination and the settled land close to the Gulf of Mexico. The settlers got free or very cheap land, of which Texas had a great deal, the companies that sponsored settlement got a percentage of the land they brokered, and the republic got settlers on its edges: it was a good deal for everyone.

A number of "colonists" came to Texas through those colonization projects. The project that included the area that would become Denton County was the Peters Colony, which eventually included all of thirteen present counties and parts of thirteen more, an enormous area.

People came to Denton County mostly from the Upper South, often with intermediate stops in places like Missouri. Denton County was a pleasant area, with sufficient water and good soil in the eastern part of the county. In the western part, the heavy clay soil was hard to cultivate until the invention of the steam plow, and in the early years, it was used mostly as grazing land.

By 1860, the colonization project had ended. In that year, the county had slightly more than 5,000 people. When the Civil War broke out in 1861, the sympathies of Denton County went to the Confederacy, although the Secession referendum passed only narrowly. Nevertheless, most of Denton's young men marched off to war and served in a number of Texas units.

By 1860, Denton County had several small towns. The original county seat was fixed in 1846 at more or less the geographical center of the county and named Pinckneyville. Court met there under a tree. During the next ten years, the county seat moved south, first to Corinth and then to two sites in Alton (now known as Old Alton). Finally, in 1856, the Texas legislature moved the county seat to a place they called the city of Denton, which did not exist until its town square was laid out the following year.

In the decades that followed, Denton County became a prosperous agricultural area, with subsistence farming changing to a cash economy when the railroad came through the county during the 1870s. The high point of optimistic prosperity came in 1895-1897, when the county's citizens built its landmark courthouse. In the 1980s, the courthouse was completely restored to its original splendor under the auspices of the Texas Historical Commission.

In the 1890s, citizens of Denton County began the close relationship with higher education that has marked the county throughout

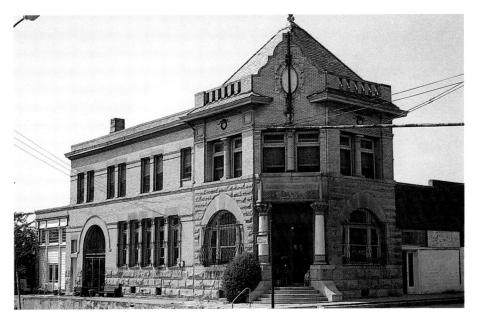

the twentieth century. In 1890, citizens of the county established Denton Normal College. After several name changes, the institution today is the University of North Texas, a major research university. Twelve years later, the citizens of the county successfully lobbied the legislature to establish the state college for women there. Accepting its first students in 1903, that school for women has prospered and become the world-famous Texas Woman's University.

Denton County became less agricultural as the neighboring great metropolitan area of Dallas and Fort Worth expanded to the north. The Interstate Highway system of the 1950s made Denton part of the modern transportation network that opened up commerce with every part of the United States and with trading partners in Canada and Mexico. Together with the Dallas-Fort Worth International Airport, just outside the county's southern boundary, and the Alliance Airport in the southwest part of the county, new modes of transportation have now largely supplanted the old railroad system.

For the last two decades, Denton County has been one of the fastest growing counties in population in the United States. Yet all of this growth has not masked the debt that Denton County and its citizens owe to their pioneer forebears who came to unturned soil and through their bravery and industry made the land bloom.

THE DRISCOLL FOUNDATION

Clara Driscoll

The Robert Driscoll and Julia Driscoll and Robert Driscoll Jr. Foundation, the Driscoll Foundation's official name, was founded by one of Texas' greatest public benefactors, Clara Driscoll, to honor the members of her family. Representing the wealth of three generations and one of the largest early Texas fortunes, this legacy is embodied by the Driscoll Children's Hospital at Corpus Christi dedicated to providing for the perpetual care of children in South Texas.

Threads of Driscoll family history can be found interwoven throughout the tapestry of Texas history. Daniel Eidersceoil or O'Driscoeil of County Cork, Ireland, who eventually shortened his name to Driscoll, came to Texas with other immigrants being organized by "empresarios" or land agents to help the Mexican government colonize the region in the 1830s, and is believed to have joined the Irish settlement pioneered by James McGloin and John McMullen in Refugio County. For serving with Sam Houston's army at the Battle of San Jacinto, Driscoll received a bounty land grant for over 1280 acres in Victoria County, the start of a vast South Texas empire. Family interests rapidly expanded from land and cattle into banking, oil and gas, and Driscoll land holdings spread from Palo Alto Ranch headquar-

ters to 125,000 acres in Duval and adjacent counties in the arid region between the Nueces and Rio Grande Rivers called the Nueces Strip. When their father died, Clara's brother, Robert D., Jr., furthered family banking interest, but the talented Princeton graduate died at the age of only fifty-eight, leaving Clara to manage the Driscoll enterprise. Inspired by her father and brother's public-spirited efforts to develop the port at Corpus Christi and incorporate the St. Louis, Brownsville and Mexico Railroad that sparked the growth of several South Texas towns, the young woman set out to become a positive force for change.

Because most early American philanthropists were male, her brother's early death gave Clara an opportunity enjoyed by few women of her generation to leave a lasting legacy. Well-suited to the task, she had gone around the world by the age of eighteen and completed her education at Miss Thompson's and Peebles School in New York with finishing school at Chateaux Dieudonne in Boronel sur Oise, France. Like many Texas women who combined strength and sensitivity, practicality and artistic flair, "Miss Clara," as she was called, had the manners of a refined Southern lady and the skills of a ranch manager, preferring to think of herself simply as "a cattlewoman." In addition to writing several novels and a Broadway play, she took an active role in supporting Woodrow Wilson, F.D. Roosevelt and John Nance Garner in national politics and developed a habit of giving gifts to Texas that preserved both the gracious estate that houses Austin's Laguna Gloria Museum and the Alamo, the most sacred shrine of the Texas Revolution.

Driscoll Children's Hospital reflects Clara Driscoll's wish that her estate be used to build and operate a children's hospital in Corpus Christi to "serve the health care needs of children." Planned with the help of her personal physician, McIver Furman, M.D., the hospital opened in 1953 just eight years after her death. Governed by three Trustees and originally organized as a tax-exempt trust, the

Foundation operated the facility for its first fifteen years exclusively as a charity hospital. The Clara Driscoll Memorial Pavilion was subsequently created for paying patients as a non-profit corporation, and in 1969 the Trustees established a board of governors to run the hospital. A new private non-profit corporation comprising the entire medical complex was established in 1988.

Today, Driscoll Hospital is a regional pediatric referral center and one of six free-standing children's hospitals in Texas. Each year, its 1200-member staff provides emergency care to thousands of children in addition to handling more than 60,000 hospital, surgical, primary and specialty patients, more than half from outside the Corpus area. Noted for its cardiac diagnostic and neonatal units, the hospital also operates one of 200 pediatric residency programs in the nation. To serve a still largely rural population, it maintains a Children's and Youth Clinic at Robstown, more than twenty outpatient clinics throughout South Texas, and a transport team capable of reaching almost any location in the region.

The Driscoll Foundation has supported other South Texas community enhancements by donating land for the Del Mar Technical and Vocational School, making land available to Coastal Bend Youth City, and assisting in bringing a Mental Health program and the State School for Mental Retardation to Corpus Christi. Working with those who later leased the Driscoll ranches, the Foundation also promotes ecologically-sound land use and the development of area resources.

Driscoll Children's Hospital

CAMP HEART O' THE HILLS/ CAMP STEWART

"Kids need more spontaneity in their lives today, and we at Camp Heart O' the Hills and Camp Stewart try to provide them with an opportunity to experience that," Camp Director Jane Ragsdale said. "In a time when children have organized play days, such as Little League, they need to have unstructured fun times."

Camp Heart O' the Hills (for girls) is located on the Guadalupe River's South Fork and Stewart (for boys), on the river's North Fork near Hunt, seven miles apart. The camps, located in rugged Hill Country settings, foster lifetime skills, social and personal, to strengthen a child's personal sense of worth and dignity, as well as hobby/avocation skills to provide a lifelong love of healthy activities. "Campers need to find their own identity. They need a safe place to discover what's important to them," she said.

Ragsdale said the camps provide opportunity "to have a blast while we work at building skills and character." She noted that Camp Stewart, launched in 1924 by E.J. "Doc" Stewart, is the oldest continually-operated private camp in the Southwest. Heart O' the Hills Camp has a history of providing a pleasant, relaxed atmosphere for its guests. It was first established in 1928 by Stewart as an inn for parents who brought children to area camps — two of which he established.

The main lodge was built on an enormous heart-shaped boulder known as the "heart of the hills." Fire swept through the lodge in November 1948, while the inn was owned by Kenneth and Velma Jones, but the hotel was expanded and restored before reopening in May 1949.

The Jones' daughters, Jan and Jo, attended Camp Mystic. Jo, who was killed in a traffic accident when she was 15, especially loved camp, and urged her parents to convert Heart O' the Hills Inn, a popular honeymoon and social resort, into a girls camp. Heart O' the Hills Camp was established in 1953 under the direction of Kitty Winter Magee, who remained through 1966. It was purchased in 1976 by the families of Whayne and Bobbie Moore, and Camp Stewart owners Si and Kathy Ragsdale. In October 1987,

the Ragsdale family purchased sole interest in The Heart.

A March 1996 article in *Family Life* magazine promotes Camp Heart O' the Hills and Camp Stewart as two of the top ten summer camps in the nation. The camps are also featured as two of the "Best Camps in the USA" in a Random House book Choosing the Right Camp by Richard Kennedy.

The camps serve youth from age 6-16, teaching traditional lore, Eastern and Western riding skills and environmental knowledge. Campers with special needs, such as limited hearing ability, or unreasoning fears, for instance, are assisted in their search for happiness at camp by one-to-one relationships with various counselors. "We walk people through their fears, helping them to face and conquer them," Ragsdale noted. Special problems are given sensitive treatment by counselors. The camp staffs point with pride to numerous men and women who have achieved more than wealth can buy from their camping experiences. "We're proud of our former campers," Ragsdale said, adding that Heart campers have achieved individual goals such as becoming physicians, judges and strong civic leaders as well as "good mothers."

Many campers who enjoy their summer stays write long and praise-filled letters to the directors. Some cite the camp as "the best experience of my life." One particular letter, entitled "Lessons Learned at the Heart," hangs in the Director's office. The writer, Michele Horn, named 42 items, including: "The Heart has taught me to have strength and confidence in myself; ... that it is ok to mess up; ... with a positive attitude I can accomplish anything I set my mind on; ...to participate in the game of life" and "... a lot about myself." She concludes, "I feel very fortunate to have been able to experience such an amazing place. Camp is my utopia."

The history of Texas is a rich and varied tale—one told not only by the stories of the men and women who lived it, but also by the places they created and the communities, neighborhoods, and buildings they left behind. Our state's past surrounds us—from the Texas State Capitol in Austin to the Presidio County Courthouse in Marfa; from the Oliphant log house in Sabine County to the classical architecture of Houston's Courtlandt Place neighborhood; from the 1830 Jesús Treviño House in Zapata County to the 1939 Fair Park Texas Centennial Buildings in Dallas—Texas history is an important part of our present. Preservation Texas works in partnership with people throughout the state to preserve this legacy, bringing together community leaders, legislators, business people, historians, teachers, and many others to build more livable communities today by reinvesting in the past and preserving for the future..

Active participation by Preservation Texas has been instrumental in saving many of Texas' historical treasures. When funding for the restoration of the Texas State Capitol was jeopardized and the state's 1858 General Land Office Building was threatened with demolition, Preservation Texas mounted a campaign of determined advocacy and reasoned dialogue to preserve the funding for the Capitol project and to ensure that the GLO Building was saved. Today, Texans everywhere can share a feeling of pride in these gloriously restored public landmarks.

Since its founding in 1985, Preservation Texas has provided training for individual citizens and preservation organizations throughout the state, providing workshops and educational forums on many topics, including fund raising, newsletter production, membership development, and advocacy training. Heritage education workshops have helped teachers learn how to use the historic places in their own communities as primary resources in designing educational programs and activities for their students.

No one wants to see beautiful and important links to our state's magnificent past slip away. Preservation Texas, dedicated to recognizing and preserving Texas' rich architectural heritage and historical identity, is organized to help Texans confront the threatened loss of valuable resources. Participation is open to all and is available through memberships for families, individuals, organizations, businesses and corporations who cherish and seek to preserve the special character of the Lone Star State.

PRESERVATION TEXAS

Above: The circa 1820 Oliphant House was built at the Sabine River crossing of the Camino Real by James Taylor Gaines, signer of the Texas Declaration of Independence and contributor to the Texas Constitution.

Above left: The 1886 Presidio County Courthouse is one of the primary defining landmarks in the west Texas town of Marfa.

Below: After a 1983 fire came close to destroying the Texas State Capitol, the largest and most comprehensive state capitol restoration project in the nation has restored this 1888 landmark to its original architectural magnificence.

RIP
NICHOLS

Rip Wood Nichols

Throughout a long and respected Dallas business career, Rip Wood Nichols was a man always eager to find the next challenge and make them into opportunities.

"He had the gift of taking something and making the most of it," said his widow, Bernice Nichols. By the time Nichols died in July 1992, at aged 76, he had formed and operated eight successful companies over a business career spanning a half century.

Nichols' talent for business was evident early. He attended what is now the University of Texas at Arlington for two years, hitchhiking to and from his Dallas home. Then, impatient to start life, he grabbed the opportunity to work at the order desk of a Dallas plumbing supply company, where his wage of 30 cents an hour was double that of his college job.

But before long, Nichols saw another opportunity. Among his duties was making sure customer orders were delivered on time. Young Nichols believed he could provide better and faster service than the delivery company his employer used, so in 1937, he borrowed $150 and launched Texas Delivery Service. It wasn't easy. For one thing, Nichols was only 21. For another, his equipment comprised a single Model A truck, which he drove himself, and a motorcycle belonging to his only employee. And the Depression was still under way.

First month sales were just $25, and second month sales were only $100. When his motorcycle deliveryman quit suddenly, Nichols took $25 from his small earnings to make a down payment on a pickup truck and hired a driver. It was a wise investment: Texas Delivery went into the black in the third month, with a grand income of $300. By year end, Nichols employed two pickup drivers, two men on motorcycles and a bicycle-delivery boy.

Business grew rapidly until World War II gasoline rationing sliced Nichols' then 30 trucks and 50 employees in half. When he returned from service in the Pacific, Nichols found only 11 trucks still running and many customers gone.

Not yet 30, Nichols set about rebuilding Texas Delivery Service, and two years later, began expansion into other businesses the rapidly growing city of Dallas needed. Ever one to spot opportunities, Nichols in 1948 expanded into heavy hauling and hoisting, followed the next year by renting material handling equipment.

One business sprouted another, until ultimately, Nichols controlled eight businesses under the Texas Delivery name. In two, the entrepreneur made his lasting business mark. In 1950, he opened Texas Delivery Warehouse, which stored extra business merchandise and company documents, and in 1954, he began Texas Industrial Disposal (TIDI), Dallas' first commercial containerized trash pickup service. Nichols was known as the consummate businessman — in the early 1950s, he even equipped an air-conditioned mobile office, complete with desk, manual typewriter, file cabinet, reference books and adding machine, so he could work productively between client calls.

"This way, he could visit clients and still get a full day of work done. That's what made him a success," remarked Bernice Nichols.

Eventually, however, running so many diverse businesses became cumbersome. Nichols analyzed the growth potential of each, then sold all except TIDI — which had burgeoned into his largest business — and his original Texas Delivery. Texas Delivery Warehouse was sold to his friend, Ned Edwards, but because Edwards wasn't interested in the considerable number of business records stored there, Nichols found he still had a third viable business remaining.

That proved fortuitous, however, because several years later when Nichols cast about for a compact business he could run with his family, he saw specializing in office records as the perfect opportunity. Selling TIDI and Texas Delivery, Nichols founded Security Archives in September, 1970.

With Security Archives, Nichols set out to create a solid, family-run business. He got his wish: the company was operated today by son-in-law Pat Clayton, while grandson Woody Clayton was vice president. In May of 1996 Security Archives was sold. Rip Nichols presence, though, is still felt through the standards and values he set for all his business operations. "He was a hard worker; he meant what he said, and his workers all respected him," said Mrs. Nichols. "Rip wouldn't say something couldn't be done. He'd always try something else until he did it. He really believed everything would work if you just find the right way to do it."

Caprock Canyon State Park.

PHOTO BY LEROY WILLIAMSON

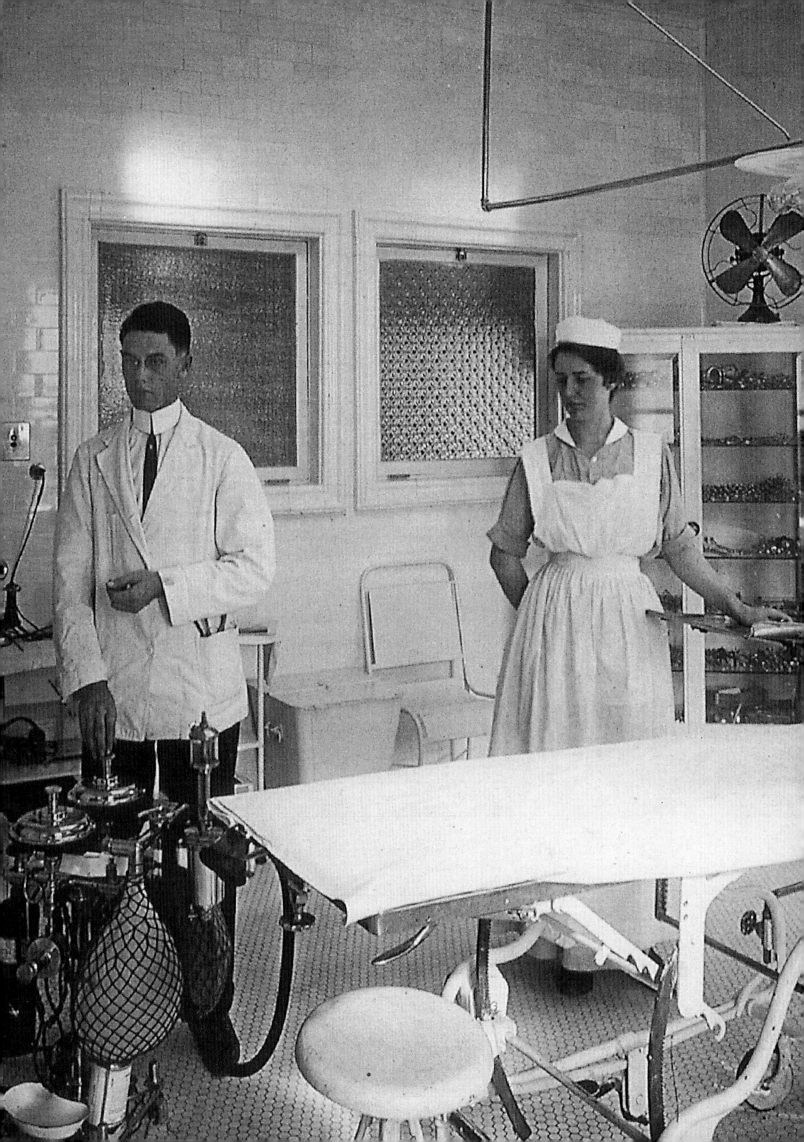

HEALTHCARE

medical and research facilities,

hospitals and clinics provide

world-class healthcare for Texans

Surgery at Scott & White Hospital in about 1914-1915.

TRINITY MOTHER FRANCES HEALTH SYSTEM

Mother Frances Hospital, 1937.

Long before most were old enough to remember, out of the ashes of disaster emerged two of the most trusted institutions in east Texas. Tested by enormous tragedy and molded by a sense of service, the two were compelled to meet the medical challenges of their communities. Over the years, following almost parallel paths, the Trinity Clinic and Mother Frances Hospital soon took their place as the medical heart of an entire region. Today, the leadership that has bound these two institutions for six decades has become the Trinity Mother Frances Health System, one of the nation's most progressive and innovative health systems.

When Trinity Mother Frances Health System began preparing for the future, there was a solid foundation in place. The hospital and clinic has long-standing histories--plus commitment to the community.

In 9134, The Trinity Clinic began as the Bryant Clinic. It was founded by two general practitioners, Dr, William Howard Bryant and Dr. Sydney W. Bradford. Mother Frances Hospital was opened only a short time later, in 1937.

Both were challenged to meet a dramatic and desperate need in their early years. A major tragedy--the New London gas explosion--struck the neighboring community. The Bryant clinic received the first call for help in Tyler. And the day before the formal dedication, Mother Frances Hospital opened early to care for the victims of the devastated town. The two institutions exemplified caring and compassion then--just as they do now.

In 1948, The Bryant Clinic changed its name to The Medical & Surgical Clinic. More recently, with the addition of the two other medical group practices, it is now known as The Trinity Clinic.

Mother Frances Hospital has changed over the years. What began as a 60-bed hospital has grown into a respected, regional medical center with more than 350 beds. A wide range of spe-cialized programs and technologies provide sophisticated care for the people of east Texas. In 1989, Mother Frances Hospital was named "Texas Business of the Year" for its significant achievements in the areas of business management, employee relations and community service.

The Sisters of the Holy Family of Nazareth, sponsors of Mother Frances Hospital, have embedded into the very core of the institution a spiritual energy. Their Foundress, Mother Frances Siedliska, Blessed Mary of Jesus the Good Shepherd, knew that faith with action would reach further than faith alone. Through years of service, the Sisters have led Mother Frances Hospital with a philosophy that is the guiding force behind the delivery of health services to the community.

The heritage of compassion and excellence in health care evidenced from the beginning is still alive and well at Trinity Mother Frances Health System. It is nurtured by a large, dedicated staff including physicians who participate in the care of their patients each step of the way.

Health care services for east Texans have never been closer-or more accessible. And that all began when Mother Frances' first regional clinic opened in 1988 in Canton. Today the system supports twelve additional primary care clinics located throughout the region in Chandler, Hawkins, Henderson, Jacksonville, Lake Palestine, Lindale, Mineola, Overton, Quitman, Troup, Tyler, and Whitehouse. Each clinic is staffed with a full time medical doctor and, in some cases, supported with mid-level practitioners. Together with nurses and other clinical professionals, these clinics provide a complete range of primary care services to patients. They are equipped to handle minor emergencies, minor surgeries, x-rays, pediatric care, women's care and general long-term family medical care. They are also able to handle job-related injuries, cardiology services, provide physicals, pre-employment examinations and low-cost mammography screenings.

Trinity Mother Frances Health Systems opened a clinic in 1995 designed specifically for seniors, the first of its kind in east Texas. The clinic offers many services to help seniors assess, manage and prevent health-related problems. Health screenings and educational programs are offered regularly. The clinic accepts Medicare, provides referrals to medical subspecialties and helps coordinate community and social services to assist with housing, financial matters and home care.

The best place for extended care and recovery following a hospital stay may be in the patient's home. Home offers comfort and convenience and many times, is conducive to healing. Trinity Mother Frances Home Care provides a full range of health care services in the patient's home. These 24-hour services range from general nursing and infusion therapy to diabetic monitoring and rehabilitation programs. Home infusion services provide 24 hour care for intravenous drug therapy. To better serve the region, Home Care offices are located in Tyler, Quitman, Canton, Kilgore, Jacksonville and Athens.

The System has responded to the concern of citizens and business groups about controlling costs of health care while maintaining quality. As a result, partnerships have been formed with east Texas industry to provide comprehensive medical benefits through a large network of primary and specialty care physicians. The networks are comprised of over 1,000 area physicians and 34 participating regional hospitals. Through these networks, employers and payors realize substantial savings. Trinity Mother Frances Health System has developed health insurance products designed to meet the needs of today's business partners. The System has developed group products for self-insured and fully insured employers; a preferred provider organization; Medicare supplemental and select products; point of service plans; risk management with a non-profit physicians' corporation;

wellness and prevention programs; corporate wellness; occupational health; and much more.

The Trinity Mother Frances Health System offers a full range of medical care in a variety of specialties with Centers of Excellence in heart and lung care, cancer prevention and treatment, spine and joint care, trauma, obstetrical and pediatric services.

In 1983, Mother Frances Hospital began building what has become a premier heart center for the east Texas region. The Heart & Lung Institute of the Trinity Mother Frances Health System surpassed national standards and was recognized by the Wall Street Journal as a leader in cardiac care. Over the years, the goal has been to develop a center of excellence which embraces patient care, research and education. Today, the Heart & Lung Institute offers an extensive service that meets a full range of clinical needs for the patient with suspected or known heart disease.

Committed to innovative technologies, Trinity Mother Frances introduced lifesaving clot-bursting drugs to the region in 1988 and the latest heart disease risk testing in 1996. Over 30,000 heart procedures have been performed since opening. That includes more than 20,000 catheterizations, over 4,000 angioplasties and over 4,000 open heart operations. In addition, the Heart & Lung Institute offers extensive cardiac and pulmonary rehabilitation services as well as patient, professional and community education programs and heart disease risk testing through the Lipid Clinic. Heart

(L-R) David Teegarden, M.D., Senior Vice President; J. Lindsey Bradley, Jr., FACHE, Chief Administrative Officer; Patrick R. Thomas, M.D., Chief Medical Officer; Ray Thompson, FACHE, Executive Vice President.

Trinity Mother Frances Health System

Disease Risk Testing is the most advanced laboratory testing available to predetermine the onset of heart disease even before major symptoms start to appear. The Trinity Mother Frances Health System was the first hospital in the nation to offer this testing to the community it serves.

In 1993, the Trinity Mother Frances Regional Wellness Center was opened, the first one of its kind in the area. The 13,000 square foot facility includes a walking track, advanced equipment and medically supervised exercise programs. the Center offers a wide variety of individualized programs including personal wellness, cardiac rehabilitation, cancer rehabilitation and corporate wellness programs.

The Spine and Joint Institute was established at Mother Frances Hospital to bring together a wide range of health professionals dedicated to this service. Institute services include prevention, education and research as well as surgery and rehabilitation. The goal of the program is to help individuals through the acute stages of injury and pain and reduce the risk of reinjury and loss of time at work or play.

Dedicated to the women of east Texas, The Women's Center offers a myriad of comprehensive services, from childbirth and infant care to diagnostic testing and surgery. The Birth Center features family-centered maternity care and offers rooming-in, as well as a sibling visitation program. Prior to hospitalization, comprehensive childbirth education is available for parents. The Birth Center provides a community-based Level II antepartum, Labor and Delivery and postpartum service with a nursing staff specially trained in identifying and responding to obstetric and medical complications of labor and delivery. The Women's Diagnostic Center is a comprehensive center for diagnostic testing offering mammography, stereotactic breast biopsy, ultrasound-guided biopsy, routine diagnostic ultrasound, bone densitometer for osteoporosis screenings, patient education including breast self exam and breast prosthesis fittings. The Center is staffed with a mammography radiologist who provides medical evaluation while the patient is in the office allowing for immediate additional testing if necessary.

Mother Frances Hospital has a long history of caring for children and the family. The Children's Center, the only dedicated pediatric facility in the area, provides a specially planned environment designed to promote the healing and recuperation of sick children. The 20-bed center includes in-room sleeping quarters for parents and a special activity center designed to support age appropriate growth and development needs.

Nursery services for healthy newborns as well as high risk infants are provided in the Level II Nursery. The unit includes: a six-bed Level II Special Care Nursery, a twelve-bed Intermediate/Premature Care Nursery, an eight-bed Admission Nursery, four separate well baby nurseries with a capacity for 50 infants, and two isolation rooms. The staff is specially trained to care for infants and certified in advanced pediatric life support.

Trinity Mother Frances Health System opened the FamilyCARE Center to provide pediatric health care and prenatal care to the uninsured women and children of east Texas. Over two years later, the Center has grown to two locations increasing the physician staff to support them. The FamilyCARE Center OB/GYN Services provides prenatal, preventive and primary women's health care. The FamilyCARE Center Pediatric Services provides health care services for newborns through adolescents, including chronically ill children. Some services include immunizations; early periodic and developmental screenings; and medical site for the Child Abuse Intervention Program.

The CancerCare Institute of the Trinity Mother Frances Health System has the ability to care for all types of cancer. The Institute offers surgical intervention, chemotherapy, radiation therapy, support services and rehabilitation therapy. The CancerCare Institute hosts monthly Tumor Conferences and provides professionals with prospective, multi-disciplinary management of oncology cases. A cancer registry provides analytical data on incidence, treatment and survival to physicians, administrators, Texas Department of Health and National Cancer Database. Education and emotional support are provided to cancer patients and family members through targeted support groups.

Emergency and trauma services are provided 24 hours a day through the Emergency Care Center, Flight for Life Emergency Helicopter and Ground Emergency Medical Service. Staffed 24 hours a day with emergency physicians and other professionals, the 24-bed Emergency Care Center is the busiest emergency center in the region, caring for patients of all ages and levels of urgency. The Level II Trauma Center at Mother Frances Hospital provides coordinated care throughout the trauma patient's course of treatment. The Flight for Life helicopter, Emergency Care Center, Trauma Operating Room suites and a high-tech surgical trauma intensive care unit support services provided by the trauma professionals. Board certified trauma surgeons, members of the flight team and other professional care givers help assure a complete continuum of care for patients. The Level II Trauma and Emergency Service offered through Trinity Mother Frances Health System is a well-organized system of people and resources designed to provide optimal care in critical situations.

TeleCare Plus, The Professionals at Trinity Mother Frances Health System, is a free community service offering health information and physician referral over the telephone. Callers can discuss health-related questions with registered nurses, request health information, register for community seminars and schedule appointments for health screenings.

Mother Frances Hospital has offered eye care since it opened in 1937. The first eye surgeries at Mother Frances were performed by eye, ear, nose and throat specialists during the 1950's. In 1949, the first ophthalmologist joined the medical staff at Mother Frances Hospital. Today, the Eye Institute provides a full spectrum of services ranging from trauma to delicate lens repair. The specially trained staff provides a high level of care and concern for inpatients and outpatients. About 1,400 eye surgeries are performed each year in the Tyler Square Outpatient Surgery Center and operating rooms at Mother Frances Hospital.

When Trinity Clinic and Mother Frances Hospital were founded more than sixty years ago, the current network and partnership were beyond imagination. Today, the organizations are vastly different than in the 1930's; however, a unified mission remains unchanged--to enhance community health through service with compassion, excellence and efficiency. The philosophy is perpetuated by collaborating with those who share the vision, values and future of the system. Built on a proud history of service to the region and motivated by respect and compassion, Trinity Mother Frances Health System continues to meet the needs of the people through quality, comprehensive health services.

The physicians, hospital and professionals have been trusted friends for 60 years and are the same people east Texans trust and rely upon today. In this tradition, the people of Trinity Mother Frances Health System are truly a large part of the history of the Lone Star State.

The Heart and Lung Institute has been nationally recognized as a leader in cardiac care.

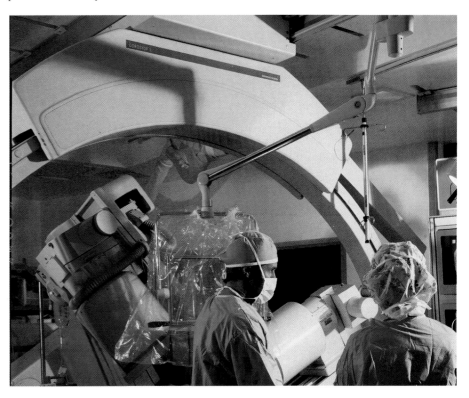

TEXAS MEDICAL CENTER

Texas Medical Center is a comprehensive medical complex which was organized in the mid-1940's as a means for coordinating medical and health education, patient care, and related research — all in a not-for-profit setting. Today, it stands as a major health care resource that also provides extraordinary opportunities for students to obtain a broad base of professional experience. The institutions in the Texas Medical Center are supported by gifts of philanthropy, trusts, government, and by religious and fraternal organizations. Much of the Texas Medical Center can only be described as "unique."

There are more than 48,000 full and part time employees, and it is Houston's largest single-site employer. The concentration of buildings make it a medical city in itself. Over 4.2 million patient visits a year are recorded. The 18,500 students attest to its being one of the major medical and health research centers in the nation.

The 42 member institutions include two medical schools; four schools of nursing; schools of dentistry and public health; one of the largest medical libraries; a high school for the health professions; a junior college offering health careers and related technology courses; and many other educational facilities awarding both degrees and certification in all the medical and health fields of knowledge. Also, there are hospitals which are among the largest in the United States—such as the VA Medical Center, The Methodist Hospital, St. Luke's Episcopal Hospital, Texas Children's Hospital, Hermann Hospital, Ben Taub and

Lyndon B. Johnson county hospitals—to small specialized facilities such as The Hospice at the Texas Medical Center. Other member institutions include TIRR (The Institute for Rehabilitation and Research), The Institute of Religion, Shriners Hospitals for Children - Houston, LifeGift Organ Donation Center, the Gulf Coast Regional Blood Center, and the Joseph A. Jachimczyk Forensic Center — the Harris County office of the medical examiner.

The University of Texas has a number of units in the Texas Medical Center campus, most grouped as the UT Houston Health Science Center but also the UT M.D. Anderson Cancer Center, recognized all over the world for its outstanding treatment and research of cancer.

The acclaim received by many of the hospitals in the Texas Medical Center comes, of course, from patients and doctors, but they are also nationally recognized. One such well-known listing is the annual U.S. News & World Report survey which ranks six of the Texas Medical Center hospitals as "best in the nation."

The history of the Texas Medical Center is the recording of the generosity and vision of several early Houstonians—notably Dr. E.W. Bertner, a medical doctor; George Hermann, who farmed land that continued to grow in value at the edge of Houston; and, perhaps most importantly, Monroe Dunaway Anderson, a cotton broker who left his millions of dollars in a trust to be administered by friends for the good of mankind.

Dr. Bertner was the one who from the beginning believed that a Texas Medical Center was possible, although even he could not have dreamed how large it would become. Dr. Bertner practiced medicine in Houston throughout his lifetime, and many of his patients were among the most influential people in Houston. He served as president of the Harris County Medical Society and later, the Texas Medical Society. Dr. Bertner had traveled across the United States and throughout Europe, and much of what he saw he brought back to help plan for the Texas Medical Center. He worked steadily and successfully towards his goal of a world-class medical complex, and he lived to see his dream come true.

George Hermann was a bachelor who left much of his estate to the City of Houston. Hermann Hospital, Hermann Park and Hermann Square are all name in his honor. Hermann

Hospital was built at the edge of what had been Mr. Hermann's farm, far south of downtown Houston. It has always been a sparkling jewel as a medical facility with its graceful architecture and near-tropical garden setting. The new Texas Medical Center was sited next to it, and the hospital and the center have been closely linked ever since.

As to how the Texas Medical Center actually came to be is more the story of Monroe Dunaway Anderson. At the conclusion of World War II, after Mr. Anderson's death, the newly formed Anderson Foundation offered to match funds set aside by the State of Texas Legislature to build a state cancer treatment and research hospital. The offer of money from the Anderson Foundation helped locate the facility in the newly formed Texas Medical Center.

At this same time, Baylor University voted to move its medical school from Dallas to Houston, partially because of the offer of land from the Texas Medical Center corporation. So, the new state hospital for treatment and research of cancer and the long-time distinguished medical school became the first two member institutions in the medical center which was to grow spectacularly.

Through the years, the rules for an organization joining the Texas Medical Center have been straight-forward and simple. Generally, in return for a gift of land on which to build, and at times some other considerations, the institution declares it will remain not-for-profit and engage in the highest caliber of medical and health education, patient care, and related research. Some members, like Hermann Hospital or the VA Medical Center, joined, bringing with them their own land. But the mandate of "not-for-profit" remains the binding agreement for all the members of the Texas Medical Center.

The dream of the early Houston leaders has continued to grow for the more than 50 years there has been a Texas Medical Center, and this medical complex is truly "Houston's gift to the world."

THE METHODIST HOSPITAL

Methodist Hospital, Houston, circa 1924.

The Methodist Hospital today, flagship of The Methodist Health Care System.

The tradition of excellence in medical care which began at The Methodist Hospital in Houston almost 80 years ago has established Methodist as a leading health care institution in the Bayou City and around the globe.

The hospital's roots go back to 1908 when Dr. Oscar L. Norsworthy, a prominent physician, built a 30-bed health center in downtown Houston to accommodate his growing practice. Eleven years later, he and his wife sold the facility to the Methodist Episcopal Church for less than half its appraised value — on condition that the church would agree to erect a new hospital building.

The new Methodist Hospital opened in April 1924. During its first year of operation, it admitted 1,620 patients, who paid $3 a day for a bed on a ward or $6 daily for a private room with a bath and closet. Within three years, its patient census had almost doubled. By 1929 the hospital was filled to capacity and forced to turn patients away.

Then the bottom fell out of the stock market, ushering in the Great Depression. Since few people could afford to pay for health care, the hospital found itself in desperate financial straits. Still, it continued operations and opened a school of nursing in September 1934 to meet the growing demand for graduate nurses.

The facility's financial picture began to brighten, and by 1943 Methodist was debt-free for the first time in its history. In late 1944, the M.D. Anderson Foundation, which managed the $20 million estate of cotton magnate Monroe D. Anderson, offered land to the institution in the newly created, 134-acre Texas Medical Center on what was then the outskirts of town. A $1 million gift from Houston oilman Hugh Roy Cullen and his wife Lillie, followed by a $500,000 challenge grant from M.D. Anderson Foundation trustees, financed construction of a hospital on the site.

The Methodist Hospital's reputation took a major leap forward in 1948 with the arrival of Dr. Michael E. DeBakey, a noted heart surgeon who became chairman of Baylor College of Medicine's Department of Surgery and began practicing at Methodist. In June 1950, Methodist and Baylor agreed to affiliate. After Methodist moved into a new 300-bed facility in the Texas Medical Center in November 1951, it quickly filled to capacity as patients arrived from around the world to benefit from its cardiovascular capabilities and other technological advances.

By 1954, the hospital had a regular staff of almost 300 physicians. Its annual patient census had grown to almost 16,000, and once again it was forced to turn patients away for lack of space. Although a new wing was added in 1963, the hospital was again operating at capacity within a year.

As The Methodist Hospital's reputation for excellence continued to grow, even more space was required to meet the expanding service demand. The Herman Brown and Ella F. Fondren buildings, totaling 273,000 square feet, were opened in December 1968 to house the Fondren and Brown Cardiovascular and Orthopedic Research Center.

By the beginning of the 1970s, The Methodist Hospital had 1,040 patient beds. The decade saw substantial growth in such areas as teaching, research, and outpatient services. As part of a $100 million expansion that began in 1972, the hospital built a Neurosensory Center to house the institutes of ophthalmology, neurology, otolaryngology, and expanding special services offered by the hospital. A $2 million contribution from the Alice and David C. Bintliff Foundation financed construction of the Bintliff Blue Bird Building within the Neurosensory Center to accommodate the hospital's growing pediatric neurology clinic. In 1980, the Total Health Care Center, which includes Scurlock Tower, its garage, and the Marriott Hotel, was opened, offering facilities to meet the needs of patients and their families outside the hospital. The 1978 construction of Alkek Tower, a four-floor addition to the Brown Building, was made possible by a $3 million donation from Mr. and Mrs. Albert B. Alkek of Victoria, providing space to house research facilities and services for cardiovascular inpatients. A $7.4 million grant from the Fondren Foundation in 1976 financed the six-floor expansion of the Fondren Building to add patient beds and more research and medical service facilities.

By the next decade, rising medical costs, increased competition, falling patient census figures, and growing government involvement in the health care field encouraged hospitals to share facilities and expertise. In October 1980, The Methodist Hospital board authorized formation of a community hospital network. By 1984, 15 hospitals with a total of 3,840 beds had joined the network. Methodist eventually purchased San Jacinto Memorial Hospital in Baytown, one of the original 15 in the network.

Continuing its expansion, in November 1984 Methodist launched a $196.9 million construction project boosting the bed total in its Texas Medical Center facility to 1,527. The three-phase endeavor included a 10-story hospital facility, the 25-story Smith Tower professional building, a 1,400-car parking garage, and renovation of the original buildings and concourses to link the buildings in the Methodist complex. In addition, a matching grant from the Cullen Trust for Health Care and a gift from The Hamill Foundation funded construction of a Multi-Organ Transplant Center. Concurrent with this physical growth, researchers at Methodist and Baylor continued to make major medical advances. Achievements including the development of ultrasonography for imaging prostate tumors, research into the chemical treatment of Alzheimer's disease, and experimentation with Tissue Plasminogen Activator, a drug for treating heart attacks, enhanced the institutions' reputations as research leaders.

Growth of the hospital's physical space and services continued into the mid-1990s. During this period, it acquired neighboring Diagnostic Center Hospital and the Visiting Nurse Association, and opened the Baylor Sports Medicine Institute and the Institute for Spinal Disorder in Scurlock Tower.

Today, The Methodist Hospital has more than 4,000 employees and 900 physicians on its active medical staff. It ranks among the most distinguished medical institutions in the world, with a reputation for excellence in such vital areas as cardiac care, cancer, neurosensory, and orthopedic care.

In response to a rapidly changing health care environment and the need to curb medical costs, The Methodist Health Care System has shifted focus from treating people who are sick to keeping people well. With this in mind, Methodist has entered into contracts with almost every managed care organization in the greater Houston area as well as two major health maintenance organizations. The system has also begun transition into an integrated delivery system addressing the full spectrum of community health care needs. All these efforts are aimed at furthering the organization's objective of making quality health care available to as many people as possible at the lowest cost through the provision of more preventive, primary, and home care services. The formation of the Methodist Health Care System - a network of area hospitals, health and medical centers, a primary care physician group, a secondary health maintenance organization, and VNA a home health care agency - will allow Methodist to take its high quality of care into communities outside Houston.

Throughout its history, The Methodist Health Care System and The Methodist Hospital have remained true to their mission to provide high-quality, cost-effective health care that delivers the best value to the people it serves in a spiritual environment of caring. The tradition of excellence that has characterized the organization for almost 80 years will continue as it strives to achieve its vision — to be Houston's leading health system.

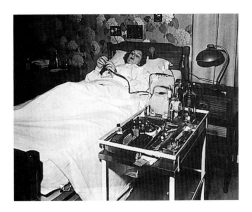

All the comforts of home? State-of-the-art patient care used to mean long hospital stays and cumbersome machinery.

Today, home care can make treatment a walk in the park.

St. Luke's Episcopal Hospital/ Texas Heart Institute

A Legacy of Quality

For more than four decades, St. Luke's Episcopal Hospital in Houston has offered an environment of health care excellence by blending quality medical care with compassion.

In 1954, Bishop Clinton S. Quin and the Episcopal Diocese of Texas founded St. Luke's to provide quality health care for the benefit of the community. Their vision was to advance medical care and enhance human life through education and research. Several years later, the Texas Heart Institute was established at St. Luke's—and an ambitious research program was combined with excellent patient care.

Today, St. Luke's builds on this vision. St. Luke's Episcopal Hospital is a nonprofit, 946-bed, acute-care multispecialty hospital, governed by 23 trustees from the community. Year after year, St. Luke's and Texas Heart Institute have been named among the top 10 cardiology centers in the nation by *U.S.News & World Report.*

1954 - St. Luke's Hospital

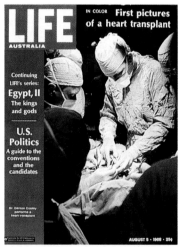

1968 - First successful heart transplant

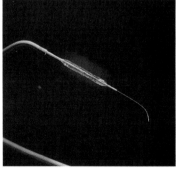

1985 - Laser angioplasty

1954

St. Luke's opened its doors as a 341-bed general hospital dedicated after nearly a decade of planning and hard work. St. Luke's became the 68th Episcopal hospital in the nation and the first new general hospital to be built in Houston since 1927.

1954

St. Luke's Auxiliary of 400 volunteers was founded by Mrs. Walter J. Kilpatrick and numbered more than 1,000 by year's end.

1960

Supported by donations from a former patient and her husband, St. Luke's formally dedicated the Linda Fay Halbouty Premature Nursery, which had grown from eight beds to 50 bassinets and isolettes.

1962

Cardiovascular surgeon Denton A. Cooley, MD, established the Texas Heart Institute (THI) at St. Luke's for the study and treatment of diseases of the heart and blood vessels.

1968

The world learned that the first successful heart transplantation in the United States had been performed at St. Luke's/THI by Dr. Cooley.

1969

The world's first total artificial heart implantation was performed at St. Luke's/THI, proving that a mechanical device could be used as a bridge to a heart transplant. The original heart can be seen in the Smithsonian Institute in Washington, DC.

1979

The first balloon angioplasty procedure in Texas was performed at St. Luke's/THI.

1984

To control costs of cardiovascular surgery, Denton Cooley, MD, introduced the concept of fee bundling, an efficient billing system for physician and hospital services. St. Luke's signed the first of many managed care contracts as large corporations and insurance companies took advantage of this innovative program.

1985

The first laser angioplasty procedure in the U.S. was performed at St. Luke's/THI.

1986

The world's first implantation of the battery-powered HeartMate, a left ventricular assist device used to sustain patients waiting for suitable donor hearts, was performed at St. Luke's/THI.

1988

The Hemopump—a tiny, manmade device designed to pump blood for a failing heart—was first implanted in a patient at St. Luke's/THI.

1988

St. Luke's dedicated its new, spacious Cardiac Catheterization Laboratories—still the largest and most fully equipped in the world.

1990

St. Luke's Medical Tower—a 29-story medical office building connected by skybridge to the hospital—opened. Expanded ambulatory surgery facilities reflected the changes taking place in the delivery of health care. The Tower's twin beacons have become the landmark of the Texas Medical Center, giving the Texas Medical Center a distinctive presence in Houston's skyline. The building has been featured in more than 40 publications, and in 1994 won first place in both the Houston and Southwest Regional divisions of the Building Office Managers Award.

1990

St. Luke's initiated its first outcomes management research program to define the best treatments for quality patient outcomes and cost control. (Now widely acclaimed, in April 1996, St. Luke's Center for Innovation hosted its Third Annual Outcomes Management Symposium. At the first symposium in 1994, close to 700 participants were enrolled, with representation from Canada, Australia, and the Far East.)

1991

St. Luke's Center for Orthopaedic Research and Education was established, with the unique goal of cultivating a molecular focus in orthopaedics.

1993

St. Luke's and Texas Heart Institute honored Drs. Cooley and Christiaan Barnard of South Africa with the Silver Heart Celebration—marking the 25th anniversary of heart transplantation.

1994

St. Luke's celebrated four decades of caring for the community. At the same time, Dr. Cooley marked his 50th year of active medical practice.

1994

The Texas Heart Institute was one of three cardiovascular centers in the nation to receive federal funding to develop a totally implantable artificial heart.

1994

Through its Stereotactic Radiosurgery Program, St. Luke's began offering the XKnife, a sophisticated nonsurgical option for the treatment of many neurosurgical conditions, including brain tumors. The program was the first XKnife program in Houston and the second in Texas.

1995

Supported by the battery-powered HeartMate, a patient returned to work while waiting for a heart transplant. Texas Heart Institute received approval from the Federal Food and Drug Administration to conduct clinical trials of the HeartMate as a permanent alternative to heart transplantation.

1995

The 600th heart transplantation was performed by physicians of St. Luke's/THI. St. Luke's is the world leader in the number of cardiovascular surgical and nonsurgical procedures performed, with more than 90,000 open heart procedures, 150,000 cardiac catheterizations, and 12,000 coronary balloon angioplasties performed since 1975.

1995

St. Luke's Cancer Program was awarded three-year approval for its community-based cancer program by the Commission on Cancer of the American College of Surgeons. St. Luke's was one of only four health care institutions in Houston to be categorized a cancer care "Teaching Hospital."

And Today...

In the current global community, St. Luke's Episcopal Hospital and Texas Heart Institute serve as a referral center for patients from across the United States and around the world. Beyond cardiovascular care, St. Luke's excellence extends to more than 41 specialties.

A major teaching hospital, St. Luke's provides an environment for information exchange among top caliber professionals from the world's medical community. New frontiers in research continue to be probed at the Texas Heart Institute and in many of St. Luke's specialty areas, including orthopaedics, oncology, high-risk obstetrics, neurosciences, urology, and digestive disorders.

Today, St. Luke's is an acknowledged leader in managed care initiatives and a designated "center of excellence" by major employers. Yet spirituality remains alive in this hospital, as its founders intended. Chaplains, care givers, and volunteers recognize the role each plays in helping a patient's spirit to heal. Art, music, humor—as well as the beauty of nature—enhance the well-being of patients and staff.

While meeting today's complex health care challenges, St. Luke's Episcopal Hospital is the center of science, talent, compassion, and quality medical care it was designed to be.

1990 - St. Luke's Medical Tower

1993 - Drs. Cooley & Barnard

1994 - Dr. Cooley

1994 - Modern technology at work

1996 - National recognition

INCARNATE WORD HEALTH SERVICES

In the 1850s, South Texas found itself in the midst of a battle with two dreaded diseases: cholera and yellow fever. Like many Texas towns of the era, San Antonio – where the epidemic was most rampant–contained a courthouse, several general stores, a drug store and most definitely more than one saloon. But it had no hospital and very few doctors. The city was under siege and the diseases took a terrible toll. The cholera epidemic alone lasted six weeks and claimed more than 600 lives. In the city with population of less than 4,000, disease was killing 25 percent of the populace. In 1860, another cholera epidemic struck. Again, the body count was high. The mayor of San Antonio and other civic leaders pleaded with Bishop Claude M. Dubuis to intercede the cultural and social force behind the Texas frontier: the Church. So Bishop pleaded to the Monastery of Incarnate Word and Blessed Sacrament in Lyons, France with the words:

Our Lord Jesus Christ, suffering in the persons of a multitude of the sick and infirm of every kind, seeks relief at you hands."

In answer to that call, the Reverend Mother Marie Angelique agreed to prepare women willing to respond to the call to travel to Texas for a ministry of health care. These brave Sisters were the first members of the religious order that became known as the Sisters of Charity of the Incarnate Word – and the beginning of what would become one of Texas' leading health care systems. Incarnate Word Health System.

Landing in Galveston after their trans-Atlantic voyage, those sisters set up a small hospital. Three years later, Mother Joseph, second superior of the Galveston community, sent three Sisters to open a hospital in San Antonio. In March of 1869, Sister Madeleine Chollet, Pierre Cinquin, and Agnes Buisson

Dr. Arthur Spohn.

left Galveston for San Antonio by stagecoach and traveled more than 280 miles. They arrived in San Antonio only to learn that the building intended for their use had burned to the ground. Undaunted by tragedy, the Sisters set out to rebuild the burned structure. After eight months of arduous effort, their first hospital was finished and named Santa Rosa Infirmary. On November 25, 1869, Sister Madeleine submitted an announcement to The Weekly Express informing the public that San Antonio's first private hospital would be open. On December 3, the day of the hospital's opening, the nine-bed hospital admitted eight patients. Through the year, Santa Rosa continued to reach out to meet unmet needs in South Texas, opening the state's first pediatric unit in 1918 which would later become one of Texas leading children's hospitals

The Sisters expanded their Santa Rosa health care services to open St. Anthony's Sanitarium in the Texas Panhandle in 1901. It has become the major referral hospital for parts of New Mexico, Colorado, Oklahoma, and Kansas, as well as the Texas Panhandle. In 1995, St. Anthony's consolidated with High Plains Baptist Hospital to become Baptist/St. Anthony's Health Care System to "create a stronger local presence for nonprofit Christian health care."

In 1905 the Sisters were asked by Dr. Arthur Spohn to staff and run the Spohn Sanitarium in Corpus Christi, now the Spohn Health System. The Spohn Sanitarium was built with the help of community leaders whose determination was so strong that nothing deterred them from getting donations to build and rebuild the much needed hospital. Prominent families such as the Kings and Klebergs were among the hospital's founding fathers and the "founding mother" was Alice Gertrudis King Kleberg who knocked on doors for six years to raise money for the original building. Then when it was leveled by a hurricane in 1919, she convinced her mother, Henrietta King, to donate five acres of land. Then, she gathered a group of community leaders, including John G. Kenedy who had already donated his house to be a temporary hospital, to help her in a second door-to-door campaign for building funds.

The Spohn Hospital continued to grow. By 1930, continued expansion and growth of staff changed the institution from a long-term illness care "Sanitarium" to Spohn Hospital with the mission of caring for the critically ill. Spohn continued its original mission to serve the middle class and poor of the region. The new Spohn Health System includes the Spohn Memorial Hospital, Spohn Bee County Hospital, a network of Spohn Neighbor Care Centers, Spohn Kleberg Memorial Hospital, and Rural Health Clinics in Falfurrias, Hebbronville, Kingsville and Bishop; also Practice Concepts (MSO) including the Gulf Coast Medical Clinic and South Texas Health Alliance.

In 1911, the Sisters began St. Joseph's Hospital and Health Center in Paris, Texas, which has become a major tertiary referral medical center for Northeast Texas and Southeast Oklahoma. St. Joseph's Hospital & Health Center also operates: TOPPS (Texas & Oklahoma Preferred Provider System), Health Solutions (MSO), and St. Joseph's Family Clinics in five Texas cities: Cooper, Honey Grove, Wolfe City, Deport, and Paris.

Most recent accomplishments at St. Joseph's include a redesigned, more efficient patient care delivery system. Also in 1995, St. Joseph became the second hospital in the Southwest to offer a new form of heart catheterization called "transradial coronary catheterization," and it completed a new radiology department with new and better diagnostic equipment.

In 1933, the Sisters assumed sponsorship of the Josephine Heitkamp Memorial Hospital in St. Louis, which became known as Incarnate Word Hospital in 1949. Originally an acute care hospital, it developed a program of services to provide a continuum of care for older adults. Then in 1995, Incarnate Word Hospital merged with Deaconess Health Center. Physician partners of the system are the St. Louis Medical Group, developed with Deaconess, and Southside Physician Hospital Organization, aligned with Incarnate Word, which together form the largest affiliated medical group in St. Louis. Deaconess Incarnate Word Health System includes Incarnate Word Hospital, St. Theresa's at South Gate and South Gate Terrace Retirement Apartments, Deaconess Medical Center-Central Campus, Deaconess Medical Center-West Campus, and Deaconess Occupational Health Center.

Meanwhile, the Sisters' San Antonio home base, Santa Rosa Hospital, has also continued to expand. Now called the Santa Rosa Health Care Corporation, it includes: Santa Rosa Hospital, Santa Rosa Children's Hospital, Santa Rosa Northwest Hospital, Santa Rosa Rehabilitation Hospital, Villa Rosa Hospital, Santa Rosa Home Health & Hospice, Santa Rosa Children's Clinics, Santa Rosa Community Outreach, and Primary CareNet (MSO), which includes Alamo Mental Health Group, Health Texas Medical Group, and Solomon/Anthony Clinic.

Today, the Sisters ministry in health care continues to provide services true to that original calling by Bishop Dubuis and in keeping with the mission shared by all of the hospitals and service of Incarnate Word Health Systems: To extend the healing love of Jesus Christ, the Incarnate Word."

Each day, the people in the hospitals and other services reach out to their communities with new medical technology, high standards of excellence, and a mission of caring planted firmly in the efforts of the founding Sisters of Charity pioneered the idea of a total system of medical care that would offer the latest preventive, diagnostic, and treatment facilities to care for the mind, body and spirit – Incarnate Word Health Services.

Spohns Hospital, Corpus Christi, Tex.

Spohn Sanitarium, 1905.

SCOTT & WHITE

Arthur Carroll Scott, M.D.

Raleigh R. White, Jr., M.D.

The story of the founding of Scott & White is the story of railroads and medicine. One of the largest multi-specialty medical centers in the United States, Scott & White began in Temple, Texas, an important crossroads town perched on the edge of the Blackland Prairie in Central Texas at a major juncture of two key rail lines. The institution, which will mark its Centennial in 1997, began in 1897, when Dr. Arthur Carroll Scott and Dr. Raleigh R. White Jr., joint chief surgeons for the Gulf, Colorado & Santa Fe Railway, formed a medical partnership for their private practice.

Expanding beyond service to railroad employees over the past century, Scott & White Memorial Hospital and Clinic has grown into one of the nation's largest multi-specialty medical centers, with approximately 460 physicians and non-physician-scientists in a group practice on its main campus and in its network of 19 regional clinics. Backed by its solid leadership of 100 years of delivering personalized, comprehensive, high-quality medical care, Scott & White is also a national pioneer in managed care.

Dr. Scott and Dr. White were responsible for overseeing medical care for railroad employees at the Santa Fe Hospital and for hiring "line physicians" who cared for railroad workers along the 1,284-mile steel network of Santa Fe track. Soon, railroaders and their families up and down the rail line felt they could trust their care to these two Temple physicians. Their joint practice was firmly grounded on the following principles:

1. Anything that will add to the safety of the patient must be provided.

2. The financial status of the patient shall never in any way modify the kind of service that patient receives.

3. Young physicians must be trained in the art as well as the science of medicine.

4. Nurses must be taught the art, science and philosophy of nursing.

5. The leaders of the institution must possess vision.

One of Dr. Scott's and Dr. White's most noted contributions to medicine was the use of the hot knife or thermocautery to treat cancer. Before antibiotics, cautery could excise tumors quickly with little bleeding and reduce the risk of infection. So deft was Dr. Scott's skill with thermocautery that he was among the first physicians in the United States to be able to remove metastatic cancer without injuring important nearby arteries and veins. Additionally, Dr. White championed the cause of patient's rights and professional ethics. In a series of speeches he exhorted fellow Texas physicians to give "a square deal for the patient" by eliminating fee-splitting and other unscrupulous practices.

From Dr. Scott and Dr. White's humble beginnings, patient registration grew each year, and they expanded into nearby buildings and property. Shortly before Dr. White's death in 1917, the hospital had developed from a mere 16 beds into a bustling clinic and 200-bed hospital with 5,278 patient registrations in one year. Patients from throughout the United States flocked to Scott & White for medical care. By the early 1920s, Temple proudly boasted its nickname "Hospital Center of the Southwest." The city also enjoyed a championship professional baseball team, called "The Temple Surgeons." In 1933, Scott & White was the first Texas institution to be accredited by the American College of Surgeons for cancer surgery and treatment. It was five years before any other Texas institution would earn that status.

Scott & White has continued to thrive with the excellent foundation established by its founders. In the late 1940s, the institution was reorganized into Scott & White Clinic and two not-for-profit entities, Scott & White Memorial Hospital and the Scott, Sherwood and Brindley Foundation. By the mid-1950s, the institution had grown into 31 buildings spread over nearly six city blocks near downtown Temple. In December 1963, the hospital and clinic moved to its present campus, a 240-acre hilltop in south Temple. The new $9.6 million building consolidated all Scott & White's services under one roof. In its first year on the hill, Scott & White had 54,900 patient visits. In 1995, more than 1 million patient visits were recorded.

By the time Scott & White celebrated its Diamond Jubilee and 75 years of service, the institution had completed a major expansion and had affiliated with the Texas A&M University Health Science Center College of Medicine. Medical students complete two years of basic science study at A&M in College Station and spend the last two years in clinical training based in Temple.

In the late 1970s, Scott & White expanded patient service into surrounding communities with a network

of regional clinics. Managed care was on the horizon, and Scott & White once again enjoyed visionary leadership. The institution now consists of the main site in Temple, and a network of 19 regional clinics situated throughout Central Texas. The Perinatal Center, designed especially for high-risk babies, serves a 21-county area.

The Scott & White Health Plan, a federally chartered, not-for-profit health maintenance organization (HMO), began in 1982. It has grown to be the nation's 18th largest group model plan. The health plan is nationally ranked in the top 10 percent of health plans for its quality of care and patient satisfaction.

These high satisfaction surveys reflect the fact that Scott & White has remained a leader in personalized state-of-the-art care. For example, in 1973, the Watson Wise Dialysis Center opened for patients with kidney disease, serving the 21-county area. To advance its diagnostic radiology services, in 1974 Scott & White was the second institution in the state to install an EMI Scanner and among the first to install a computerized tomography whole body scanner in 1980. In 1987, Scott & White put into service a magnetic resonance imager (MRI), the first in Central Texas. Also in that year it was the first Texas hospital and the second nationally to purchase a second-generation lithotripter to crush kidney stones inside the body without surgery.

In 1994 and 1996, Scott & White was ranked one of "America's Best Hospitals" in a national *U.S.News and World Report* survey which cited the institution especially for its gynecology, urology, orthopedic, and cancer services. A 1995 survey in that magazine included Scott & White as one of the top institutions in the nation for quality care in many other areas.

As a result, patients from throughout the United States and many foreign countries come to Scott & White for treatment, ranging from routine and high-risk obstetrical and newborn care to infertility treatments to up-to-date cancer treatment and care to cardiac surgery and rehabilitation, all available under one roof. More than 17,000 patients annually are admitted to the hospital, and more than 2,300 babies were born there in 1995.

Virtually all recognized medical specialties are available at Scott & White, including Allergy/Immunology, Cardiology, Internal Medicine, Dermatology, Endocrinology, Gastroenterology, General Internal Medicine, Geriatrics, Hematology/Oncology, Infectious Disease, Medical Diseases of the Chest, Nephrology/Hypertension, Neurology, Occupational Medicine, Rheumatology, Obstetrics/Gynecology, Occupational Medicine, Pediatrics, Physical Medicine and Rehabilitation, Psychiatry/Psychology, Radiology and Anesthesiology.

The Department of Surgery provides specialists in Cardiothoracic Surgery, Vascular Surgery, Dentistry and

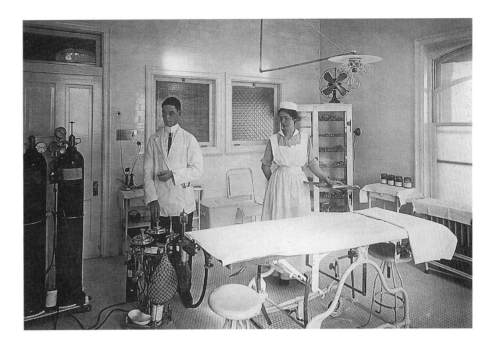

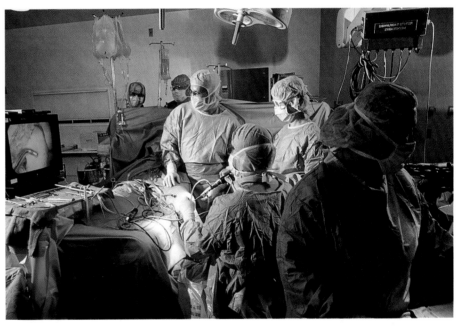

Oral Surgery, General Surgery, Neurological Surgery, Ophthalmology, Orthopedic Surgery, Podiatry, Otolaryngology, Pediatric Surgery, Plastic Surgery and Urology.

Initiated by its founders, the tradition of excellence is firmly established at Scott & White. A century ago, people needing high-quality medical care came by horseback, wagon and passenger train to Scott & White. Now, patients travel by car, train, airplane and Medivac helicopter. With its vast network of regional clinics, Scott & White can now provide primary care for other patients in their home communities.

The practice of medicine is changing radically, but Texans — no matter where they live — know they can trust Scott & White for personalized, comprehensive, high-quality care, just as their parents, grandparents and great-grandparents did.

Surgery at Scott & White in about 1914-1915 (pictured above) and modern orthopedic surgery.

HEARTPLACE

![Texas icon]

HeartPlace and the CPR Network have displayed innovative leadership in research and development by introducing new treatments and bringing together their experience, skills, and knowledge to improve patient outcomes.
Left to right: Rolando Solis, M.D., Peter Wells, M.D., Azam Anwar, M.D.

Since it was formed in 1962, HeartPlace has become the pioneer and recognized leader in cardiovascular care. With a record of innovation, quality patient care and well-planned, systematic growth, HeartPlace physicians established the first cardiology training program and the first specialized coronary care unit at Baylor University Medical Center. HeartPlace is the only cardiology practice in North Texas to significantly invest in health maintenance, primary prevention, and full-time physician specialists in cardiac rehabilitation and cholesterol-lowering therapy.

HeartPlace's 36 cardiologists specialize in diagnostic, interventional, preventive and cardiac rehabilitation and offer a full range of evaluation and treatment options. Many on staff were among the first in the Dallas/Fort Worth Metroplex to perform such procedures as cardiac catheterization, balloon angioplasty, cardiac laser and stenting, transesophageal echocardiography, thrombolytic clot-busting therapy, implantable cardiac defibrillation and electrophysiologic ablation. Some of their other milestones include: permanent pacemaker implants, radial angiography and radial angioplasty and the transradial approach for balloon angioplasty.

With 18 locations throughout North Texas and Southern Oklahoma, HeartPlace serves a large number of patients with its state-of-the-art technology. Focusing on high quality patient care, HeartPlace specialists perform more than 7,000 catheterizations and 2,500 angio-plasties annually. Its "patient-specific ap-proach" provides detailed information which is integrated into a total patient profile and, when necessary, rapid access for advanced treatment is available.

HeartPlace is committed to educating the public about the importance of adopting a "heart healthy" lifestyle through ancillary services such as health risk appraisals, stress and weight management programs and smoking cessation services. The objective is to reduce the need for end-stage surgery and cardiac intervention with the end result of lowering health care costs.

Patients receive the highest quality of medical, operational and customer service care. Services include: Same day appointments, 24-hour phone access and follow-up to post procedure care. Outpatient testing is available at select clinics and all locations offer free, easy access parking. All findings, recommendations and pertinent records are presented to referring physicians within 24 hours or as needed.

HeartPlace communicates with patients regularly and relies on patient satisfaction surveys to help maintain quality patient care and service. It also evaluates staff and physicians through its own internal Quality Improvement and Utilization Management programs.

Excellence is more than just a goal," says HeartPlace President Dr. Kevin Wheelan. "It is our normal operational standard. Everyone involved with HeartPlace realizes the importance of a well-coordinated, cooperative effort."

A centralized management system is the foundation of HeartPlace's success. This decade is seeing a change in the health care industry and the concept of a physician practice management company is a logical response to this new business environment. Cardiovascular Provider Resources, L.P. (CPR) which was formed in 1995, will become a multi-faceted physician practice management company (PPM). HeartPlace is the basis on which CPR was developed. That same pioneering force in quality patient care and well-planned growth is the underlying principle on which CPR will build. HeartPlace and CPR are shaping the future of cardiovascular services.

The Address is 3600 Gaston Ave., Suite 1157, Dallas, Texas, 75246. The telephone number is (214) 841-3800 or (800) 263-4795; Voice/TDD (214) 841-3809.

Irving Healthcare System celebrates 32 years of providing high-quality, cost-efficient health care to citizens of Irving and neighboring communities. Irving Healthcare System consists of a 288-bed acute care facility, The Irving Hospital; five medical buildings; Irving Cancer Center; Irving Heart Institute; Irving Women's Pavilion of Health; Howard Center for Behavioral Medicine; and additional medical, diagnostic, rehabilitative and surgical services.

Nestled between Dallas and Fort Worth, Irving Healthcare System has settled into a rather enviable position among its peers in the health care world. Positive achievements within the last two years have propelled the progressive organization forward into a leadership position in the Metroplex and reinforced its reputation for excellence. One of the highest possible scores from the Joint Commission on Accreditation of Healthcare Organizations (JCAHO), indicates that the hospital has achieved an exemplary standard of quality in all areas of operation.

One of the busiest emergency departments in Dallas County, Irving Healthcare System ER recently underwent a complete expansion and facelift, bringing more efficient care to the 51,000 people who seek services there each year. Completed in July 1996, the $9 million emergency department renovation features radiology and laboratory facilities and is one of only a few emergency facilities in the area to have CT scan equipment conveniently located in the department. Patients are directed to one of three patient care tracks for occupational health services, minor non-urgent care and emergency treatment, with separate entrances for convenience and efficiency.

An affiliation with Baylor Health Care System has opened the door to new services, new facilities and new plans for providing people with easily accessible health care they deserve. Signed on August 1, 1995, the agreement specifies a 20-year lease arrangement with Baylor Health Care System and the development of the Baylor western region which oversees all development in the western portion of the Metroplex, including Irving.

One of the first joint ventures between Irving and Baylor was Baylor Health Center at Irving.Coppell, located on a 27-acre tract on LBJ Freeway (Hwy. 635) and MacArthur Blvd. in north Irving. It is the first completed facility of a north campus for Irving Healthcare System, according to officials.

The 72,000 square foot building contains a day surgery facility, community education classrooms, the North Texas Center for Learning and Behavior, offices for primary care physicians and capability for future radiology and lab services. Plans are under way for further development of the property, which also fronts Highway 161 and Las Colinas Boulevard.

Some major services offered by the Irving Healthcare System include: Baylor Senior Health Center in Grand Prairie, the Osteoporosis Center and the Diabetes Lifestyle Center located within the Howard Center for Behavioral Medicine, Irving Heart Institute, Irving Cancer Program, and Irving Women's Pavilion of Health.

Other services recently added or expanded include: a new sleep lab, expanded Irving Adult Day Services, and Baylor SportsCare at Irving.

Since 1964, when it was first built as Irving Community Hospital, Irving Healthcare System has remained dedicated to the people it serves. The organization's growth and progress best benefits those people. Every service or program added, every step made toward the future is judged by the mission of Irving Healthcare System — to provide high quality health care, health education and service to the people of Irving and in the surrounding communities.

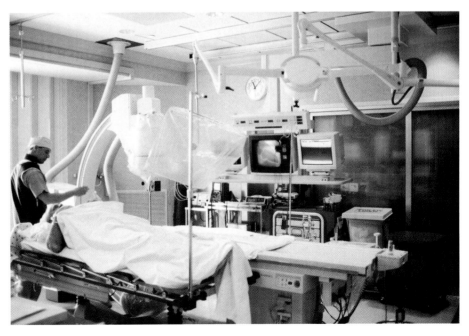

IRVING HEALTHCARE SYSTEM

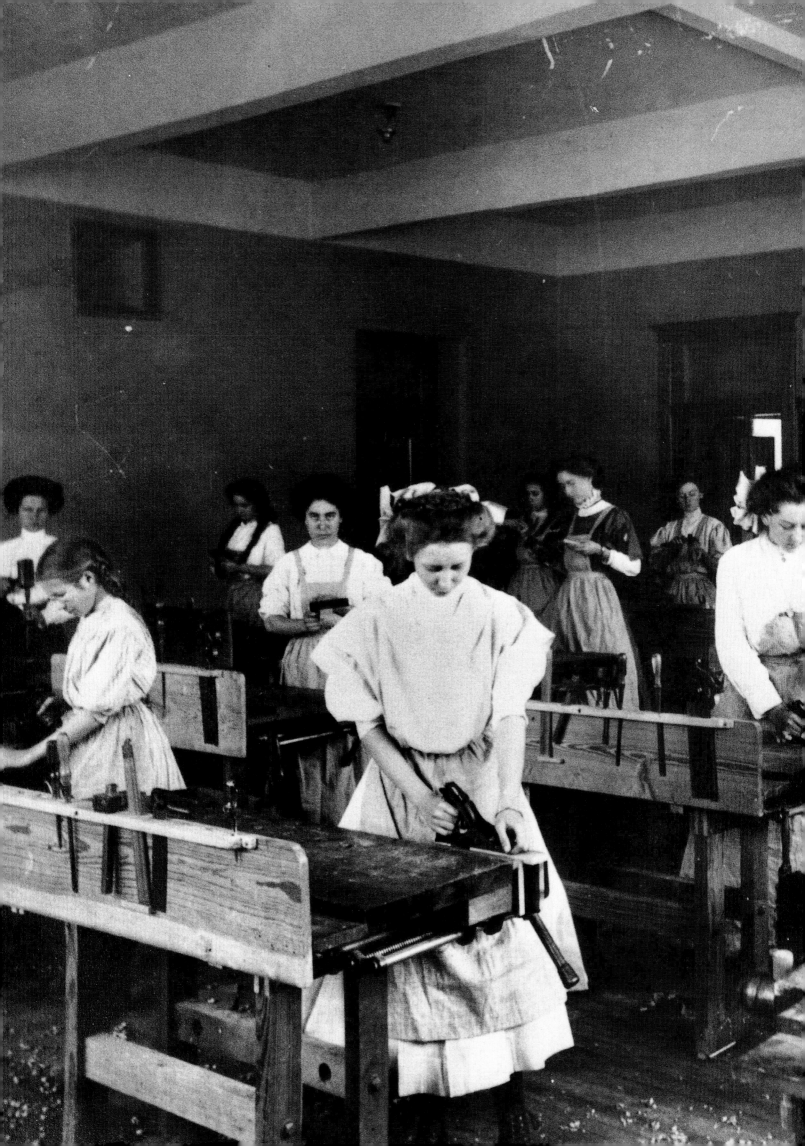

EDUCATION

institutions of higher education provide

Texans with the skills and knowledge

to lead the nation and the world

into the 21st century

Joinery Shop.

THE TEXAS A&M UNIVERSITY SYSTEM

TEXAS' FIRST, TEXAS PROUD

In a stately room of marble and oak filled with the echoing voices of Texas legislators, the people of Texas saw the concept of state-funded higher education—and The Texas A&M University System—become a reality in 1876.

With the passage of that state law establishing the state's first public college—named A&M College back then—the Texas Legislature created the beginning of the Texas A&M College System. That "system," although not officially recognized as such until 1948, is now The Texas A&M University System and remains focused on its original land-grant mission of service to all Texans, from all backgrounds, in all areas of the state.

Today, the A&M System is proud to provide a wide range of educational opportunities, from the nation's third largest university—Texas A&M University (originally called A&M College)—to our regional institutions from the Texas Panhandle to the Mexican border.

In addition to Texas A&M University, the Texas Legislature created as part of the system Prairie View A&M University, which opened in 1878. John Tarleton College at Stephenville (now Tarleton State University) joined the system in 1917.

After nearly 75 years, the A&M System experienced unprecedented growth in 1989 when three South Texas universities joined the system: Texas A&M International University (formerly Laredo State University) in Laredo, Texas A&M University-Corpus Christi (formerly Corpus Christi State University) and Texas A&M University-Kingsville (formerly Texas A&I University). In 1990, West Texas State University in the northwest Texas city of Canyon joined the A&M System and adopted the name West Texas A&M University in 1993.

The A&M System continues to grow and expand its reach in Texas. In 1995, the Texas Legislature approved the transfers of the Baylor College of Dentistry in Dallas and the East Texas State University Complex, now Texas A&M University-Commerce and Texas A&M University-Texarkana, into the A&M System, effective September 1996.

Universities Located from Border to Border

The 10 universities of the A&M System each have unique personalities and offer Texans a variety of educational environments. Whether it is a nationally known fine arts curriculum, teacher education innovations or an internationally recognized ROTC program, each of the universities contribute to the Texas way of life in their own way. However, they all share a common goal: providing the highest quality service possible to Texans of all ages.

The A&M System family includes a nationally known dental school, the Baylor College of Dentistry; an historically black university, Prairie View A&M University; Tarleton State University, the largest producer of agricultural education teachers in the nation; and Texas A&M International University, a top resource in international trade on the state's newest university campus.

In addition, the A&M System includes Texas A&M University, the third largest university in the nation and world-renowned as a land-grant/sea-grant/space-grant institution; Texas A&M University-Commerce, a premier university for public school teachers and the fine arts; Texas A&M University-Corpus Christi, dedicated to South Texas coastal and urban issues; and Texas A&M University-Kingsville, a national leader in bilingual education and top producer of Hispanic engineers.

Texas A&M University-Texarkana, an upper-level university focused on giving Northeast Texas citizens a convenient higher education opportunity, and West Texas A&M University, the northernmost senior institution of higher learning in the state, are also members of the A&M System.

As their personalities differ, so do the rich traditions and strategic initiatives of these universities. However, students—and the delivery of quality educational services to those students—remain top priorities for all.

Through traditional classroom learning and technological advancements in distance learning, A&M System universities give students the knowledge and skills they need to be successful in today's competitive workforce. For A&M System faculty and staff, inspiration and compassion come easy because their responsibility is clear. Building character and integrity in students is how the A&M System helps ensure another emerging generation of Texas leaders.

State Agencies Dedicated to Advancement

The A&M System also includes eight state agencies, focused on the areas of agriculture and engineering.

Agriculture has always been an important part of the A&M System's heritage, with the first state agency, the Texas Agricultural Experiment Station, established in 1887 and dedicated to agricultural research.

The other four agricultural agencies of the A&M System include the Texas Agricultural Extension Service, with its nationally recognized statewide outreach network serving Texas communities; the Texas Animal Damage Control

The Texas A&M University System Statewide Network

Universities
Baylor College of Dentistry
Prairie View A&M University
Tarleton State University
Texas A&M International University
Texas A&M University
Texas A&M University-Commerce
Texas A&M University-Corpus Christi
Texas A&M University-Kingsville
Texas A&M University-Texarkana
West Texas A&M University

Agencies
Texas Agricultural Experiment Station
Texas Agricultural Extension Service
Texas Animal Damage Control Service
Texas Engineering Experiment Station
Texas Engineering Extension Service
Texas Forest Service
Texas Transportation Institute
Texas Veterinary Medical Diagnostic Laboratory

Left: Each year the A&M System serves more than 85,000 students of all ages, from all backgrounds, all across the state. Each of those students is working toward a common goal—graduation day.

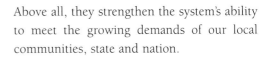

Above: Agricultural research is a top priority for the A&M System, as researchers and scientists across system universities and agencies work together to give Texans new food options, such as the 1015Y onion, the TAM mild jalapeno pepper, and the BetaSweet maroon carrot. Creative research continues in improving the nutritional make-up of crops and developing new uses for age-old plants, such as prickly-pear cactus.

Below: The A&M System devotes more than $378 million each year to research projects underway at system universities and agencies, ranging from nuclear engineering to biomedical science. Through basic and applied research, The A&M System helps answer questions, solve problems and create jobs.

Service, dedicated to protecting Texans from damages caused by wildlife; the Texas Forest Service, which develops and protects the forested areas of the state; and the Texas Veterinary Medical Diagnostic Laboratory, created to identify and prevent animal diseases, especially those transmitted from animals to humans.

Engineering research and technology transfer also have been a priority for the A&M System, with three agencies aimed at these dynamic areas: the Texas Engineering Experiment Station, dedicated to providing research and technology assistance to Texas businesses, industry and public systems; the Texas Engineering Extension Service, with its charge of developing a highly skilled Texas workforce; and the Texas Transportation Institute, created to conduct highway and other transportation-related research.

Through their service and research missions, all of these agencies have taken the A&M System's land-grant and technology transfer roles to the height of excellence in Texas and the nation. With locations and regional offices across the state and a presence in all 254 counties, A&M System research and extension agencies share the same vision and service goal of the system's universities.

The overall efforts of the A&M System's state agencies are directed toward addressing and improving the social, economic, educational, health and environmental conditions of Texans. Whether it is providing leadership initiatives for Texas youth, new crop developments, research in urban traffic reduction or job training for Texas firefighters and police officers, the agencies are dedicated to meeting the needs of a diverse Texas population.

Above all, they strengthen the system's ability to meet the growing demands of our local communities, state and nation.

LEADING-EDGE RESEARCH

The A&M System also is known for its role in leading-edge research. From archaeological excavations in foreign countries to molecular studies of subcellular particles and high-performance computing, research projects underway by A&M System universities and agencies total $378 million. Our research agencies work closely with Texas A&M University, which ranks fifth among all colleges and universities in the nation in research and development expenditures by the National Science Foundation.

The Texas A&M University System Technology Licensing Office, which assists A&M System scientists in disclosing and marketing their inventions, received more than $2 million in royalty income from licensed technologies in 1995.

From key technologies, the A&M System helps launch new companies that create jobs and stimulate industries. In fact, the A&M System tops historical technology powerhouses like Harvard University and University of California in transferring university and agency research for commercial development.

The ultimate purpose of all A&M System research is simple. The foundation of every project is to solve problems and investigate new technology to improve our economy and quality of life. A&M System agencies and universities are accomplishing that—one discovery at a time.

THE STATISTICS

The Texas A&M University System is one of the largest and most renowned systems of higher education in the nation. With headquarters in College Station and a presence in every county in the state, the A&M System offers a statewide network unlike any other.

Consider These Facts:

- More than 22,000 A&M System employees work to serve Texans.
- A&M System universities teach more than 85,000 students every year.
- The A&M System touches 3.5 million people annually through its service and

outreach mission.

- The annual budget for the A&M System exceeds $1.5 billion.
- The A&M System has been serving Texas for as long as there has been state-funded higher education—since 1876.

CONNECTING TEXANS THROUGH TECHNOLOGY

The A&M System has long been recognized as a pioneering provider and user of cutting-edge technology.

The A&M System statewide network is connected across the state by some of the most advanced technology available. Fiber optics, satellites and the Internet feed information to and from system universities and agencies in all parts of the state.

The Trans-Texas Video Conference Network (TTVN), a service of The Texas A&M University System, represents the very best in modern technology and distance communication. The TTVN, which is already one of the largest academic video conference networks in the nation, has grown from 12 network locations to more than 60 over the past four years. Facilities are available in more than 25 cities throughout the state and in Mexico City.

From El Paso to Laredo, the TTVN brings the A&M System closer to Texans in all areas of the state. A record number of 124 university credit telecourses, or distance learning courses, involving all A&M System universities were transmitted over the TTVN in 1995, providing students across the state with access to programs previously available only at specific A&M System campuses. This innovative network benefits not only A&M System students, faculty and staff, but state leaders, public school systems and the general public as well, with more than 500 videoconferences, telecourses and other broadcasts per month.

SERVING TEXANS, SHAPING THE WORLD

To achieve its goals for Texas, the A&M System continually seeks ways to increase educational quality and access throughout the state, obtain more state and federal funding and private support and expand collaborative efforts with universities and industry. The system also strives to achieve an ethnically diverse student, faculty and staff population;

improve national and international competitiveness and manage fiscal resources with continued efficiency and accountability.

The A&M System's vision is to be a premier source of education and training, leadership development, knowledge, and technology, based on a growing synergy and sense of family among members of the system. Combining resources, talents and expertise to work together with Texas communities for positive change is a top objective.

At the heart of all university and agency initiatives is the one reason the A&M System exists: to serve the people of Texas. Through its service mission, whether it is educating and developing Texas youth to be world leaders, conducting leading-edge research, or assisting in technology transfer for economic and industry growth, The Texas A&M University System is focused on the future and ready to lead Texas into the next century and beyond.

The A&M System's guiding premise is that education is about providing access to a better life for every Texan. That's why the accomplishments of A&M System universities and agencies are measured in increments of one—one student, one family, one community at a time.

SOUTHERN METHODIST UNIVERSITY

When the first students walked up the broad front steps of Southern Methodist University's Dallas Hall in 1915, they saw the promise of a fine university represented in the building's audaciously grand rotunda, inspired by Thomas Jefferson's design for the University of Virginia. However, when they turned around, they looked across a prairie of wild Johnson grass spreading for acres around them.

That first year there were 706 students — twice as many as expected — and 35 faculty members. Those pioneering students and professors were the direct beneficiaries of the bold vision of SMU's founding president, Robert Stewart Hyer, and the Methodist Education Commission that established the university. Competing with other Texas cities, Dallas won as SMU's location after civic leaders donated money and land for the campus. The city of Dallas was six miles south.

"SMU grew out of the Dallas soil," said R. Gerald Turner, SMU's 10th president and a Texas native who took office in 1995. "We've inherited the city's energy and its high expectations. Today, we have a beautiful campus in a quiet neighborhood with the vibrant city of Dallas on our doorstep. We've grown with Dallas, and we continue to expand that partnership."

From its beginning, when Dallas Hall housed the entire University, SMU has grown to include 75 buildings on 16.3 acres and offers a comprehensive curriculum nationally recognized for excellence. In its national rankings, US News & World Report termed SMU a "best value, " based upon institutional quality and financial aid.

SMU's more than 5,000 undergraduate and nearly 4,000 graduate and professional school students pursue degrees through six schools — Dedman College of Humanities and Sciences, Edwin L. Cox School of Business, Meadows School of the Arts, School of Engineering and Applied Science, School of Law, and Perkins School of Theology. SMU offers bachelor's degrees in 68 fields, master's degrees in 42 areas, doctoral degrees in 17 disciplines, and professional degrees in 16 fields.

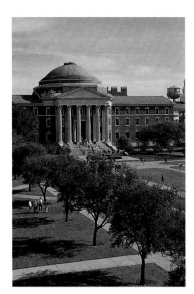

Dallas Hall through the years.

The University is fulfilling the promise seen by its first students because, from the beginning, its mission has been clear. When the University was chartered in 1911 by what was then the Methodist Episcopal Church South, its founders wanted to create a major Methodist university west of the Mississippi River — that is, a great university which happened to be established by the Methodist Church. Although SMU would "cherish the spiritual and moral values of the Church," it would above all be committed to free and open inquiry as the basis for intellectual pursuits, President Robert Hyer said. "Perpetuating a narrow, sectarian point of view falls far short of the standards of higher learning." SMU's mission was, and is, nonsectarian academic excellence. This openness is reflected in the religious diversity of the student body — 20 percent of SMU students are United Methodist, 19 percent are Roman Catholic. Other students represent Protestant denominations and other religions such as Judaism, Buddhism, Greek Orthodox, and Islam.

SMU's educational philosophy is also grounded in the liberal arts — the humanities and sciences that broadly educate students "so they can meet the challenges of the future understanding the perspectives of the past," President Gerald Turner said. Of the undergraduate classes, 71 percent have fewer than 25 students, and even the most senior-level, endowed professors teach first-year classes with enthusiasm.

SMU also attracts and molds leaders. "Our students are not only successful academically," he said. "Many of them come to us as leaders in their high schools and communities, or they develop leadership skills here through SMU's more than 150 student organizations. Our students also are active volunteers in the

Dallas community, strengthening that historic partnership."

Over the years, SMU's nurturing environment has launched many leaders in a variety of fields. Among them are former Dallas Mayor Robert Folsom, civic leaders R.L. Thornton and Ruth Collins Altshuler, oilman Ray Hunt, international industrialist Jerry Junkins of Texas Instruments, businessman Robert H. Dedman, Texas state treasurer Martha Hess Whitehead, and numerous members of Congress. SMU graduates have won the Nobel Prize in physics (James Cronin), the Pulitzer Prize in drama (Beth Henley) and reporting (Craig Fluornoy), the Academy Award for best actress (Kathy Bates), and the Tony Award for acting (Scott Waara). The inventor of the dynamic random access memory chip found in virtually every computer in the world is an SMU engineering graduate, Robert Dennard. About 60 percent of SMU alumni live in Texas, where they hold many of the state's top civic, corporate, and other professional positions.

As SMU prepares for the new century and millennium, its new president is building upon the University's founding vision to keep SMU moving higher into the nation's top tier of institutions. "Today, more than ever, we need a recognition, reaffirmation, and reformulation of those two bases that provided for the existence of SMU: leadership and partnership," said President Turner in his Inaugural address in September 1995. He outlined several priorities, among them increased globalization of the curriculum to prepare students for the global economy and Dallas' important role as a gateway to that world. One goal is to establish a Center for International Programs to serve SMU's international students as well as participants in the University's 14 study programs throughout Europe, Asia, and Australia.

Impetus behind increased globalization is spurred by the international scope of many major companies headquartered in Dallas. SMU leaders, committed to meeting the special needs of the region, believe educating students for corporate leadership in Dallas also will "prepare them for a potentially international life," President Turner said.

"A great training ground for understanding global, cultural, social, and political issues resides within the growing diversity of the American population — and of the SMU stu-

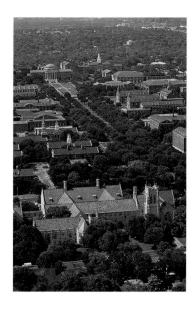

dent body," he said. "Tomorrow's leaders, at home and abroad, must be able to work effectively with people from different cultures, and fully appreciate the value of coalescing people from diverse backgrounds to work as a team."

SMU's progress in this regard is noteworthy. In 1987, total minority enrollment was only nine percent. In 1996, minority students make up 19 percent of the student body and 20 percent of the first-year undergraduate class. SMU students come from every state and more than 90 countries. Seventy-two percent of undergraduates attend SMU with some form of financial aid.

SMU also recognizes other changes in student demographics — the escalating number of nontraditionally aged students who seek higher education or retraining in mid-career or later. In addition to its popular evening Master of Liberal Arts and bachelor's degree programs on campus, in 1995 SMU started a Master of Divinity degree program in Houston and Galveston. The School of Engineering and Applied Science opened a center in the Telecom Corridor of north Dallas to serve professionals needing advanced training. The Engineering School transmits courses directly into company offices and military bases nationwide. For those who cannot attend classes on the Dallas campus, SMU will look for other ways to bring education to those who seek it, where they need it.

Future priorities include strengthening academic programs along the entire spectrum of communications — from writing skills at one end of the process to mass media and

Campus life.

telecommunications at the other. SMU plans to enhance its traditionally strong science programs "to become a, if not the, major per-medical and pre-health care educator in the area," President Turner said.

To remain faithful to its founding principles — nonsectarian, but church-related and thus value-centered — SMU knows it cannot ignore the unprecedented ethical challenges accompanying the social, cultural, and technological revolution of the past 30 years. Numerous courses, from science to law to business, include the study of ethical issues in those fields. And in 1995, SMU opened the Cary M. Maguire Center for Ethics and Public Responsibility to develop courses, sponsor seminars, and conduct research that can be applied to contemporary ethical issues.

Another new center of expertise will help the University enhance understanding of the unique past and potential of its region. The William P. Clements Center for Southwest Studies, part of the Clements Department of History, opened in Fall 1996. SMU's longtime strengths in Southwest studies include extensive library collections and a campus near Taos, New Mexico, which includes an archaeological dig of a 13th Century Anasazi Pueblo.

"Whether our students are on the Dallas campus, learning through internships with

our many corporate supporters, or engaging in field research in the mountains of New Mexico, the hallmark of their education is the personal touch," President Turner said. "We will keep our offerings up-to-date by meeting emerging needs and by using technology as a teaching tool, but we will never diminish our traditional focus on the individual. That's what sets us apart and helps our students stand out and become leaders in the community and partners in our continuing progress."

To those who wonder what the culmination of that progress will be, President Turner quotes Robert Stewart Hyer. Asked when the University would be finished, Hyer replied "After the city of Dallas is completed."

St. Mary's University is the oldest university in San Antonio and the oldest and largest Catholic university in Texas and the Southwest.

Located on a 135-acre campus about 10 miles from downtown San Antonio, St. Mary's is the only southwestern university founded on the Marianist tradition, the essence of which is nurturing students, coming from all faiths and backgrounds, and inspiring in them a sense of civic and moral responsibility. The Marianists are the Society of Mary, a teaching order of priests, sisters and brothers.

In 1996, for the third consecutive year, *U.S. News & World Report's* "America's Best Colleges" issue ranked St. Mary's as one of the best universities in the West region (sixth for discount price, seventh for sticker price and 14th for quality).

In addition to being the first university in San Antonio, St. Mary's was the first four-year university to bring doctoral-level education to the city. St. Mary's School of Law is the only accredited law school in San Antonio, and St. Mary's Graduate School has the only Catholic School Leadership degree program in the Southwest. In 1994, the university established the St. Mary's Service Learning Center, the only clearinghouse of its kind for community service projects in San Antonio. The center provides students, faculty and staff with community needs information and volunteer opportunities.

St. Mary's graduates are accepted into American medical schools at twice the national average, and law schools accept more than 80 percent of St. Mary's pre-law graduates. The university's fully accredited undergraduate programs in pre-medicine, pre-dentistry, pre-law, engineering, teacher education and business administration include a liberal arts core curriculum designed to educate students to a global vision though study of philosophy, languages, literature, history and the social sciences.

Although St. Mary's had humble beginnings, its tradition of fostering spiritual growth and community spirit along with intellectual achievement has directly impacted the lives of more than 22,000 individuals and indirectly shaped the education, life and destiny of a regional population.

In 1852, four Marianist brothers began teaching 12 boys in a Military Plaza livery stable. Construction of St. Mary's College on the banks of the San Antonio River was completed in 1853 and by 1891, St. Mary's College downtown had 448 students. Because the students needed a

quieter environment and the college needed to expand, the Marianists were offered a 73-acre tract in the Woodlawn Hills of Northwest San Antonio for $1 by the West End Town Company on the condition they would build a college within a year. St. Louis College opened for classes in September 1894. The old St. Mary's College campus is now a San Antonio Riverwalk landmark hotel, La Mansion del Rio. St. Louis College was chartered by the State of Texas in 1895 as a junior college, and offered regular collegiate degrees in 1904. St. Louis College became St. Mary's College in 1923, and was admitted to the Association of Texas Colleges as a senior college in 1925. It was chartered as St. Mary's University of San Antonio, Texas, in 1926, and is one of 39 members of the Independent Colleges and Universities of Texas.

Although the university continues to grow, it strives to maintain a close-knit, family environment in which personal interaction is encouraged due to a student-faculty ratio of 18 to one. In addition to their academic pursuits and community involvement, students on men's and women's athletic teams compete in 10 varsity-level sports.

In 1993 St. Mary's was one of two U.S. universities focused primarily on undergraduate education to receive the National Science Foundation's Institutional Achievement Award for outstanding education and training of minority students and faculty in science, engineering and mathematics.

St. Mary's students can enroll in more than 65 degree programs and participate in nearly 60 clubs and organizations. Each year, the St. Mary's Alumni Association sponsors the Fiesta Oyster Bake, drawing about 60,000 people and benefits student scholarships and university programs.

"More than 144 years ago, four brothers of the Society of Mary began this educational mission — a mission that continues to live on today," says St. Mary's University President, Rev. John Moder, S.M. "Now with modern technology in our classroom and lecture halls, St. Mary's University has kept pace with the transformations of our highly technical, ever-changing world . . . Although traditional teaching tools are being replaced or augmented with modern technology, the individualized teaching by our professors remains fixed. For it is in keeping with the Marianists' mission that we continue to strengthen our community as we move into the 21st century and beyond."

ST. MARY'S UNIVERSITY

St. Louis Hall, c. 1893, now an administration building.

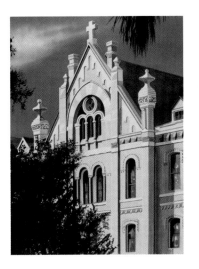

RICE UNIVERSITY

Right: Lovett Hall.

Below: Student life.

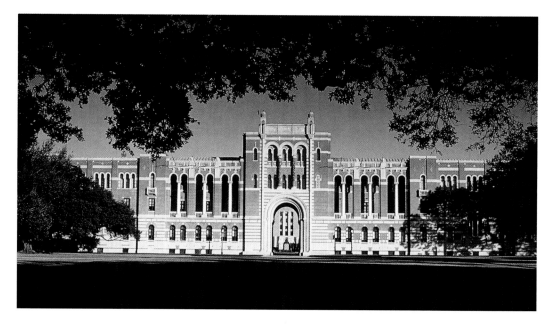

The history of Rice University, the premier private research university of the Southwest, is a story of foresight, resourcefulness, and dedication to the highest academic ideals. Yet it is a history that nearly failed to come into existence because of an elaborate scam to defraud its benefactor's estate. The Rice Institute for the Advancement of Literature, Arts, and Sciences was incorporated in 1891 by merchant William Marsh Rice. Mr. Rice, a native of Massachusetts, came to Houston in 1839, made a fortune, then retired to New York City. Childless, appreciative of the opportunities Houston had provided him, and contemplating what he might do for posterity, Mr. Rice decided to establish an academic institute.

He secured the incorporation with a note of indenture, gathered a group of trustees, and specified that after his death they should proceed with establishing the school. But an unscrupulous lawyer, Albert Patrick, had other ideas. Patrick devised a scheme to write a fake will giving himself most of Mr. Rice's fortune and have an accomplice murder Mr. Rice in September 1900. An alert bank officer noticed a discrepancy in a check and telegraphed Captain James A. Baker, Mr. Rice's Houston lawyer and chair of the trustees. Baker rushed to New York, spearheaded an investigation that resulted in Patrick being convicted, and saved Mr. Rice's fortune for The Rice Institute.

The endowment became available in 1904, but the trustees were very deliberate in planning the new university. In January 1908, at the urging of Woodrow Wilson, Edgar Odell Lovett, a mathematician and astronomer at Princeton University, was appointed president. Lovett was an inspired choice, and he soon set forth on a trip around the world visiting universities, interviewing scholars, and publicizing The Rice Institute. A noted architect was hired to design the campus, an international academic convocation was organized to celebrate the opening, and classes began on September 23, 1912, with seventy-seven students and ten faculty hired from famed centers of learning. From the beginning, Lovett envisioned Rice as a world-class university, with outstanding undergraduates, distinguished graduate work (the first Ph.D. was granted in 1918), and research and scholarship of the highest order.

If President Lovett could visit Rice today, he would be gratified at the ways in which the university has developed while, at the same time, adhering to his founding vision. After a period of austerity in the 1920s and 1930s, Rice entered a phase of expanding facilities and graduate programs in the late 1940s and again in the late 1950s. William V. Houston, president following Lovett's retirement in 1945, oversaw these developments. Kenneth S. Pitzer became president in 1961, and he increased the size and quality of the graduate programs and enhanced the humanities and social sciences.

Norman Hackerman took the reins in 1970, consolidated the gains of the previous decade, slowly expanded the enrollment, and established the schools of administration and music. George E. Rupp, the first president without a science background, led Rice from 1985 to 1993. He promoted interdisciplinary research institutes, further raised the academic ambitions of the faculty and board, and elevated the national and international recognition of the programs at Rice. Economist Malcolm Gillis became Rice's sixth president in 1993; he is a strong advocate of the interdisciplinary centers, is aggressively strengthening the diversity of the campus, and is internationalizing Rice's teaching, scholarship, and outreach programs.

Rice today has over fifty architecturally consistent buildings shaded by stately live oak trees on a campus of three hundred acres. The ensemble of buildings, characterized by arches, red tile roofs, and detailed brick work, is widely recognized as one of the nation's most handsome campuses. Because of its architectural beauty and academic distinction, Rice was chosen as the site of the 1990 Economic Summit of Industrialized Nations.

Rice enrolls approximately 2,700 undergraduates, all members of eight residential colleges—there are no fraternities or sororities—and 1,400 graduate students. An honor code is a cherished part of student life. The student body is among the most select in the nation, with the highest percentage of National Merit Scholars of any college or university. The middle 50 percentile of students have S. A. T. scores between 1350 and 1510. Rice's endowment in 1996 stood at $1.7 billion. Rice is the smallest university competing in Division IA sports, but its academic prowess is large.

Full-time faculty exceed 450 and include many who are internationally acclaimed. Rice's traditional strengths in the sciences and engineering are well known, but its schools of architecture and music are equally distinguished, and the programs in the humanities and social sciences are renowned. Rice graduates include a Pulitzer Prize–winning novelist, a Nobel laureate in physics, and seven astronauts.

From the very beginning, Rice has sought to balance teaching and research, technical and humanistic scholarship, pure research and service to society. Recent developments demonstrate a continued devotion to excellence. In 1991, two major buildings were completed, the prize-winning George R. Brown Hall for Bioscience and Bioengineering and the acoustically perfect Alice Pratt Brown Hall for the Shepherd School of Music. Just completed is a stunning building for computational engineering, a new approach to engineering in which Rice is a world leader. Under construction are a major facility for nanoscale science and technology, an innovative field in which several of the most important discoveries—such as the carbon molecule named buckminsterfullerine, or bucky balls—have been made at Rice, and a building to house the James A. Baker III Institute for Public Policy, where academic scholars and leaders from government and business will interact to study public policy issues ranging from international relations to health care. Additionally, a significant augmentation of Rice's Fondren Library is being planned.

These new facilities and the programs and resources they house illustrate the remarkable dynamism of Rice University today as it fulfills its mission of scholarship and teaching. A major research university with a commitment to the highest standards of achievement, Rice is a asset to the entire state of Texas. As President Edgar Odell Lovett envisioned in 1912, Rice is taking its place among the world's leading academic institutions.

Above: Campus life.

Below: Rice is known for its beautiful campus.

Baylor
College of
Dentistry

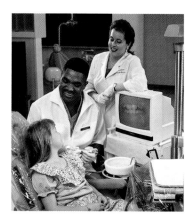

Baylor College of Dentistry is known for its extensive patient-care activities and its transfer of technological advances to students and practicing dentists.

PHOTO BY RICK MCDANIEL.

Below, Times and technology were different when Dr. Fred Reynolds, a 1915 Baylor College of Dentistry graduate, established his practice in the Texas Panhandle.

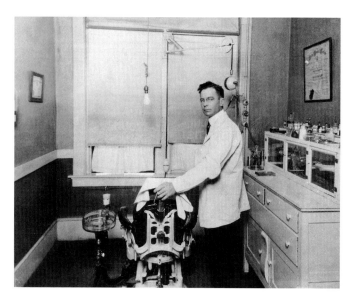

Dentistry needs no longer to conjure visions of painful drills and frightening forceps followed by painful pulling. Advanced technology in the field treats problems at their onset or even prevents them altogether.

Baylor College of Dentistry (BCD) offers dental education which can lead to health of body as well as mouth. The college is a leader and innovator in oral health issues affecting diverse areas of health care.

"The mouth is essential to the health of the rest of the body," said BCD president Dominick P. DePaola, D.D.S., Ph.D. "Beyond tooth decay and gum disease, it often mirrors a person's overall health and exhibits signs and symptoms of more serious health problems such as oral cancer, diabetes, developmental abnormalities, chronic medical conditions and immunological and auto-immune diseases such as HIV.

"Thus the dentist has become a critically important individual and a first line of defense as a primary health care provider," he explained.

Baylor College of Dentistry has sought, since its inception in 1905 as State Dental College, to equip dentists for front-line defense. Today, it is a recognized leader in dental education and research that has strong clinical applications as well as great relevance to other medical specialties.

"Scientific and technical advancements, changing demographics, the evolving profile of oral disease and the closer relationship between dental medicine and general medicine are exciting challenges for all medical educators," Dr. DePaola said.

BCD, which became a part of Baylor University in 1918, was chartered by the State of Texas as a private institution in 1971. On September 1, 1996, BCD merged with The Texas A&M University System. The community benefits from the college's commitment to total health. Today, it is the largest single provider of oral health care services in the Dallas/Fort Worth area, with more than 105,000 patient visits, 45 percent of which benefit low-income individuals. Oral health care services, including nearly $3.3 million annually in uncompensated dental care, are provided on-site at BCD's Dallas campus or through area hospitals and community centers.

Students at BCD receive a broad-based dental and medical education enabling them to effectively treat persons of all age groups as well as those with disabilities

and infectious diseases. The college offers a four-year program leading to a Doctor of Dental Surgery degree; a two-year program offered to junior-level college students leading to a bachelor's degree in dental hygiene; several master's degree programs; a Ph.D. in biomedical sciences and postdoctoral programs in the dental specialties. Advanced training is available in oral and maxillofacial surgery, periodontics, pediatric dentistry, orthodontics, endodontics, prosthodontics, dental public health and general dentistry. An M.D. program offered in collaboration with Texas Tech University Health Science Center at Lubbock provides unique educational opportunities.

"The college is a major player in this new professional era," Dr. DePaola said. "We are dedicated to education, research and service and to serving as a key component in the state's academic health and higher education community."

His statement is borne out in many ways. Baylor College of Dentistry was recognized as one of the top four dental institutions in the United States for periodontology, endodontics and geriatric dentistry by *American Health Magazine*. A poll conducted by *US News & World Report* ranked the college among the top 15 dental schools nationwide. Research initiatives at BCD include studies of the impact of aging, trauma, surgery and replacement procedures on the functions of the mouth, and the involvement of a calcium-binding protein in neurodegenerative diseases such as Parkinson's and Alzheimer's. Other research activities include the efficacy of laser therapies for various dental procedures, and the role of citrus products and coffee in inhibiting oral cancer.

To support such research and to assist practitioners and patients, BCD has a variety of highly specialized centers. The Stomatology Center facilitates diagnosis and treatment of patients with unusual and debilitating problems of the mouth. The Craniofacial Research and Diagnosis Center is a national leader in the study of craniofacial growth and developmental disorders. The Oral and Maxillofacial Imaging Center offers CAT scans and the latest in 3-D imaging to advance treatment planning for the head and neck region. The Salivary Dysfunction Clinic serves patients suffering pain and distress caused by disorders or damage to the salivary glands.

"Dentistry has changed forever," Dr. DePaola explained. "Our areas of concern have evolved tremendously from the old days of simply dealing with cavities. Today's cutting-edge research and technology clearly show us that good oral health care is a key factor in overall health."

Baylor College of Dentistry will continue to seek the frontiers of technology to prevent and treat oral disease. The State of Texas can only benefit from BCD's commitment to total health.

Celebrating 30 years of providing accessible, affordable and high quality educational opportunities, Dallas County Community College District has evolved over the years, reflecting the ever-changing needs of its students.

Dallas County Community College District began in 1966 with one college, El Centro, and a modest enrollment of 4,000 students. Today, the district's seven colleges, its economic development center and telecommunications center sustain 47,000 credit student and more than 48,000 non-credit students, earning it the distinction of the largest institution of higher education in Texas and a place among the six largest community colleges in the United States.

Conveniently located throughout Dallas County, the district's campuses include Brookhaven in Farmer's Branch, Cedar Valley in Lancaster, Eastfield in Mesquite, El Centro in downtown Dallas, Mountain View in southeast Dallas, North Lake in Irving and Richland in northeast Dallas.

The district's curriculum has more than 100 technical/occupational programs leading to a one-year certificate or two-year associate degree. Courses and programs reflect the changing needs and lifestyles of the student population, which now averages 29 years old. According to Lyle Henderson, public information officer, more adults than ever are going back to school to earn a degree or attending college to learn new skills for their jobs. DCCCD offers today's students what they need and want -- hands-on, practical learning experience in an accelerated format. Classes are

offered in a weekend format, fast-track or mini-semester to better accommodate the adult students job and family responsibilities. The distance learning program has three types of instruction and learning that rely on the latest telecommunications technology -- computer modem classes, telecourses and live televised classes.

DCCCD is fortunate to have the benefit of two distinctly different business and educational centers, the R. Jan LeCroy Center for Educational Telecommunications and the Bill J. Priest Institute for Economic Development. With its alternative learning programs such as Going the Distance, The LeCroy Center at DCCCD is a major supplier of telecourses to the PBS Adult Learning Service and Canadian networks, with its courses having enrolled more than one million people around the world.

Within the Bill J. Priest Institute for Economic Development, The Edmund J. Kahn Job Training Center offers short-term intensive vocational education and training in computer software, medical office services, auto mechanics/engine repairs, customer service and accounting. The Business Incubation Center supports young companies during their first four years of business providing professional business services, management assistance and training. The Small Business Development Center programs help entrepreneurs build their businesses from the ground up, including providing assistance with government contracting, international trade, and development of new technology. Business and Professional Institute (BPI) offers customized assessment and training programs to businesses to help their employees improve job performance.

High quality education is top priority at DCCCD and according to a recent poll by the Texas Higher Education Coordinating Board, the DCCCD has the lowest tuition rate among community colleges in the state, making it the best educational bargain in Texas! Scholarships, loans, grants and work programs make an education attainable for most students who need financial assistance.

The mission of the DCCCD is "to equip students for successful living and responsible citizenship in a rapidly changing local, national and world community." Through its advanced learning technology, its evolving variety of educational opportunities and the continued support of the business community, Dallas County Community College District remains true to its high standards and to those of its students.

DALLAS COUNTY COMMUNITY COLLEGE DISTRICT

HUSTON-TILLOTSON COLLEGE

Huston-Tillotson College is looking ahead to the 21st century as Texas celebrates 150 years of statehood.

The college on the high ground east of the State Capitol is the oldest institution of higher learning in Austin. Its foundation stands on the solid bedrock established by its founders more than 120 years ago. Tillotson College was founded in 1875 by the Congregational Church after the Rev. George Jeffery Tillotson, a retired minister from Connecticut, chose Austin as the site.

Samuel Huston College was established by the Methodist Church in 1876. It was named for Samuel Huston, an Iowa farmer, who donated $9,000 toward erection of its first building. Although a merger of the two colleges was first broached in the 1930s, the trustees of the two colleges didn't agree to the final details for two decades. The trustees of both colleges signed the document creating Huston-Tillotson College on Oct. 24, 1952.

The college always has welcomed students of all ages, races, nationalities and faiths.

As Huston-Tillotson College retains its strong heritage, the administration, faculty and staff are currently making improvements for future generations of students. The college's vision statement — "Focused on the Future" — aptly describes its mission to educate a diverse, multi-cultural community of students for leadership and service in the 21st century. That ideal reaffirms the founders' beliefs in the power of education to inspire and uplift individuals and transform society.

Students today gain an excellent liberal arts education at the institution that is accredited by the Commission on Colleges of the Southern Association of Colleges and Schools.

The college receives more than $3 million in annual, private gifts and grants, including more than $1 million from the local and national campaigns of The College Fund/UNCF. Additional gifts come from The United Methodist Church, United Church of Christ, other churches, foundations, corporations, alumni, and individuals.

So as the 21st century approaches, Huston-Tillotson College is drawing upon the strength of its roots in the past and the resourcefulness of its leaders today to meet the demands of tomorrow as an institution that is "Focused on the Future."

Huston-Tillotson College students receive hands-on education for 21st century careers.

The Administration Building stood at the former site of Samuel Huston College in Austin.

Students pose on the steps of Evans Hall after its construction in 1911-12 at Tillotson College.

The bell tower at Huston-Tillotson College, Austin's oldest institution of higher education, is a city landmark.

The National Institute of Technology, a Corinthian school, provides vocational and technical training programs to serve the changing needs of business and industry. The school teaches specialized skills in high demand in three principle areas: allied health fields, electronics, and business. Its objective is not only to give students the necessary skills and knowledge to become proficient in their chosen careers, but to help them find jobs in the shortest possible time. Graduates rapidly enter the workforce in banks, accounting firms, government agencies, medical and dental offices, laboratories, industrial plants and military installations with the help of job assistance and placement services that support the transition from classroom to workplace.

Unlike some larger colleges and universities, the NIT offers small classes and promotes student-instructor interaction in a professional atmosphere. Instructors are professionals in the occupations they teach, and classes simulate work environments and use up-to-date equipment that students will find on the job. Each program provides students with a foundation as well as practical training in their chosen field.

Electronics students learn the fundamentals of computer theory, solid state circuitry, analog and digital electronics, microprocessors, and computer software and hardware as well as the practical installation, maintenance and repair of computers, cable television, and other electronic equipment. These graduates work for Texas employers including H.E.B., Texas Business Machines Company, Tandy, Mobil and the U.S. Air Force.

Business students preparing for jobs in major corporations and industries study secretarial science, sales, and management methods, as well as accounting, spreadsheet methods, word processing, desktop publishing and other telecommunications skills. These individuals have been hired by such firms as Wal-Mart, AT&T, San Antonio's La Mansion del Rio, K-Mart, H.E.B., Sears and the Alamo Title Company.

Responsive to rapid changes in the health care industry, students in allied health fields gain administrative and clinical skills to prepare for positions in clinics, hospitals, health maintenance organizations, offices and laboratories across the state of Texas. These students may specialize as technicians in areas ranging from cardiopulmonary or chiropractic medicine to pharmacology or veterinary science.

As the nation strives to develop highly skilled workers to keep up with global competition, many believe that business should become more involved in education. It may come as a surprise, therefore, to discover that the National Institute of Technology has been a business enterprise in the field of education for over fifty years. When it began in 1935, the institution was one of a series of RET Electronics Schools whose graduates sought jobs working mainly in radio, the newest innovative technology of an era when young men aspired to the genius of Thomas Edison. Subsequently, as in other operations into nationwide networks to expand and increase their market share. In 1978 the National Education Corporation acquired several RET schools, and in 1983 changed the name of the San Antonio facility to the National Education Center-National Institute of Technology Campus.

The school moved to its present location in 1987, and subsequently expanded its curriculum to include both its medical assisting and business programs. Located on Fredericksburg Road inside Loop 410, the current San Antonio campus consists of a single modern air-conditioned facility with over 28,000 square feet of space, including twenty-three classrooms and a library. The owner of the business is Corinthian Schools, Inc. of Santa Ana, California. At that time, Corinthian acquired sixteen schools from the National Education Corporation, including its San Antonio school operation.

With the majority of its students drawn from the local community, the NIT student population has totaled as many as 450. In 1996, training for medical assistants, electronics repair and maintenance or basic business skills took from seven to nineteen months at a cost of between seven and thirteen thousand dollars.

Accredited by the Commission of Career Schools and Colleges of Technology, NIT offers students access to numerous government funding programs including the Federal Stafford Loan Program (FSL), the Federal Parent Loan for Undergraduate Students (FPLUS), Federal Perkins Loan, Federal Pell Grant and Federal Work Study (FWS) programs, and Federal Supplemental Educational Opportunity Grant (FSEOG). The school is also authorized to enroll non-immigrant alien students and is approved for the training of veterans and eligible persons under the provisions of Title 38 of the US Code.

Students in National Institute of Technology's Allied Health Fields program get "hands-on" training at giving inoculations.

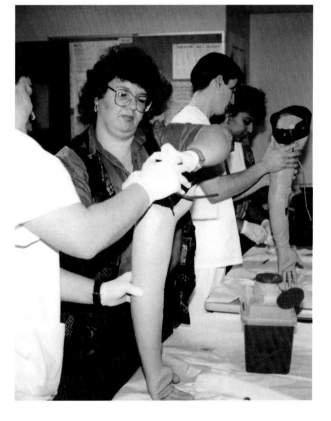

Our Lady of the Lake University

The Gothic spires of Our Lady of the Lake University's buildings symbolize its graceful times past, and they guide the eye upwards to symbolize the university's unlimited vision for the future.

Founded by the Congregation of Divine Providence as Our Lady of the Lake Academy, a high school for girls and a teaching academy for the Sisters, Our Lady of the Lake University observed its centennial during the 1995-96 academic year. The first 100 years showed a vision for the needs of the community, which led to innovative education, expansion, and several "firsts" in area academic achievement. Our Lady of the Lake University was the first institution of higher learning in San Antonio to be fully accredited. It started the first school of social service in the Southwest, and was first in the area to offer a doctoral program in counseling psychology.

The university is located on a 72-acre, tree-shaded campus about three miles from downtown San Antonio, next to Lake Elmendorf, and it has been affectionately nicknamed "The Lake." Its architectural styles, which range from Gothic to modern, reflect the many changes that have occurred at The Lake in response to the changing needs of the community it serves.

By 1911, Our Lady of the Lake Academy had doubled the size of its original Main Building and started a liberal arts school for women with only one student, who received private lessons. The State of Texas approved Our Lady of the Lake as a junior college in 1918 and, in 1919, authorized the college to award four-year degrees. To accommodate students seeking teaching certificates, an elementary school, St. Martin Hall, was built in 1929.

In 1950, the Department of Education began offering a master of arts in education, and the State Board of Education approved its teacher education program in 1957. The high school closed in 1966 and a major change occurred in 1969 when The Lake became co-educational. In 1975, the college became Our Lady of the Lake University, reflecting its more complex structure and expanded course offerings.

The success of Our Lady of the Lake University's Weekend College is an outstanding example of the university's tradition of responding to community and student needs with innovative programs. In 1978, The Lake introduced the first Weekend College in South Texas. It added a master of business administra-

tion degree in 1983, then opened a Houston branch in 1986 and a Dallas branch in 1994. The Houston Weekend College began offering an MBA degree in 1992, and a second Houston branch opened in 1995.

More than 3,300 students are enrolled at The Lake in more than 40 undergraduate, graduate, doctoral, and professional programs in the College of Arts and Sciences, the School of Business and Public Administration, School of Education and Clinical Studies, and the Worden School of Social Service. The Lake has 115 full-time and 100 part-time faculty; about 67% of the full-time faculty hold doctoral or other terminal degrees. The student-teacher ratio is about 16:1. While the majority of students are from Texas, 23 states and 14 foreign countries are represented. About 450 students live in the residence halls.

Bachelor's degrees include Bachelor of Arts in about 25 fields; also Bachelor of Science, Social Work, Applied Studies, and Business Administration. Also offered are: prelaw, premedical, pre-medical technology, and prenursing programs; interdisciplinary majors in 11 fields; a dual-degree engineering program that leads to a B.A. in liberal studies and a B.S. in engineering; also, teaching certificates in bilingual, elementary, secondary and special education. A Bachelor of Applied Studies degree is offered to students having 18-30 hours of credit in a technological specialization from transfer courses, life or work experience, or credit by examination. The most recent curriculum additions are an Electronic Commerce degree program and a Master of Arts in Sociology, with emphasis in Sociological Practice.

Reflecting on The Lake's 100 academic years, University President Sister Elizabeth Anne Sueltenfuss, CDP, Ph.D., said, "Our Lady of the Lake University has a proud heritage, adapting to changing times and differing student needs, building an inclusive educational community, and leading the way in serving both traditional full-time students and the non-traditional older student."

TSTC, then James Connally Technical Institute, was created in 1965 by the Legislature to meet the evolving work force needs of Texas business and industry. The looming need for a special institute for technicians had been a pressing issue for state leaders and the soon-to-be-abandoned James Connally Air Force Base in Waco was the ideal location for the top-quality technical institute they had planned. Governor John Connally predicted the institute would be, "the most sophisticated technical-vocational institute in the country."

In January 1966, JCTI began to fulfill the vision of state leaders by offering hands-on instruction in advanced programs such as metrology, chemical technology, and industrial design and drafting. The following year, the Legislature approved a second campus for the South Texas region. The Harlingen campus, also built on an abandoned air force base, immediately found strong support and rapid growth. In 1970, the Legislature approved additional campuses on former air force bases in the Panhandle region at Amarillo and in the West Texas region at Sweetwater. As demand for quality technical education grew, TSTC extension centers were approved for McAllen (1983), Abilene (1985), Breckenridge (1989), Brownwood and Marshall (1991).

The year 1991 brought exciting change and opportunity for Texas State Technical Institute. As an institution of higher education, the Legislature officially recognized TSTI as a college and changed its name to Texas State Technical College System. Since then, the TSTC System has had an enrollment increase of about 1,400 students between 1991 and 1996 (at present locations). In 1993, Texas voters approved a proposition which placed TSTC under the Higher Education Assistance Fund (HEAF).

Today, Texas is reaping the rewards of an established, world-class technical education system. TSTC, with its statewide role and mission, is efficiently and quickly reshaping the face of Texas to meet the high-tech challenges of today's global economy. TSTC's high graduation rate, strong relationship with business and industry, and state-of-the-art laboratories are providing productive and responsible graduates for employers across Texas.

Among the strengths of TSTC's success are an emphasis on "learning-by-doing," where students are provided hands-on opportunities to apply technology; residential campuses which permit students from across the state to attend full-time; and a student-centered philosophy:

"We believe in people. We believe people desire to be responsible and productive citizens. ...We believe technology is a force to be explored and channeled by people in a productive and responsible manner for the benefit of all mankind. ...Therefore, we believe all people should be provided with the educational opportunity to learn the skills necessary to perform meaningful work and thereby pursue their goals as responsible citizens contributing to the welfare and success of their family, community, state, nation and world."

The Texas State Technical College System is a state funded coeducational two-year institution of higher education, offering an associate of applied science degree or certificate in technology fields. TSTC has an outstanding history of graduating Texans from diverse cultural and socioeconomic backgrounds in technical programs critical to the economic development of Texas. TSTC's telephone numbers are: in Harlingen - 1-800-852-8784; in Sweetwater, Abilene, Breckenridge, and Brownwood - 1-800-592-8784; and in Waco and Marshall - 1-800-792-8784.

TEXAS STATE TECHNICAL COLLEGE SYSTEM

(Left) Nationally recognized for its high graduation rate and boasting a job placement rate of 88 per cent, TSTC emphasizes laboratory experience.

(Below) Industry partnerships are vital to TSTC's success. Semiconductor Manufacturing students use a robotic wafer sorter donated by Advanced Micro Devices. The average starting salary in this field is $30,000.

WILEY
COLLEGE

Wiley College, founded in 1873 by the Freedman's Aid Society for the purpose of providing an education for newly freed men and women, is a four-year private, coeducational institution.

Following Wiley's 1882 charter in Marshall, Texas, the Freedmen's Aid Society became the Board of Education for Negroes, which merged with the Board of Higher Education of the United Methodist Episcopal Church.

Currently the culturally diverse and growing enrollment of over 600 students represents 23 states and seven foreign countries.

Wiley College, an open-admission institution, offers 23 degree programs and a student-teacher ratio of 15 to one in a Christian environment.

The commitment of the college is to provide a broad liberal arts and career-oriented education facilitated by a faculty of 60-percent earned doctorates. Wiley emphasizes the power of inquiry, the command of language and insight into ethical thought. To enable each student to function effectively in a pluralistic, highly technological and rapidly changing global society, the college fosters the development of critical thinking and the search for values embracing contemporary society's emphasis on innovation and competition across disciplines.

In 1932 under the leadership of President M.W. Dogan, Wiley College became the first of the Negro Colleges west of the Mississippi River to be granted the "A" rating by the Southern Association of Colleges and Secondary Schools. In 1960 Wiley was reaf-

firmed under the new SACSS standards. Today Wiley maintains full accreditation by the Commission on Colleges of the Southern Association of Colleges and Schools to award baccalaureate degrees. As an institution of the United Methodist Church, Wiley maintains a state and church-related accreditation by the Texas Education Agency and the Commission of Black Colleges of the University Senate of the Board of Higher Education and Ministry of the United Methodist Church.

Under the leadership and vision of Dr. Lamore J. Carter, the 14th president, Wiley College is on course to achieve the goals of the Five-Year Plan approved by the Board of Trustees and designed to prepare Wiley for the year 2000 and beyond. Currently the college is pursuing a $10,000,000 Capital Campaign and seeking to meet the Mabee Foundation Challenge of 2.65 million dollars for bricks and mortar projects.

With enthusiasm Dr. Carter is often heard speaking of Wiley's future, "The best is yet to come." The vision for the college is to be a highly-ranked academic institution drawing from the wisdom of time as stated in the Alma Mater refrain, "Oh, Lord, we pray, may our dear WILEY stand a beacon light shining o'er our dear land. And may her sons with steadfast purpose true; go forth inspired glorious deeds to do."

The wooded, 63-acre campus is located 145 miles east of Dallas and 38 miles west of Shreveport, Louisiana. Off I-20, follow Exit 43 North. Turn north on Rosborough Springs Road. The Wiley campus is at the first intersection of the first traffic light.

Rattlesnake. *Oil on board, painted by De Forreset Hale Judd. Snake, rocks and cactus painted in cubes and planes of color.*
COURTESY, THE TORCH COLLECTION, HOUSTON, TEXAS.

THE MAKING OF *HISTORIC TEXAS*

Historic Texas: An Illustrated Chronicle of Texas' Past is the fortuitous convergence of disparate forces during 1995 and 1996.

The first, and foremost, force was the desire by Preservation Texas, Inc. to strengthen its private sector voice for historic preservation in Texas. The *Historic Texas* project has allowed Preservation Texas to dramatically increase its name recognition dramatically, particularly within the Texas business community. Simultaneously, it has provided an opportunity for the organization to earn new income to help carry out its ambitious and varied agenda of historic preservation.

The second force was the decision by a specialized publishing company, Lammert Publications, Inc. of San Antonio, to expand into the publication of art-style illustrated history books. In 1995, our 23-year-old company established a subsidiary, Historical Publishing Network, whose mission is to help preserve in print some of the nation's invaluable local historical narratives. *Historic Texas* is the first major endeavor of the new entity.

By extending an opportunity to select corporations, communities and organization to share their own corporate history as a part of the book, Historical Publishing Network has made it possible for Preservation Texas to place its name on a new illustrated history of Texas without having to capitalize the project, and to earn income and expand its base of members and benefactors. The income received from these "corporate sponsorships" funded the writing, research and production of *Historic Texas*.

The third force was a belief shared by many of us with a love for the rich story of Texas, that a new comprehensive history of the state, with a focus on the visual, made good sense and was especially timely in light of the book's commemoration of the 150th anniversary of statehood.

The fourth force was the desire of Dr. Archie McDonald, one of Texas' most eminent history scholars, to write a new and distinct history of the state. In his manuscript, Dr. McDonald's challenge was to revisit the old story of Texas, keeping in mind that his words would need to complement and expand on the hundreds of illustrations and photographs planned for the book. He did an admirable job of meeting that challenge.

The fifth was Dr. McDonald's introduction of Dr. R.G. Dean and Ouida Dean to Historical Publishing Network. The Deans accepted the formidable task of collecting the hundreds of illustrations, maps, paintings and photographs used in *Historic Texas*. They traveled the length and breadth of the state, visiting archives, libraries and museums. When *Historic Texas* began to take shape in our design department, Dr. and Mrs. Dean had identified over one thousand images to be considered for the book. Only about one-fourth of those found their way into the final version. The Deans also wrote the captions for the images, many of which can stand alone as history lessons in miniature.

The sixth force was the impetus given by the Cowboy Artists of America and the Cowboy Artists of America Museum in Kerrville to put us in contact with artist Gordon Snidow. Snidow's cover painting of *The Last Star Mill* was the perfect image to capture the spirit of Texans and how they experience their past.

The seventh and final force was the enthusiastic willingness of the Texas corporate world to support the concept of *Historic Texas*. The corporate sponsors in the "Sharing The Heritage" section of *Historic Texas* took advantage of a once-in-a-lifetime opportunity to be a part of Texas history in a uniquely positive and productive way.

As a team effort, the production of *Historic Texas* involved dozens of individuals in addition to those named above. Two stand out in particular: Charles "Chuck" Newton, operations manager for Historical Publishing Network, who designed and laid out art and copy for *Historic Texas*; and Margie Elliott, vice president of Preservation Texas, Inc., who provided support throughout the effort and in the final editing of the manuscript and captions.

The individuals who spent the most time making *Historic Texas* a reality are Project Manager Barry Black and his team of project representatives: Barbara Frank, Helen Carr, Sydney McNew, Gene Peeples and Jim Heath.

We were most fortunate that Dr. and Mrs. Dean encountered dozens of helpful and willing photo and illustration resources. We are particularly appreciative of the cooperation of the Torch Collection of Torch Energy Advisors Incorporated of Houston and the Stark Museum of Art of Orange for allowing *Historic Texas* to feature many of their priceless paintings and drawings.

The confluence of the forces that shaped *Historic Texas* has resulted in a product in which we take great pride. We hope you share our enthusiasm and that you relive the Texas adventure often in the pages of *Historic Texas*.

Ron Lammert, publisher
San Antonio, November, 1996

The total list of photo sources used in *Historic Texas* is:

Adventure Cycling Association, Missoula, Montana

Bush Presidential Materials Project, College Station

Center for American History, The University
of Texas at Austin

Connie Thompson, Pollock

Corpus Christi Public Library, Corpus Christi

Cushing Memorial Library A&M University,
College Station

Dallas Museum of Art, Dallas

Dallas Public Library Historic Photograph Collection,
Dallas

East Texas Research Center, Stephen F. Austin
State University, Nacogdoches

Gillespie County Historical Society, Inc.,
Fredericksburg

Harry Ransom Humanities Research Center,
The University of Texas at Austin

Image Crafters, Nacogdoches

Institute of Texan Cultures,
The University of Texas at San Antonio

Leroy Williamson, Bartlett

National Museum of American Art,
Smithsonian Institution, Washington, D.C.

Panhandle Plains Historical Museum,
West Texas A&M University, Canyon

Southwest Collection Tech University, Lubbock

Southwestern Writers Collection,
Southwest Texas State University, San Marcos

Special Collections Division,
The University of Texas at Arlington Libraries

Stark Museum of Art, Orange

State Preservation Board, Austin

Sterne-Hoya Museum and Library, Nacogdoches

Stone Fort National Bank, Nacogdoches

Texas Confederate Museum, United Daughters
of the Confederacy Division, Austin

Texas Department of Transportation, Austin

Texas State Archives Prints and Photographs
Collections, Austin

The Torch Collection of Torch Energy Advisors, Inc.,
Houston

Tyrrell Historical Library, Beaumont

Of course *Historic Texas* would have been quite impossible
without the support of our corporate sponsors:

Aeromexico

Baylor College of Dentistry

Camp Heart of the Hills/Camp Stewart

Casita Enterprises, Inc.

Catering of Central Texas

Coastal Securities

Conquest Airlines Corporation

Continental Airlines, Inc.

Dallas County Community College

Denton County Sesquicentennial Celebration

Dr Pepper/Cadbury North America

Driscoll Foundation

El Fenix

Fairmount Hotel

Filling Station Restaurant & Bar

First Valley Bank

First Victoria National Bank

Fuel Resources, Inc.

Heartplace

Hines, Inc.

Huston-Tillotson College

HWC Distribution Corp.

Incarnate Word Health Services

Input/Output, Inc.

Irving Healthcare System

Menger Hotel

The Methodist Hospital

Mobil

National Institute of Technology

Rip Nichols

Our Lady of the Lake University

PGS Exploration

Pilgrim Pride

Prestige Ford

Ramada Inn Bayfront

Randalls Food Market

Rice University

Safeco Land Title

Scott & White

Southern Methodist University

Southwest Airlines

Southwest Securities

St. Luke's Episcopal Hospital/Texas Heart Institute

St. Mary's University

Stewart Title

Stoneleigh Hotel

Taylor Publishing Company

Texaco

Texas A&M University System

Texas Medical Center

Texas State Technical College

Trinity Mother Frances Health System

Walter Oil & Gas Company

Walter P. Moore & Associates

Wells Fargo Bank

Wiley College

Wilsonart International

INDEX